AUTOBIOGRAPHY OF A
GHOST

I0110853

AUTOBIOGRAPHY OF A GHOST

The Making of a Mystic Mind

By

Glen A. Just

First Edition

© Copyright 2009 by Glen Arthur Just

The Library of Congress has cataloged Autobiography
of a Ghost as Registration Number TXu 1-618-943.

Cover photograph by the author

All rights reserved. No part of this work covered by the copyright
hereon may be reproduced or used in any form or used in any means
without the permission of the author and publisher

Published by Eagle Entertainment USA
130 Teton Lane #2
Mankato, Minnesota 56001
Website: www.eagleentertainmentusa.com
ISBN # 978-0-615-39562-3

WHAT'S INSIDE

PROLOGUE

INFANCY

My unusual memory contains snippets of recall starting with nursing and crib confinement. Both neglect and abuse are extensive during these early months of life, continue throughout childhood, and are painfully remembered. My schizophrenic mother used smothering and physical violence to control normal but unwanted infant behaviors. I survived many such episodes, but two of my four sisters were sent to early graves. At two years of age I was pronounced dead by our family doctor and approached by angels to be taken to Heaven. I refused Heaven and consciously returned to my lifeless body, my heart started beating, my breath returned, and my long journey to the pages of this story began.

Visual memory permits me to recall scenes and faces starting within months of my birth. My mentally ill mother left me in my crib soaked in urine and feces as she sought the sexual pleasures of other men. This pattern of neglect continued until I was to become self-sufficient somewhere between four and five years of age. During much of my childhood, a loving extended family provided nurturing that surely meant the difference between my living or dying. My drunken father's brutality is balanced with genuine moments of concern during his more sober moments.

My story is one of life-long efforts to understand and become whole. It is a story of infant survival, childhood trauma, adolescent struggle, and adult triumph. My combination of emotional, physical, sexual, and verbal abuse combined with felonious neglect is unusual only in its magnitude and combinations. My world is a world that many children both living and dead have experienced. Many times my little body stubbornly refused to die. Out-of-body experiences became an important part of my childhood and continued through my adult years. My Guardian Angel provided solace shortly after this death experience and has stayed with me until now. The ability to cry and feel normal pain or emotion was lost at age two and not regained for forty years. "Ghost" chronicles my struggle to understand mystic experiences, the physical presence of my Guardian Angel whom I named Moses, different haunting ghosts and spirits, endless nightmares, and diagnosed mental illness.

HOPE IS ETERNAL

My life has been unique in many ways. My unusual memory of trauma is not common. Horrible experiences often remain hidden behind each one of our conscious psyches, never to surface, but still hauntingly plaguing our daily lives from their unconscious depths; this has not been my experience; traumatic memories and associated pain have been my frequent companions. The message I most want to share is a message of hope; I believe without question that we can overcome tragedy. Growth is ours if we will only rise to the challenge one small step at a time. Each step of new awareness and integration gives us added strength to take another, even if we must stop for a breather now and then. To breathe on, to have courage, and to keep trying is to become something we never dreamed possible. To end one's blind, unforgiving, life in incomprehensible anguish is not an option; despair is not an option; suicide is not an option. I encourage all desperate readers who think there is no hope to look beyond their immediate pain to find this hidden strength. I believe most sincerely that insight into life's meaning; being loved and gaining acceptance wait for each one of us. I know that answers are often not immediate, but we can tease answers from a slowly growing tapestry of threads that bind us to a brighter future. The dark anguish of the moment can become our sunlit days of future joy. Each one of us must learn to believe in his or her self and who we can become.

Being given a second life has indebted me to humanity. I have lived a full life and I've been allowed to grow, I know and have known love, and I am healed. I know that healing is a process that opens new levels of fulfillment and happiness. Each level is worth our efforts; each level opens a new world of meaning; each level slowly removes our sense of hopelessness as we replace pain with understanding, loneliness with new friends, and despair with joy. I experience my life as if it had a predestined purpose. I feel deeply spiritual, but have disdain for those who preach a dogma that prevents any individual from realizing his or her full potential. Dogmas of hate, self-destruction and self-limitation are so easily taught by the wicked craftsmen of the world and its errant teachers.

As I learned to explore ever growing expanses of my inner world, I was gradually renewed and attached to larger segments of humanity and this incredible universe. I now live in a small world where little differences that we call skin color, gender, intelligence, religion, and ethnicity simply become embellishments for our wonderful oneness as human beings. It is my wish that this little book will help connect tattered threads of personal history that readers may have lost from their own lives, and, in these connections, dare to take another step into a brighter future. These small steps of growth and discovery can take the reader to the beginning of time, and the fullness of the universe; this has been my good fortune. May it be yours!

MYSTICISM UNVEILED

Over the course of my life's journey I attempted to explain the mystic experiences in my life and thereby discovered the root causes of astral travel, speaking in tongues, spirit possession, automatic writing, channeling, reincarnation, false memory, and Zen driving. My road to discovery started in my teen years when I taught myself hypnosis. I later enhanced these techniques as a university student to gain total body and mind control. Self-analysis in my early 20s was combined with self-experiments as I matured into my adult years. One path along this journey that I call Dream Programming reveals our natural human capacity to create both false memories and experience reincarnation. The mysticism of shamanism and its counterpart found in major world religions is identified as being simply part of our normal brain capacities. I used this capacity to consciously heal myself and explore the altered states of my core personality; states that go by various mystic names in different religions. Struggle became discovery, discovery became awareness, and I then used this emerging awareness to explore intra-psychic worlds that revealed the basis of different religious interpretations of these altered realities. In this process, the fine line between mysticism, mental illness, and much of traditional philosophy disappeared.

Through **Autobiography of a Ghost** I present many aspects of the classic American immigrant struggle with all its pain, family dysfunction, and stubborn human will to survive. It is my story of personal triumph with many unusual twists. My spiritual quest matured when Eastern Mystic "nothingness" was merged with modern physics and the out-of-body exploration of thirteen billion years of cosmic evolution. Memory droplets start months after my birth and miserly water a fragile skeleton struggling to become real, whole and bloom. These final words are written in a wonderful world of love and harmony. Peace that was long-sought but never mine in America became a reality in the incredible dynamics that represent the growth of modern China. Words on paper that were not possible in my homeland finally emerged and provide closure to a lifelong struggle to be whole as I pulled them slowly from the depths of memory in the land of the Middle Kingdom.

APOLOGY

I want my children, family and friends to understand why I have often been blind or insensitive. I cannot reach back in time and change my past, but I can seek forgiveness for my own sins and short-comings. Apologies to those I've hurt is not enough. I am seeking understanding that only comes from integrated wholeness of self and spirit. I have tried to unite both in a manner that communicates, in a way that transcends mere ink on paper. My goal is to share this awareness with you as I move between the multiple levels of reality that unfold autobiographically; our common humanity can so easily transcend time and place. Our shared humanity can create insights that transcend and triumph, where rational objectivity, dogmatically taught and learned, simply continues our ignorance. Each one of us creates and chooses our own reality - knowingly or unknowingly. We usually let our culture shape our realities and we thus come to be defined as normal; but when our family history is abnormal we are easily categorized as being crazy, a mystic, or just an undesirable person. I have been classified as all three.

I do not feel righteous or angry about my life. It is my history, and I am eternally grateful that I had a second chance to live it. My life has been full of accomplishment, personal joy, deep trauma, anger, but most of all a chance to grow and more fully experience the bountiful fruits that life has to offer. Death experiences are said to leave lasting impressions on those of us who live through them. This is true for me. "Autobiography of a Ghost" has more than one hidden character; the ghosts and spirits are all part of who I am. Some are explained, some are not! I am committed to as much self-honesty as life has slowly given me. I most earnestly seek to discover the next level of awareness and insights that this journey offers.

I was compelled to write "**Ghost**" as closure to that part of my life that was either dominated or controlled by spirits and traumatizing memories. Part of my psyche demanded this story be put on paper in order for me to feel complete. Consequently, it was necessary to revisit experiences in which I struggled to understand my own history – a final step of self integration. If I simply threw "**Ghost**" in the wastebasket it was worth the effort. It has brought forth new insights and what it is that I share with almost every other person on this planet.

Often as I listened to the children and young adults in treatment programs that I developed or administered, I wondered how they could endure and survive the endless acts of fellow human cruelty. As I came to appreciate their miseries, unwanted nightmares and mystic visitations, I was forced to re-experience my own. Shared stories of young traumatized victims forced me to confront my own memories. I had worked hard to leave these experiences in intellectual boxes where there was no pain, a cognitive level of manipulation that I learned at the university – one of intellectual gymnastics. In these forced re-visitations I gained additional insight into who I had been and who I was becoming. Most sincerely, I am trying to reach across time, distance, and the riddles of human misery to share a lifetime of personal seeking, growth and understanding. Hundreds of survivors have shared their stories with me over the years, and given me strength; I hope to give back one small fraction of their gifts.

In my quest to understand who I have been and who I was becoming, I was forced to think about many of my own mystic experiences. In this way I discovered my dualistic side, and confronting this dualism, a dualism that is both dark and light, I have achieved a wholeness that I once thought to be impossible. I discovered the other person hidden behind the mask of my fragmented self, a fragmented self that I presented to others much of my life as being authentic. Self-discovery, I discovered, is a universal quest. The quest to know myself has been like a haunting ghost – bothersome, tiring, demanding, irritating – but at the same time rewarding.

Writing "**Ghost**" is a way for me to affirm who I am, and in so doing, to more fully understand myself. I have learned that to understand others, I must first understand me. Self understanding demanded that I first become whole; a fragmented self only experiences other fragments. The intellect that lives in compartments only knows the compartment that it is currently locked into. I believe that unless one knows who they are, really knows who they are in the sense of "know thyself," the rest is just intellectual gymnastics. A first step in personal growth is to realize which compartment of life we are living in; next to see the separate compartments side-by-side as a whole; and finally to bring them together in true integration: the house that an integrating self builds. We are fully adult when we take this last step; it is not easy; it is not common, but it is worth all our struggles and efforts.

SISTERS

My sisters, Carol and Donna, lie in their graves at Lakeside Cemetery, mute, and without ability to tell their story of neglect, trauma, and death. There are untold numbers of children like them in America and across the world; children who are commonly diagnosed as perishing from unknown causes, crib-deaths and other polite sounding terms, or children who simply stop breathing. As one child who stopped breathing mysteriously, was pronounced dead and then given life, I wish to add my thoughts to these silent voices. I cannot speak for most children, but I can speak for my mute sisters, Donna and Carol; and now as I write these final words, for my beloved sister June who is finally free of all her earthly pain.

Multiple deaths within families like mine can be easily prevented. Something as simple as visiting nursing services can eliminate my type of family histories. My living was either an accident, or perhaps divine intervention. My two sisters who survived into adulthood experienced the same living family hell that I experienced. My good fortune, or at times I thought misfortune, was an exceptional childhood memory that collected trauma the way misers hoard money. Blocked memory has been both a timely salvation for my surviving sisters as well as a curse; a curse that frequently demanded perpetual obedience to a twisted childhood. But I know from experience that as our memories return, our souls can become whole if we will only rise to the challenge.

SISTERS ARE LIKE SOUL FOOD

I evoked the Mind of all that is,
and found your thoughts, mine, and His.
I stretched my hands in wonder o'r,
and found your gentle touch once more.

I searched for love so sweet and dear,
and found your caring spirit near.
The kind acts of nature brought me health,
which you enhanced with home and self.

The inner sadness I could not hide,
you took away and left my pride.
When lonely feelings brought forth fear,
away you chased with smiles and cheer.

You brought joy and laughter to my mood,

your inner thoughts I shared like food.
When silence came and voids remained,
your acts recalled became refrains.

Beijing 2008

CHAPTER 1

REFUSING HEAVEN

I am now a little over two years old and about to join my two dead sisters. I had no real knowledge of life's joys or the meaning of death; no knowledge of angels or heaven; only knowledge of my earthly hell. Dad told me when I was in my teens that mother had called him in a panic from the hilltop house saying that I had stopped breathing. He later asked her why she hadn't just called the doctor, telling me that he was perplexed by her odd behavior. Dad explained that he placed towels soaked in cold water on my head and how I finally began to respond. I don't remember any of this, and I don't remember going to the hospital. My first memory of the hospital was dying and meeting the angels.

My hospital bed was on the second or third floor, first room looking into the stairway. The hospital sat next to Beaver Dam Lake – wooden frame, and three stories. In its better days it had been a lumber baron's symbol of new wealth before being converted. When my hospital door was open, I could see people's heads appear as they came up the stairs. Soon their bodies would follow, but the bed was so placed that I never saw their feet. It was like magic lying there in bed; people just floated into view through the open door.

I have this picture clear image of three people standing by my bed. At my head was a nurse in white uniform, next dad, and third, the doctor. I didn't know the doctor's name then, but he was gentle and spoke softly. In the back, near the room's closed door, was a faceless figure; none of its features were visible as it stood in the shadows of this dying room. I remember hearing the doctor tell dad that I was gone. Next, the sheet was pulled over my face, and I could no longer see light. I didn't like the darkness that followed, but it didn't last. A moment later, I found myself standing between my father and the nurse looking down at my lifeless body. I don't recall how I got out of bed. I was just standing between my father and the nurse. This happened instantly! I was amazed at how tall I was standing there. I was standing shoulder-to-shoulder between my father and the nurse. Or, was I floating shoulder-to-shoulder between my father and the nurse? We were all looking down at my corpse.

As I contemplated my dead body and how I could be this tall, a series of lights appeared in the distance, grew brighter, and moved toward me. The view of the hospital room and my bed faded away, and my total world consisted of approaching, twinkling lights. The lights came from a great distance and dominated my visual field – they were rapidly moving toward me. As the lights came nearer, they were transformed into a group of warm, smiling faces, and then their attached bodies appeared. Five or six people approached me. I don't recall the exact number, but they were both young men and women. Their arms were outstretched, and I knew they were going to take me to Heaven. I didn't know any of them, and Uncle Gus was not with them. But they were all about the same age as Uncle Gus. None of the angels were old like grandpa or grandma. None of them had wings; they just floated through space effortlessly. Their smiles made me feel warm and wonderful as they came nearer. At first I was eager to embrace them. A sense of peace and happiness was totally enveloping me. They started to reach for me, and I knew I was about to leave Earth forever. The gate to Heaven was opening for me.

A moment later, I stepped back from the angels. I consciously decided that I was not ready to go to Heaven. It was a strange moment of choice, and I have always remembered it as an option that was given to me. Why? Why would the choice of life or death be given to a not yet three year old? I seemed to know that going to Heaven meant never seeing any of my family again, but more than anything else was the feeling that I was not yet ready to leave. I turned my back on the angels, and waited. I thought they would grab me and make me go, but they didn't. I am sure I would have gone if Uncle Gus had been with them. I liked Uncle Gus. I looked down at my sheet-covered form as I again became aware of being suspended between my dad and the nurse – a vivid picture in my mind that always stays with me. Next, I very consciously got back into my body. The sheet didn't seem to be a problem and I passed through it without effort. I didn't like being covered by the sheet, unable to see, and remember trying to get it off.

Dad told me later, when we talked about my dying in the hospital, that the doctor pronounced me dead and began placing the sheet over my face. Dad then asked to have my nose tube and arm IV taken out. The doctor removed the tube and IV, covered me with the sheet and pronounced me dead. A little while later dad said I started to move. I never told him that I had watched myself die, or anything about the angels. He would recoil from any attempts on my part to discuss other worldly experiences, and made it clear that they were just nonsense. I learned before I was three years old that people in my world would accept any crazy explanation for things not understood rather than discuss life's mysteries. By the time I was five or six, I quit trying. Life-long mystic experiences simply became part of my private life, and I would not be confident enough to share them at any length with others until I was middle-aged.

As I began to breathe and stir, the shadowy figure by the far wall moved into the light. It was mother. I felt a strong sense of fear, and was filled instantly with terror, a feeling that I would have many times through the years as I grew older. How strange that I should feel such terror when only moments before the angels had made me feel totally loved, safe and at peace. My young and growing mind would experience these contradictions, with their vivid memories and recycled pains, over and over again for decades. I often felt this was my penalty for staying on this less than perfect planet, and refusing Heaven.

I returned home with dad and mother only to find that I could no longer walk or talk. The crib once more became my daytime jail, and it was more confining now than it had been when it was exclusively mine. I don't remember where my sister June slept. She would have been about one year old, and this single family crib was her usual sleeping place. Although, she probably just traded places with me, taking my bed and me hers. There is a blank space in my memory, but eventually I went to Grandma's and to the safety of her loving arms.

Returning home, the old farm house routine started all over again, I had to learn how to both walk and talk a second time. I recall being put back in the crib, I was bigger, but my muscles were weak. I was not strong enough to pull myself up and over the crib's bars. I was totally imprisoned. Feces and urine once again caked me and the unwanted diaper as it would dry to my skin during the long day as if glued. I remained urine soaked much of the day, but it too would usually dry before my mother, Madge, returned. I was unable to forage for food, and frequent hunger and thirst returned as I tried repeatedly to leave my unwanted confinement. I was once more alone in the dark; the eternal dark that I both loved and hated. The dark was my friend at night and my enemy during the day. Eventually my strength returned, once more I started walking, and my ability to talk gradually came back as well. My reacquired ability to use the toilet was a gift that most adult memories can only speculate about. Finally, I was once more free of crib imprisonment, free from stinking feces and urine, free from red, raw skin, and free from immobility. However, what mother called epileptic fits followed me for a number of years, ending in fainting spells when I was about eight years old.

It was still summer weather outside, and I would often meet my brother coming home after school. He would fight with neighbor boys – all Italian. He did not like Italians, and called them Wops and Dagos. Bud would beg me to get mother as the Italian boys would not let him into the house as long as he kept calling them names. I never wanted to leave. I wanted to stay and help him fight because he was my brother, but Bud would demand that I get mother. I would eventually, and the Italian boys would run home. My brother taught me early that Wops were mean. He never used their names; they were not real people, just Wops and Dagos.

Once I was free of the crib, got my strength back, and could walk again, I was not as lonely as I had been before going to the hospital. I could leave my body whenever I wanted to, and I did this often. I was afraid to fly very high in case I might fall. I didn't know how I stayed up in the air and this made me fearful of flying above the clouds. I practiced flying close to the ground, and never went too far from the house, or out over the water. I was afraid of getting lost, too. I enjoyed flying above solid earth and would let my body float gently down to contact, but I was afraid of landing in the lake and drowning because I didn't know how to swim. Reality was such an easy thing to create. Later, I would learn, creating reality is what makes us human, and, how we create reality is the key to understanding who we are.

My muscles attached themselves to my damaged brain once again, and I was soon walking and talking – everyone gave me attention for trying. After hospitalization, I had an expanded sense of freedom. I could fly whenever I wanted to, and leaving my body was pleasant – a little like talking to the angels. It was very peaceful being out-of-body, and these experiences were some of the happiest moments of my early years. I tried to explain flying to mother, but she would just place her finger over her mouth and shush me up. I was walking better than ever, and was once again in control of toilet functions, walking and talking. I was happier than I had been before I died, and remember laughing often. Sometimes I would laugh at the smallest things, and just keep laughing and laughing until Madge physically made me stop. Laughing was a fun place to be; my cares would float away and I would be in a world where only laughter existed, a world where pain was blocked and nonexistent. I liked other children, and fear of ordinary things was something I no longer had. Fear was a feeling I saw on the faces of others, not something that concerned me. I had trouble understanding it. I was free of fear, and I loved this new sense of well-being. People were afraid of so many things; falling, getting hurt, death, and physical pain. I would not understand the intensity or meaning of these feelings for many years, and for some, not for decades.

IDES OF MARCH: BIRTH

Blowing snow, large wet flakes splattering against the windshield of the 1935 or maybe it was a 1936 Buick, wind sliding the car like a giant hand as Doc fought for control. Doc always bought a

5

new Buick every two years, and continued this practice when I knew him during my later teen years. The trip from the hospital to Upper Lake Vermillion would have demanded everything his pneumonia-racked body could muster. A blizzard that intense, that late in the season, dictated a home delivery. Wet, sticky end of March blizzards combine snow, freezing rain, and ice crystals that cling like glue; they paint the trees and landscape like diligent gods and everything becomes a fairyland. Doc would have fought against the slope of the narrow blacktop highway; a highway transformed into a treacherous skating rink not fit for day or night adventure. A chuck hole, or frost-heaved mound of ice could instantly spin his seat-belt-less car into the ditch, or worse, leave him immobilized, out-of-sight, slowly freezing. Transporting a pregnant woman under such severe weather conditions was unthinkable. This was Madge's fifth child; two living, two dead. Her second baby had survived less than one month after delivery, her third less than six months. Vonna was her fourth birth baby and the second child to live. The odds: this new baby had a 50-50 chance of making it. And so it was 50-50!

Doc should have questioned his sanity. Driving half-blind over treacherous roads was not something he would have advised his bed-ridden pneumonia patients, yet there he was, with rasping lungs risking his own life to ensure the arrival of a new country bumpkin. Turning back most certainly would have ended the life of this soon to be plucked fetus; pink flesh struggling to become free and live. Flipping the Buick into a desolate farmer's ditch with his own inflamed lungs would have been suicidal. Doc should have remained in bed, but instead he drove on because that is what country doctors did. It was a fact of rural life in Northeastern Wisconsin and much of the Midwest. Medical people lived with the elements and the poverty – they were part of the community, one of the people. The pressures put on a country doctor, who was on call twenty-four hours, seven days a week, created a special toughness of mind and spirit, while at the same time the body almost daily begged for relief from this unremitting routine.

Heading east from Island City on Highway 48, the road to Upper Lake Vermillion is known to locals as being at the bottom of the first deep valley, the lake being just a short distance south of the intersection. In later years, I always looked for this valley in inclement weather when I drove to my brother's farm. Doc would have known most of the county roads well, the way he knew each family and their children, and later their children's children for miles around. Ten years of practice in Barron County, in the depths of the Great Depression, taught many lessons. Hard liquor was one of them, and it got Doc through many days, and many years of rural medical servitude. Alcohol prohibition for country folks had been as effective as telling birds not to eat worms. Doc was from the old school and felt a commitment to his patients the way some preachers feel an umbilical connection to their flocks. He wore the same tired face of local farmers scratching out a meager living during the desperate days of the 1930's.

Doc was never a drunk in the traditional sense, but did imbibe multiple martinis during the dinner hour. Some folks tossed their drinks down, but not Doc. Doc imbibed. Doc's martinis had the slightest hint of vermouth with the olive rubbed round the ring of his glass before being gently dropped into the liquid itself. Doc drank his martinis slowly savoring the mixture of gin and olive juice as he carefully rotated his martini glass with each sip, thereby enjoying the same mixture of gin, vermouth and olive juice until the glass's rim was traversed and the container emptied. This ritual was repeated with each subsequent martini; it was an operation equal to the removal of a hot appendix. Only God knows how many knife wielding operations he performed after these acts of alcohol surgery. The locals would comment knowingly about how well Doc could hold his liquor, while they were equally thankful for his sober or inebriated attention. Doc never staggered, slurred his words, or showed obvious signs of being intoxicated. He could hold his liquor as well as any of the locals, which of course meant practice.

My delivery was uneventful as mother later described it. Dad heated water and stood by nervously as Doc brought new life into this desolate farmhouse. The storm made it impossible for a nurse to be in attendance. When I asked her to tell me about my home delivery, Madge said deliveries were easy. The mental image I formed was one of her spitting babies out the way children spit watermelon seeds at a summer picnic. Sister Vonna would be two years old in six weeks, and Bud would be six the following week. The gap between Bud and Vonna belonged to sisters Carol and Donna who had died mysteriously in their infancy – hushed deaths that were only discussed by relatives in private conversations. Out-of-mind deaths that parents never, but never talked about unless prodded to do so, and the prodding was always longer than the response.

Bud would have been responsible for much of Vonna's care during the first weeks after my birth, as he did not start first grade until the following September. When we talked over the years, Bud said that finding food for Vonna, my other sister June, and me had been a challenge for him when we were little. Mother's frequent absences presented a survival problem for all of us. Our collective memories swirled through neglect and abuse like maggots through rotten meat whenever we forced discussion of these early years, and that was almost never. These discussions began to emerge routinely at my promptings after we had all become middle-aged adults. Repression of our traumatic childhoods had been a collective response, which was increasingly broken at my insistence as we siblings passed through what was to become my rebirth and renaissance.

Whenever I asked mother about my birth, the storm, delivery, and how she handled the stress, her responses would be without feeling or emotion; similar to the way one talks routinely about what's for dinner. Thoughts that shared deep emotions did not become words that she openly expressed, if they ever did occupy her mind, and if they did, emotional intimacy was out of the question. She lived in the present. I came to experience Madge over the years as someone who thought tears were for simple souls who did not know how to exploit either pleasure, or other people. Tears were reserved for beatings when dad found her sleeping with other men, not for death. And I can't imagine she had them for new, burdensome children.

I have this mental picture of her attending her infant daughters' funerals totally dry-eyed. Children happened – some lived, some died. That was fate! Throughout my life, and up to the time of her death, I felt that Madge's inner core of nurturing had been scrambled like eggs with the demonic half of her schizophrenic self. Whether one got egg white or yoke depended on the moment. Whether children lived or died depended on Madge's mood.

My first memories of her were those of nursing at her breasts. Madge taught me that nursing was something that she controlled. Nursing for her was painless. Uncomfortable nursing was not permitted. The solution was simple – she pressed my face tight into her breast until my sole effort was focused on trying to breathe. The vivid memories of her calloused, firm hand against the back of my head as I struggled to stop my aching lungs from screaming remain like ugly scar tissue one can see on a pock-marked face. My body would go limp, and my mouth would release its grip before I was permitted to resume feeding. Nursing was a time when getting air was often more difficult than getting milk. Madge's anger took time to subside, as did her grip on my head, and oxygen was once more permitted along with nourishment. It is the oxygen deprivation that lingers in my memory as my nursing would have ended within fifteen months, or sooner with the birth of Sister June.

These were my two overpowering first memories of the person I called mother. Memories of my struggle to breathe during the early months of life still make me pause, take deep breaths, and relish the wonderful feeling of free flowing, oxygen filled air. Madge was a master at using suffocation as a behavioral re-enforcer, so easy to use, and it was totally effective on me. This simple method of child control would have come naturally to her. She could go to anger in a split second, and react without any consideration of the consequence, and I remember many of those moments well. Combined with her dual personality, our lives as her children became probabilities.

Being without food throughout the day, forced to accept dried feces and urine as glued-on body attachments, all made me appreciate her care when it was finally offered. I hated diapers, feces, urine, and the confinement of the crib. My diaper would dry slowly to my body during the day as hunger and thirst built. My first memories of the crib were of high prison-like walls that kept me confined. I would sit up, grab the bars, and peer into the semi-darkness that was my frequent daily companion. In some ways it is strange as I write these words, the visual images of looking out through the crib's bars are as vivid as the computer screen on which these words are written.

The memory of earaches is especially strong during my early months of crib seclusion as similar earaches would follow me through puberty. Mother's punishments when I cried out in pain remain equally as clear as the crib's walls of confinement. I cried-out in pain only as a final act of desperation, especially during those moments before the right eardrum would begin to ooze liquid. I would wait for it to break, and then the pain would subside. When I was older and could express myself in words, requests for earache help would be followed by hot milk poured directly into the ear's opening. Sometimes the milk's temperature exceeded the burning point, but in either case, burning or not, the helpful effort was complete and Madge could return to whatever it was that occupied her mind or body. Sometimes the remedy worked, sometimes it didn't. It was the effort – the ritual – that counted. Madge believed in ritual, not in infant or childcare.

As hunger and thirst grew during Madge's absence, I would gradually become braver, grasp the side rail of the crib, and carefully lower my body as far as my arms would extend. First, I remember that before I could walk I was not able to reach the floor, and had to drop the short remaining distance to the boards below. Later, I was just able to touch the floor by extending my toes, and this gave me a greater sense of security. My sister June would have inherited the crib fifteen months or so after my birth, hence, all of these early memories are spotty and mixed, except the crib's bars and oxygen-deprived breast feeding. I was old enough to crawl when I first started gaining freedom from the crib, or at least that is my association. I never remember falling, or hitting the floor hard enough for it to be painful when I pulled myself over the crib's bars, and I seem to be unusually good at remembering painful childhood episodes. It is as though my second gift of life created a permanent space in my mind to re-experience these simple moments of childhood.

Some of my other early memories include being able to stand, and walk by holding onto objects around me. The second floor of the old farmhouse by Lake Vermillion had large steps that required me to descend like a four-legged puppy. I navigated the stairs the way rock-climbers conquer mountains. I remember crawling to the stairway in the darkness, finding the first step, and one-by-one, navigating each huge platform downward one after the other. I don't recall sitting on the steps and "bumping" down the way my own children would later do. I recall festering wood splinters being a strict teacher that encouraged careful movement.

The room my crib occupied was in semi-darkness during the day. The shades were thick light blockers that contained dad's cigarette smoke and the lifeless yellowing of years gone by. Shades were pulled shut when Madge was away from the house on her frequent jaunts. Small streaks of daylight would come through their cheap unapproachable cracks throughout the day, offering just enough light to see the room in outline. This slowly moving company of light gave me something to watch hour after hour as the sun passed overhead: warm, ethereal, and inviting! The larger world beyond that weathered farmhouse was inviting me out to play while the crib cruelly locked me in. My lifelong love of the outdoors was born from crib imprisonment. Years later this old farmhouse burned to the ground, and I thought the ghost of my first birth was finally at peace.

The steps were different. By the time I was halfway downstairs, the light from the cracked shades was gone. Nearer the door, another sliver of light would appear at my feet. This small soft glow was like a magnet, it meant freedom and a room full of light, food and comfort when the door was opened. I was like a frog in hot water with the temperature slowly rising; I waited quietly and hoped for relief. The frog cooked; I pined. The frequent ritual of food and water deprivation drove me to repeatedly attempt this awkward climb. Almost always, the door at the bottom was locked, and I would lie down on the last step and wait. The climb down would refocus my thoughts and help reduce my hunger, but it also increased my thirst. I learned early that water was something that went with food. Over the next two years, I repeated this journey of steps in the apartment above Erickson's Main Street store, and in the old house near the hospital.

My brother reminded me that we had lived in another rental near what is now the Corner Bar, but I have no memory of this place. I only recall living in three houses by the time I was two. One set of steps was like the next – wooden with a locked door at the bottom. I could hear Madge returning home through the locked door by Lake Vermillion. Sister Vonna would appear like magic when Madge finally opened the door. Brother Bud would find his way back from school, but he always seemed busy playing outside.

Sometimes Madge would respond to my turning the knob and pushing on the door. Mostly, the door would open when food was being placed on the table, or she was ready to have another child in her life. Crying was something Madge didn't respond to unless she was trying to nap, and then she would become enraged. Crying was like aggressive nursing – she would painfully retaliate, but mostly, crying was a waste of good liquid tears. It was like throwing money into the wind with nothing to show for my expenditures. I learned to save my tears the way ocean castaways conserve water.

Patience, patience! How difficult it was for me to wait those last few minutes for food and drink. Such good training though! I was learning to feel only when and what I wanted to feel. If I was good and didn't make noise, or if dad was home, mother would set food within reach of my highchair. This I devoured immediately. I remember dad remarking on his death-bed that I was such a great cheese lover. Mother's ploy with cheese always worked. Cheese was easy; a couple quick strokes with a knife and the kid had a happy, busy face when he got home. Dad thought I was the ultimate cheese lover, and routinely put cheese on the table when I visited him over the years. He thought children were women's work, and never once looked in my day-long empty stomach when I was a child. I would have devoured raw turnips with as much enthusiasm.

I was learning self-control; crying was becoming infrequent, and day long hunger and thirst were removed by bed time. Mother no longer had to peel off the caked dried feces from my bottom as I embraced toilet training with a passion. I had to overcome this strong repulsion of dirty diapers after the birth of my first son. It was a contest of timing, manipulated by my nurse-wife who laughed at her squeamish spouse. Her calculated absences forced me to respond. I would have exchanged the initial experiences for ten whip lashes if I had been given the choice. Repulsion is such a mild word! Red, raw skin scrubbed clean of caked dried feces with the tenderness of a lion eating fresh kill; now, that's repulsion.

FINDING FOOD

I learned how to open the door at the bottom of the stairs in the house by the hospital. It was a wonderful old house without door locks, and when Madge forgot to prop a chair against the door, I could get free; but most of the time I wiggled the door repeatedly until the chair fell away. It was summer and I knew how to find Aunt Olga's house. Aunt Olga lived three blocks from our house, next to highway 63. She was a major source of food, baked cookies, and she always had milk. I just walked the three blocks, opened her unlocked back door, pushed a chair up to the entrance cupboard, climbed on the chair, climbed up on the cupboard, sat down and started eating cookies. Pushing the chair made noise and Aunt Olga would come and help me by adding milk, sometimes even sandwiches. I learned early that food was where I could find it. I just had to figure out where to look. People never refused me food, and I don't remember how I got back home from these forages. I just remember that it was a long walk to Aunt Olga's and I had to be careful when crossing the streets. These early journeys of world exploration to Aunt Olga's have stayed with me throughout life. Travel remains an adventure, not a loss of familiar comforts. I would find something exciting at the other end whether it's three blocks for cookies or three thousand miles for pristine Mexican beaches, but when I travel I always look for food. Food by itself is an adventure of wonderful tastes.

Mother kept certain foods hidden. She needed sweet treats, special foods, and exotic morsels that would help keep her weight down. I couldn't find her hidden treasures when I was small, she kept them high up in the cupboards away from little hands. I would see her munching greedily in the evening when she was cleaning the kitchen. When I got older, I noticed her devouring these treats any time during the day. Once I reached the age of eight or nine, I knew where she hid them. She got extremely angry if I took the chocolate or candy, and I didn't like the dry toast that she nibbled on between bites of sweets.

By the time I was ten years old, I just stopped looking. Mother stressed that these were her foods; foods that helped her stay thin. I still like to think that chocolate is non-fattening. The luxury of Aunt Olga's cookies and milk didn't last. We moved to the south end of town on the hill overlooking the bottom of Beaver Dam Lake. This part of the lake is opposite the canning factory, and turns green in late summer. The house was near the top of the hill facing northwest. It commanded a view of two parts of the lake cut by Second Street, as the street meanders out of town and turns into a country road.

ISLAND CITY

Island City, Wisconsin, was a sleepy town of 1800-odd souls in 1936. Seven blocks took one from the south end of town to the combined high school and grade school on the north side. The last glacier's retreat eight thousand years ago had dumped a moraine of sand, gravel, and rocks across this part of North America. Beaver Dam Lake sits on the south side of the moraine separating good farm land from sandy soil that is best used for growing grass and trees. The lake is of the finger variety, long and narrow at seven miles with a loop that goes around Island City itself. The lake has been cut numerous times to the west by road fill, and at least four times around the city. The town is now only surrounded by water on three sides. Highway 63 comes up from the south, angles east a mile into town, and then turns north. The east-west road that shares Highway 63 as it approaches Island City is Highway 48. As the highways pass through town, one is reminded that most of the core buildings sharing transit are well over a hundred years old. The town struggles to be modern by pasting on a new hospital, school, and a few other necessary items needed for it to live in the 21st Century. It is quaint, livable, friendly, but mostly stuck in an earlier place of times gone by. History doesn't talk in Island City; it whispers.

Tourists are struck by the state's natural beauty as they drive through these gentle rolling hills, lush green landscapes, and watery waysides. A great variety of trees block the traveler's view in all directions. Lakes appear continuously along one's driving route. Eagles are commonly seen, deer crossings must be paid attention to, and every kind of animal from fox, wolves, to bears roam freely. Locals call this God's country. I don't know about God, but I do know that angels spend considerable time visiting their country cousins. Island City is blessed with this beauty and one knows immediately why its citizens yearn to keep the town unspoiled, natural, and at peace; every national brand chain store destroys history, smothers the beauty of nature with things like yellow arches, and spoils nature's painted landscape. Little of this exists in Island City.

The railroad came through in the late 1800s to transport both logs and agricultural products to more distant markets. Italian laborers had followed the steel horse by the thousands as it extended north into what was then a wild, wooded, lake filled state. Italians settled out in large numbers along the rail line as they saved enough money to buy land or property. They were like all other immigrants, a people working hard to create a new life for their families and help reshape this still unspoiled beauty called Northeastern Wisconsin.

In addition to Italians, the mixture of immigrants was European with Germans, Swedes, Norwegians, Dutch, Swiss, Poles, Russians, and a number of other less numerous nationalities added in. Prejudice toward the Native population was extreme, as extreme as the immigrant's ignorance of them. Physically Native people looked and acted strangely as seen from the perspective of these new European colonizers. They spoke languages none of the newcomers understood, were isolated on the most unproductive land, and were viewed as being racially inferior. Northern European immigrants thought that Italians were darker skinned and therefore shared some of this inferiority. They experienced a lesser, but still strong discrimination from many of their Northern European relatives. This pattern of discrimination lasted until a complete generation of children had experienced each other in school. By the time I entered high school in 1950, Italians were simply school mates, and many Italian girls were beautiful; dark hair and brown eyes easily competed with yellow hair and blue eyes. However, native people were not welcome in white schools; they were pushed out, and made to feel inferior. Job-wise, they were only permitted to perform the most menial tasks for their white employers, or try to subsist on government handouts.

Island City was one of three notorious logging communities in Northeastern Wisconsin by the 1900s. It was filled with brothels and bars where loggers often squandered their hard earned dollars. An old saying, "Island City, Hayward, Hurley, and Hell," was still verbal currency amongst old timers in the 1940s. In 1950 when I delivered papers door-to-door, only one house of prostitution and five bars remained. The prostitute was the only person that gave me a tip when I collected for her newspaper subscription, and it was usually a dime. The Lady would come to the door with a large practiced smile, pay me for the subscription, watch my reaction, and then offer the tip. I thought she was nicer than my mother, and I didn't know why town's women said such bad things about her. Townsmen never spoke openly of her in the presence of children or wives. I never, but never, saw this woman on the town's streets in all the years I lived there. She must have shopped and spent her leisure time in one of the neighboring communities where she could be just another woman out for the day.

FAMILY

When I was born, the Great Depression still racked America and dad managed an Erickson gas station one block south of the old high school on Main Street. Radio broadcasts were everyone's source of news.

President Roosevelt's New Deal was all the talk. He was going to save America. I liked Roosevelt, he sounded like a kind-hearted grandpa to me. Everyone listened to him on their radios. He had this funny sounding Eastern accent. I liked his accent, it was softer than grandpa's, and he talked slower. Roosevelt was going to put two chickens in mom's cooking pot. I hoped it would happen soon. I liked chicken.

The other talk on the radio was about Germans. Dad, grandpa, grandma, and all of my aunts and uncles spoke German. Their voices were soft when they talked about Germany and Hitler, especially when strangers were nearby. Uncle Fritz, Uncle Eric, and dad said they would fight Hitler – Hitler was a very bad man. Grandpa said that Stalin was a bigger tyrant then Hitler because he was killing all of our family in the old country. Dad believed that Stalin had killed more than one hundred of his cousins in the Ukraine. Stalin also killed an estimated 1.75 million German-Ukranians in one of the world's least known genocides. The German-Ukranian history being well documented by one of its sons: Joseph S. Height, "Homesteaders on the Steppe: The Odyssey of a Pioneering People," Tubingen, 1975.

Great Grandpa Samuel had disappeared in the Ukraine with a loaded wagon at age 91 and was never heard from again. He sent grandpa a picture of himself, his horses and wagon piled high with all his life's belongings and then tried to outrun the Russian Revolution. Reds and Whites of the emerging revolution came to German-Ukrainian villages slaughtering whole families, or taking them away to labor camps. Letters exchanged between America and the Ukraine became fewer and fewer and ended with great grandpa's disappearance. Afterwards, the only contact with our European family was from relatives still living in Germany. Eventually, all our German-Ukrainian family lost contact as the new Soviet Union sucked out their life-blood and most of our family swirled into the oblivion of unrecorded genocide. I didn't understand this talk, but knew that the world was full of bad people, and I had to be on the watch for them. German-Americans had formed groups, "bunds," in Northern Wisconsin that initially supported Hitler's Third Reich. Our family was caught in an awkward position, both hating Hitler and Stalin. This was not a comfortable place to be as America went to war against the "ubermenschen" while allied with the Soviets.

Uncle Eric came back home briefly before shipping out to Europe and the German campaign. I remember his visits well because they were full of surprises and treats. He knocked at the front door, something family never did, and when it was opened, presented a large box. I ran to look in the box and was amazed at what I saw. The box was full of candy and chocolate. He had bought all of these hard to find sweets in the Army PX. My eyes must have been standing two inches in front of my face when he picked up the box, handed it to me, and said it was all mine. I grabbed the box, ran upstairs to my room, and squirreled everything under my bed. I returned downstairs to find my parents and Uncle Eric laughing. I had to bring the box of candy back and share it with the whole family. Uncle Eric always did special things for us; he was like a second father to me. I visited him regularly until he died in Island City's nursing home in 2004.

Uncle Eric fought the Germans through Normandy and up to the end of the German Campaign when Hitler committed suicide. He came back home briefly before shipping to the Pacific to fight the Japanese. Uncle Eric had his stomach blown out by a Japanese torpedo off the Philippine Islands, but survived the trip back to the states and years of subsequent stomach surgery. Uncle Fritz was shot by three Japanese snipers in the early months of his Pacific service; a story that my cousin says he fabricated. He described what sounded like an old Wisconsin squirrel shoot as he carefully and systematically shot each sniper out of the trees and to their deaths. He told me he was severely wounded in this encounter, but Cousin Gus says it's not true. Dad was too old to be a soldier, but he often talked about being rejected by the draft board when trying to enlist. A story I thought was fabricated to make him appear patriotic or cover up his guilt for letting his younger brothers provide fighting support from our family. German-Americans, like all other American soldiers, returned home wounded or at war's end, the bunds were forgotten, and America was free. The war to end all wars was won. We were one nation, proud of having saved the world from tyrants, and full of stories that taught us children the righteousness of American wars, a righteousness not to be forgotten, a righteousness repeated endlessly, a righteousness never forgotten.

CHAPTER 2

UNCLES AND GRANDPARENTS

I first remember Uncle Gus in what must have been the house by the old hospital, as one could look directly into Beaver Dam Lake from our backyard. He had a tumor surgically removed from his brain, and often visited our home. Uncle Gus was a gentle soul struggling to recover from this operation. I remember very little about him except that his tumor grew back, and my dad and uncles tried to convince him to have more surgery. Uncle Gus was adamant; he would rather die than go through the pain of brain surgery a second time. In my mind's eye I see him shaking his head no, and refusing the collective efforts of his brothers to convince him otherwise. Persuasive attempts for him to have his head cut open again were forceful enough to leave a lasting impression on my young memory.

Uncle Fritz, Uncle Eric, and Uncle Gus often came to our house and drank whiskey with Seven Up. This remained dad's favorite alcoholic drink throughout his life. I refused it no matter how thirsty I was, and it was often offered to me when I was a child.

The second story of our house was open from my crib to the stairway. There were different beds in this large un-walled room - more attic then bedroom. I remember navigating the stairs and trying the locked door at the bottom. The stairway was enclosed in darkness but a slit of light showed at the bottom. When the door opened, my eyes were flooded with blinding light. I stood up, walked into the glare, and gradually focused. All the adult men were holding glasses, and dad offered me his. I took a deep sip and spit the liquid into the air. The taste of whiskey overwhelmed the soft drink mixture. It was my first memory of whiskey and Seven Up. Everyone laughed uproariously, for this was a hilarious scene for intoxicated adults.

I don't remember Uncle Gus's funeral, but I remember dad and my uncles drinking afterwards and revisiting their failed attempt to get Uncle Gus to have more surgery. They talked about Uncle Gus going to Heaven and not having any more pain. I knew Heaven was a good place for him because I had met some of the angels. I felt he would be happy there. My dad and uncles talked endlessly about how they wished he would have undergone another operation; the pain of brain surgery was far better than death, they said. I didn't think so. I knew Uncle Gus was happy and at peace in Heaven. I never tried to visit Uncle Gus in Heaven even though I was pretty sure I could. I was afraid to visit Heaven because I thought the angels would not let me go back home again.

Uncle Gus was dead, and once more I went to live with grandma and grandpa on their farm. Grandpa and my dad and uncles had cleared much of the land when they first moved to Wisconsin. Dad told me stories about dynamiting stumps and hacking out tree roots with an axe. He complained until his deathbed how hard grandpa had made him work. It was an excellent piece of land, but land that at the time needed all the hands of ten children. Uncle Bert nurtured the land into a modern farm and retired from it in the 1980s. Dad was the oldest son, and should have inherited the property according to family tradition. But, he was "wild" in his early years and didn't like working with Grandpa, or following Grandpa's rules. Dad adopted Grandpa's stern style with his own children, and saved gentleness for his grandchildren. Intergenerational blindness being in the male genes of our family was something that I naturally inherited.

Like most old two story farmhouses, Grandpa's had steep wooden steps with a large landing at the top that served as a storage area. There were three bedrooms upstairs – two facing east and one to the north. The bedroom on the first floor was the master bedroom for Grandpa and Grandma, and later for my Uncle Bert and Aunt Ethel. When Uncle Gus died I got to sleep in the north bedroom between Uncle Eric and Uncle Fritz. When I tried to crawl over Uncle Eric at night, he would get up and guide me to the night potty near the top of the stairs. It was always Uncle Eric that helped me. He slept on the outside of the bed away from the wall where Uncle Fritz slept. The outside sleeping position was the privileged spot for older brothers.

The many years I shared a bed with my brother, it was the same. In beds that were shared, one's spot was either on the right or left, or possibly in the middle for larger families, and wasn't changed nightly. My spot in my uncles' bed was in the middle; I was less than two years old when I first started sleeping there. The second time I remember staying on Grandma and Grandpa's farm was some time after my refusing to go to Heaven. I don't remember having regained the ability to walk yet, and I couldn't go up or down steps by myself; I remember the steps being too steep and too difficult for me to navigate. One of my uncles carried me to bed, and they must have carried me down in the morning. But, I have no memory of how I got downstairs. I never had any bad memories about living in this house when I was little and learning how to walk again, and I didn't have nightmares there until I was in my teens.

I helped grandma bake bread in the morning when I became stronger. This is my fondest memory of her. Grandma had ten living children, two others she had lost during the hard years before she came to America from the Ukraine. Baking multiple loaves of swartzbrot was an affordable way to feed a large family. The oven would be full of dark rye bread every morning, and the aroma would make my mouth water in anticipation. I stood on grandma's right side in order to be away from the oven and the area were wood was put into the stove. I would stand with my left hand clutching her dress. Her dresses, like those of most farm women, were made of coarse cotton. Flour was marketed in sacks with various colored prints that working people used for clothing. Flour sacks made dresses for females, and cotton shirts for males, and a dozen other clothing items. Women liked colored and floral patterns on their sack-clothes, and men liked solid colors for their shirts.

Grandma, at about five feet one inch, towered over me like a giant bread maker. The first loaf would come out of the oven all golden brown. By that time, I could taste the warm bread and butter just from its aroma. Grandma churned butter herself and added a little salt to make it taste better. She would lift the hot bread out of the oven, place it carefully on the breadboard, and cut off the end. This was called the heel and its crust covered the entire bottom and sides of the first slice. Homemade butter was spread carefully over every inch of the slice. The butter would melt into the warm bread soaking it down to the crust; Grandma was always generous with butter. She would blow cool air over the hot bread long enough to make it the right temperature, and carefully hand it to me. To this day when I spread butter or jam on bread I cover every inch of it the way Grandma did.

By the time Grandma handed me the bread, warm and with that special aroma that only fresh baked rye has, I would be dancing in anticipation – shifting feet back and forth like a child playing hopscotch. I don't recall sitting down, but I do remember using two hands to hold the piece. I didn't eat the bread, I devoured it. It went down as fast as I could chew and swallow. Life-long hot rye bread directly from the oven, smothered in melted butter, competes with any food I have ever eaten. But, I have never found anyone, or any bakery that makes it taste quite as good as Grandma's. Whenever I think of her, which is often, I always think of this special moment by the old wood stove, clutching her dress with my left hand and waiting for nature's most divine food to appear. Most likely, grandma is still baking rye bread in Heaven, and I bet it still tastes the same.

CRYING

The yard in front of Grandma's farm house was part garden and part strawberry patch. Many good things came from this rich black earth: fresh strawberries sprinkled with sugar, strawberry shortcake, strawberry pie, every kind of northern grown vegetable, and a mixture of memories. The first time I recall being lonely enough to cry it was morning and I was eating rye bread with Grandma. Suddenly, I was overcome with sadness. I ran out into the yard near the strawberry patch, laid on the wet grass, and remember sobbing totally out of control. This is the only time I recall crying at her house. Crying was not something that I could do near Madge and feel safe. That moment was completely incompatible with hot rye bread and being with

Grandma. She was always tender with me, but this time her voice was unusually soft and somehow different. She picked me up, sat on the wet grass, and held me tight. Grandma always knew how to make me feel better.

But that moment was different! This feeling of being lonely at Grandma's farm came out of nowhere. It was a strange but still familiar experience. A decision was being made in my mind of its own volition. This moment of transformation would stay with me for many decades. As Grandma held me and rocked back and forth on the wet lawn by the strawberry patch, I came to feel totally cared for and protected. In retrospect, she became my mother of unconditional love and security. Whatever it was that I was missing was permanently erased by Grandma's loving arms.

In the following days, months and years, crying became a feeling that was beyond my emotional capacity. I was about two years old. Giving up crying that day at Grandma's was not the same as making a conscious decision the way I did during my adult years. It was more like placing this part of me in a room and closing the door. Even more accurately, I double locked the door, and bolted it shut.

For the next 40 years I would get tears in my eyes if I had intense pain, but my voice and facial muscles would remain detached and unmoving. Pain and strong emotions took place in my body – not my brain. My eyes would shed a tear or two if I broke a bone, or got hit in the wrong place playing sports, but I never cried. Tears at these times were like sweat. They happened spontaneously. They were a physical not an emotional part of me. I learned to cry with a therapist friend when I was 42 and going through my first divorce. It was a single session, and it was one of the most difficult growth experiences I would have in my entire life. The sensation of crying was totally alien, much like finding my voice speaking a foreign language that I had heard but never studied.

My therapist friend was familiar with much of my childhood background and suggested that I should learn how to cry. I trusted her and agreed. I felt foolish trying, the first attempt was totally artificial, and I wanted to discontinue the effort. She insisted and kept coaching me step by step. At her prompting, I flexed my throat muscles to emit a noise like crying, closing my eyes and forcing tears, and emotionally letting myself go back to the front yard of grandma's house. The process took about an hour with one failed attempt after another. Eventually, disconnected parts of my brain began to merge, and a tear or two came out with muffled cries. The sounds were like something one hears through a thick door, muted – not clear or distinct. The sounds belonged to someone I did not know. The boxes in my brain were reduced by one.

Permission to feel and express past pain through tears gradually came for a few seconds. It was not a flood of long suppressed tears, but I was actually crying. A small sense of relief followed, but most importantly, there was a realization that a part of me had rejoined the world, but I did not yet have a sense of wholeness. What I took away that victorious day was a sense of accomplishment; like finding and placing a difficult piece in a maddening puzzle that had been sitting on the kitchen table for weeks, but, aware that the puzzle was still very incomplete.

When I returned home from the hospital after meeting the angels, I was a happier child. I was changed permanently. In many ways this was my second birth. Over the years, I mentally returned to the hospital numerous times, and relived meeting God's messengers. I thought about myself as a re-born child as I tried to make sense of who I had been and who I was becoming. A new more pleasant inner world with peace of mind began to emerge. I had loving aunts and uncles, and great grandparents, and out-of-body experiences that provided a wonderful sense of freedom. I could escape earthly bounds when I wanted to, and I often did.

Dad told me many times that he had paid for seven different divorces from Madge; that was only one of two names he used to refer to her in my presence, the other being "your mother." He never attached swear words to her name when angry, but demonstrated related negative facial distortions accompanied by intense efforts. They never lasted being separated long enough for the legal waiting period in Wisconsin to take effect. Cohabitation voided their divorce application. On average, these dissolution proceedings were initiated every two years until I was 15. I don't remember consciously ever missing Madge. I missed the meals she offered, when they were offered, but emotionally there was nothing there but a hollow emotional shell. I would live with Grandma and Grandpa during these weeks of separation. I was reunited with Mother-Grandma when I went to the farm, and there enjoyed some of the happiest days of my childhood.

GRANDPA

Grandpa was a gruff and stubborn man. I understood this from being with him so frequently as a child. He was never wrong about anything when talking to Grandma, or my aunts or uncles. But to me and his other grandchildren, he was a different person. He was gentle, kind, and as attentive as Grandma, except he didn't hold me or feed me rye bread. Grandpa had been in the Russian Army at the time of the Russo-Japanese conflict. He was with one of the cavalry units at the war's front when struck by pneumonia. The Japanese had taken Port Arthur, now the modern Chinese city of Dalian, and were pushing across Manchuria toward Harbin. The Japanese had superior radio communications and military strategy compared to General Kuropatkin's forces. Some Russian troops marched into battle in formation, lined up like puppets before the unbelieving Japanese, and were mowed down like sheep in the barnyard. Many of the superstitious Russians believed that holy crosses around their necks would make them immune from Japanese bullets. The Japanese keep a room full of these crosses in one of their Tokyo war museums.

There is a vague tale in my memory of Grandpa walking back to safety through part of Manchuria. I picture his horse being shot out from under him and Grandpa walking back through tall red sorghum, common at the time, to Russian lines. Grandpa came down with pneumonia while deployed and it probably saved his life, thereby creating my story. I don't know if this memory is accurate or not, but he was returned to Moscow and fulfilled the rest of his military commitment there.

Grandpa was an excellent horseman and could jump over the animal from back to front by only touching the saddle once in transit. As a six foot tall soldier, he met the requirements to become a member of the Czar's personal guard in Moscow. I loved his stories even though grandma objected that they were inappropriate for a three year old. I don't recall him telling me stories before I was three, although he probably did. All of the men in our family thought they were born storytellers. This was how farm people passed their time before the days of television and home movies. Family members, like all storytellers, competed with each other to improve the telling of their stories with one more version and attention getting twist. The best stories often involved tricks that were played on family or friends, or something that was presented as real but well beyond belief.

My favorite Grandpa story is one about a notorious murderer who had been imprisoned in Moscow. I didn't understand how Grandpa got to know this man, and I no longer remember the criminal's name. Nevertheless, they knew each other by sight. The criminal had escaped from the Czar's prison after Grandpa had returned to the Ukraine from his tour of duty. Grandpa was in Kiev's open market and recognized the notorious felon in the crowd. Worst of all, they recognized each other. Grandpa knew the desperate man would try to kill him as he was the only person in the Ukraine who could provide positive identification. Grandpa lived in a small German-Ukrainian farming village between the atomic disaster site of Chernobyl and Kiev. Close enough to Kiev to go to and return by horse in the same day.

Grandpa returned home that afternoon by horse and wagon in order to do his evening chores. He was in the barn after milking when he saw a man's shadow appear in the moonlit barnyard. I understood that milking was finished, and Grandpa was just pretending to be busy caring for the cattle. Grandpa had been watching for the criminal to come, and when he saw the man's shadow, he grabbed the pitchfork that he had placed behind the barn door and waited for him to enter. I was poised breathless at this point waiting to hear what happened when Grandma interrupted. She told grandpa that I was not old enough to hear such stories, and insisted he stop. He protested and argued for a moment or two, but gave in to her demands. When Grandma left, I asked Grandpa what happened. He looked at me with that serious expression he had when thinking deeply and said, "You know."

Yes, I knew. I am sure that if I go to Grandpa's old farm in the Ukraine, and could locate his barnyard, I would find the bones of one of Russia's most notorious criminals slowly turning to dust. Grandpa was full of great stories, and I would sit in rapture listening to tales about this strange world and the far-away places that had made up his former life. Grandpa was 69 or 70 years old at that time, and left the heavy work to his sons. I got to spend most of the day tagging after him. We were "two peas in a pod," as I remember Dad and the uncles describing our relationship. Teasing Grandpa, they said that we were each capable of the same amount of work. Grandpa never smiled at these comments, but neither did he offer an alternative interpretation. He would just motion to me with his head and away we would go to find another distraction free of cryptic comments.

Summer turned into fall and we were living on the hill near the south end of Beaver Dam Lake. Brother Bud was in school, and I would have been three years old. I didn't cry anymore, I had given up being lonely, and I could fly. The world was now mostly a friendly place. The only bad people in my life were the Wops and Dagos. These were people my brother frequently fought with after school. When my brother wasn't around, the younger Wops were nice to me and we played together. My brother didn't like this and would make me go home when he caught us playing together. I only knew they were Wops or Dagos when he told me; our English was the same, we liked the same games, and many other people had brown eyes. In fact, I don't even remember noticing eye color when I was little, and I surely didn't notice any difference in skin tones. As children in those days, we all lived out-of-doors. That is where play happened, not in front of computers or TV sets.

GRANDMA

By the time I was three years old I had lived in five different houses. That is, if I don't count the times I lived at Grandma and Grandpa's farm. Grandma was always more like my mother than Madge. She was gentle, loving and stayed home every day to take care of me. I never remember being hungry or thirsty at Grandma's. She was an amazing person; she never raised her voice to me, and I never said no to her. I could sit and talk to her for hours. Talking about nothing special at all with Grandma was similar to lying in the sun on a warm summer day. My cares would simply float away as I experienced the contentment and unconditional love she offered. If you had met Grandma on the street or in a store shopping you'd think she was just an ordinary farmer's wife raising children and trying to lead a good life; an ordinary person who quietly sets foot on this planet, leads and uneventful life, and just as quietly fades into the bland history that is the fate for most of us. You would have been wrong!

My favorite grandma story is about wolves in the Ukraine. Grandpa was away in the Russian Army and Grandma was at home with three little children. A pack of wolves had surrounded her small isolated winter cottage on the Steppe, and were threateningly jumping at the window glass. When she told me this story it came with all the drama of tightened body and facial muscles, with the intensity of reliving an experience that was permanently etched into her visual memory, a survival lesson that she would never forget. Grandma had this magical way of saying things without actually saying them. She was like a grandmaster of the theatre to me, pausing at the right moment, able to convey deep thoughts with a simple but subtle glance, or slight turn of her head. I studied Grandma when she told me stories the way hungry children study bakery goods through store windows.

Grandma said she knew that the wolves would eventually break through the single glass barrier and was racking her brain for some way to keep them at bay. She didn't have a gun, only kitchen utensils to meet their attack. I remember how she paused and thought about what items she had in her small hut, but I can't remember what they all were. Finally, grandma explained how she heated water until it was boiling hot, slowly and carefully opened the door and threw the scalding weapon on the pack's leader. The scourge of the Ukrainian Steppes fled from gentle Grandma's cruel act of survival, howling in pain with the rest of the pack in obedient pursuit. Throughout grandma's story I could see and feel her reliving the moment. Memory is so much more vivid than the silver screen.

Grandma had special ways of doing everything. She never bragged and in fact made it clear that what I thought were heroic acts were simply everyday events – for Grandma, they were. Her stories, like Grandpa's, were special in the telling – thick German accents punctuated with pauses that often meant a search for that hard to find English word, as German learned later in life was carefully translated into English for her grandson. My aunts and uncles couldn't tell stories the way Grandma and Grandpa could, their English held no hint of mixed German-English sounds that required careful listening, listening that added mystery to stories of a strange world with hidden meanings. Recalling my grandparents' stories clears my brain of foggy thoughts and cobwebs the way a good shower cleaned my body after a dirty sweaty day of physically working the good earth in days gone by.

Other times, Grandma told me about her struggle to survive while Grandpa was away saving Mother Russia from the Japanese. She never talked about hard times in a complaining voice and I don't think she was even capable of sniveling tones. She described the bleakness of the Ukrainian winter landscape, her struggle to provide food for her children, and her dreams of coming to America. Dad's short stature, compared to his brothers, was attributed to the near starvation he had experienced as a child during those lonely years on the Steppe. When grandpa came back from Moscow after his tour of duty had ended, and the first time she had seen him since his being inducted into service, he had been persuaded by the Czar's propaganda to move to Siberia. Grandma was determined, she thought Siberia was a bleak, god-forsaken place, and refused to go. Siberia, I knew from her voice and physical posture, was even more remote and isolated than their bleak, isolated Steppe farm, which demanded endless labor for day-to-day survival. Grandma's stories were as interesting as Grandpa's and often they were just as exciting.

Dad was six years old when our family came to America. He would sometimes talk about the Ukraine, his memories of the boat trip, and first impressions of this new land. He told me of eating various "weeds" when he was a child in Ukraine –

dandelion tops and their cooked roots, constant hunger, and day-to-day struggle to survive until Grandpa returned, the clandestine train ride to Bremen, Germany, from Kiev in the middle of the night, their wait for boat transportation to America, money sent from Iowa for passage, the stench of cheap boat passage, and limited small portions of food. Dad's memory was always much better than mine. His memory was like a printed computer screen as he could just look up and read whatever he wanted to; there was no waiting period. He never had to turn pages the way I still do.

My grandparents could not afford transportation to America in 1908. Times were hard in Russia and early revolutionary protests and uprisings had occurred during the time of the Russo-Japanese War of 1904-1905 while grandpa was away saving the Russian people. Grandpa was a great horseman in my eyes and he spoke with pride about his affection for the Czar and the royal family. However, ethnic conflict was often played out through internal struggles with one group taking revenge on the other for real or imagined mistreatment or privileges. Jews were attacked by Russian Nationals; whole German-Ukranian villages were destroyed while additional conflicts were common amongst worker groups tossed into the ranks of the unemployed. As suicidal passion built for revolution in Odessa and Kiev, the most elemental conditions necessary for our Ukranian relatives' survival gradually evaporated.

My grandparents got travel money from Grandpa's sister in Sheldon, Iowa, took the train from Kiev to Bremen, Germany, and arranged ship passage to Ellis Island New York. Dad was six years old when he first stepped off the boat in New York, but in hindsight my grandparents seemed as naive about America as he was. Various dockside vendors were hawking their wares and one of them gave each member of our family a piece of pie; a rare delicacy to weary travelers fresh from the stinking conditions of cheap boat passage. America was a wonderful place, a land of opportunity, and a new home where dreams became real, a place where delicacies such as fruit pie were given away. Then the vendor demanded money, the pies had been eaten, and payment was to be made. Fortunately, the man had not befriended the family by offering to help them with their luggage; a sad fact common to many immigrants who lost their total life possessions this way. But unfortunately, the pies were too sweet in contrast to the limited, bland food eaten in transit; everyone's stomach rebelled and the pies were lost.

All that remained of their passage money when they arrived in Sheldon by train was a few Russian coins, coins which I still have tucked away with thousands of old memories. They were now a family of five people, and were totally dependent on sibling generosity. Using her sister-in-law's German-English dictionary, Grandma began to teach her family English – one word at a time, and when dad told me this story he emphasized – one word at a time. Dad started first grade with this handful of English words; undoubtedly patched together with his native German. He told me how he was physically hit and beaten by his young classmates almost daily until he was able to converse in their language. Real Americans spoke English, and everybody else was fair game; a language ritual still common across America, and only less frequently played out when I was a child.

The paranoia that accompanied foreign language speakers in America was not only real to dad but to my grandparents, aunts and uncles. Whenever I would attempt to speak German as a child, my German-Ukrainian family would stop me. I remember how forceful Grandma was – with wagging finger she would say: "You're American, speak English!" And so it was, I spoke English and corrupted German beyond what is acceptable to polite intercourse. This language ritual was repeated by countless immigrants across America, and is still present in the "English only" ranting that even now frequently occur; even the physical encounters prevail – only now they are more ruthless and often gang motivated.

Grandpa knew six languages before being forced to learn English, and had been offered a full-time job in Bremen, Germany, as a translator. In 1908 he was 39 years old, and small Iowa towns had little use for translators who didn't speak English. Grandpa got a job working on the railroad and the family started saving money for its own American dream; land of their own, land that no one could take away, land that was free of revolutionaries, land that could be passed on to sons.

Before grandpa went to work on the railroad, he had interviewed with a local Sheldon, Iowa, farmer for a job. Everything Grandpa knew about farming with horses was still done the same way in 1908 in Northern Iowa. Desperate Grandpa was satisfied with the farmer's explanation and readily accepted the job. He asked where he would sleep and was told the haymow. That was fine, said Grandpa in what would have been excellent German, "But where does my family sleep?"

"To hell with your family," was the farmer's reply.

"To hell with your job," was Grandpa's.

This story retold to me years later became: "To hell mit yur yob."

Grandma was a library of information about the family. She knew every child, rarely had to look up a birthday, and proudly reviewed each of her sons and daughters children, their children, and in her final years, their children. In my last two years of high school, I would put the lawn mower in the trunk of dad's car and drive over to mow her lawn. Grandpa was dead by then having died of colon cancer. I would just stop the car by the road, take out the mower and start working. When the lawn was done, Grandma would appear at her front door and wave me in. This meant cookies, homemade breads, or some kind of special treat. She kept a reserve of different "goodies" just for these special moments.

Grandma and I would talk until I had to leave for work, the same way we always talked – me hanging on her every word. Her favorite activity in her final years was to show me pictures of all the family. The last time she went through this routine she stopped at 132. "I know I have 132 children, grandchildren…great grandchildren, and great-great grandchildren," she said. This time, however, her face became troubled. She paused, confused, and said, "I don't know."

"What don't you know, Grandma?"

"I don't know how many there are."

For the first time in all my years with Grandma, I realized that she had failed her duty as the family's matriarch – to keep track of every family member. Her greatest maternal responsibility, knowing every person in her lineage had become muddled and was at risk. I couldn't help her, and went to work struggling to find a way. I had never seen Grandma this troubled before, and it was the last time she ever showed me the family albums.

CHAPTER 3
FIRST WASHINGTON TRIP

Dad liked muscle cars, the bigger and faster they were the more he liked them, but the first car I remember was a meek Model A, and this would have been in 1938. At least I thought it was a Model A, but my brother corrected my memory. It was a Graham model from about 1930. It had four doors with the back doors opening against the wind, suicide doors, a design that tossed dozens of careless children like me into ditches along the roadside. I once started to open the driver's side back door while the car was gliding to a stop. Fighting with both hands and braced feet to stay in the car as it again picked up speed, the wind was winning the fight when my brother grabbed the door handle and pulled it shut.

I never felt the wind when I flew over the countryside. Being out-of-body was as carefree as lazy thoughts effortlessly passing through my relaxed brain, so the wind's force on the door totally caught me by surprise. There was a thin line between nature's reality and that of my young mind.

I could see over the back seat if I stood on the drive train hump in the middle of the floor. I wasn't able to enjoy my bird-like perch for long as it meant that I was blocking the view for my eight year old brother and four year old sister; mostly my eight year old brother's. Anyway, it was a great car specially built for someone just my size. I often stood up, expectantly peering down the road looking for the next great adventure, while my brother and sister looked out the side windows or slept.

Little sister June was about one year old and rode up front between Madge and Dad. As we drove down the highway, her diapers would air dry tied to the passenger side rearview mirror where they didn't interfere with Dad's driving. June always had clean, dry diapers as they were washed out in the streams along the side of the road, or at gas station restrooms. The rural folks heading west in "The Grapes of Wrath" had nothing on our family; we were resourceful people – survivors – and we traveled light.

There were tramps everywhere during the Great Depression. Mother never said no to tramps when they begged for food; always made them sandwiches, or gave them something else to eat. They'd come to our house and beg for food, but it was scary at night when they came after dark. They didn't ask, or at least I don't think they did, but often slept in the barn, sheds, or other buildings on our properties. Our dog would bark into the blackness when the tramps made noises in the outbuildings. Dad often tended bar at night, and this particular time we were living in another old rental house south of Island City on County Highway T. Mother's voice was filled with fear as she peered into the night. I was hanging onto her dress and she kept asking over and over again, "who's there," and noises kept coming from the shed out back, but no one answered. Mother was afraid of tramps and she was afraid of the dark, but that night her fear driven voice kept demanding an answer from the tramp, an answer that never came. She was like a moth drawn to a flame.

"Who's there, who's there?"

I stood with my left hand, always my left hand, clutching her cotton dress with the little comfort that cloth-in-hand provides a frightened child, and locked the moment into memory.

WASHINGTON

In 1938 dad decided to move to Washington State. Leaving Wisconsin made us all feel happy, and dad said there were good jobs in Washington. His restless mind demanded only the smallest speck of information to justify these cross-country moves. Mother was happy to get away from the scary tramps that crept through the night, happy to get away from one more isolated stretch of country road, the drudgery of washboards, and four unwanted children. Dad heard about work constructing a new dam on the Columbia River; work that paid good wages, maybe even enough money to think about a future beyond filling the mouths of hungry children and providing a meager living for an unhappy wife. The rumors were correct, and he quickly got a laborer's job helping pour cement high on the dam's rim.

Living at the construction site below Grand Coulee Dam was like watching a concrete mountain being pushed skyward. We lived in what was called a "worker's shack" at the base of the dam. The shack was made of rough hewn boards; floors were the same, and the shack had one moveable wooden step by the front door. Nothing was painted either inside or out. From this wooden step, I could either walk out front into the common area, or stand on the step to watch the dam's construction. Welding lights flashed almost continuously from the face of this stone monster, and I was instructed not to watch them, because somehow the flashing lights would burn holes in my eyes. This I didn't understand, and more than once I went to bed with little needles stuck in my eyeballs. The common area in front of our shack was either mud or dirt depending on the rain – or maybe it was water from the Columbia. I preferred mud; I liked the feeling of it squishing between my toes as the cool mud carried away the heat of Western Washington's summer sun.

Dad didn't stay at Grand Coulee long. He had been working high on the dam when another worker just like him fell into the fresh cement as it was being poured and was swept away. I asked him how they got this guy out, and dad said they couldn't; the man would always be part of Grand Coulee. He was squashed to nothing by the heavy concrete and would be part of the dam forever – an instant worker burial. Dad said there were other workers who had fallen into the cement. The dam was their tomb, a monument to cheap disposable labor. Their bodies were sucked into the liquid stone as they gradually disappeared. After this incident, whenever I looked at the dam, I had the impression of ghost like figures floating through the cement, and being projected off its face for all to see. To my young mind, they floated in and out of the concrete, haunting Grand Coulee as long as their tomb remains.

I still visualize these ghost-like images after all these years. I thought about this poor construction worker not being able to breathe in this human quicksand; freshly poured concrete choking off his breath, his mouth and ears filling up, and then his body being crushed. Being reduced to a grease spot by tons of cement was extremely frightening to me, but the thought of the man struggling to breathe as fresh cement filled his lungs was even scarier. I didn't like to think about anyone dying from cement-suffocation, and suffocation was the one thing I feared. It wasn't fun watching the dam being built after that, and happily Dad decided to leave. His eyes projected fear of the dam; a giant come to life ready to devour any careless or overly tired worker making a wrong step. Dad was afraid of death, and his entire demeanor conveyed an image of the grim reaper stalking him high on the dam. Dad and Madge packed up the car a few days later and we all left for Everett. Undoubtedly, the wait depended only on pay day.

Our earthly goods easily fit into the car's trunk in 1938; the only items in our car were Dad's coffee, makings for sandwiches and drinks, and June's diapers. Our moving mostly depended on having enough gas money, and a couple extra dollars for bread and peanut butter, and always a little for Dad's whiskey when we got to our destination, and both chewing and smoking tobacco.

We lived a few blocks off what is now Everett's Interstate 5 North Exit. My brother Bud showed me where the missing house used to be when we visited there in 1994. We lived on the second story with our front door and stairway descending directly to the street. I don't remember much about the inside of this house; the front stoop overlooking the street was my main source of entertainment.

There was a black man who walked by almost every day. I asked him if he was a Nigger, because that's what white folks called black people in 1938. He was the first black person I had ever seen. The old man carefully walked halfway up the steps and in a gentle voice told me that Nigger was a bad word and I shouldn't use it any more. He didn't try to scare me, and was like my own grandpa except he was black and didn't have an accent. I decided not to call him Nigger after that and stopped. Nigger was a word like Wop and Dago, words that just got people in trouble. Afterwards, he waved to me as he walked by while I sat searching the world and the street for whatever excitement it had to offer, or maybe I was just waiting for him to wave.

Ebe Slough is just across Interstate Highway 5 and old State Highway 99 on Everett's Eastside, but Interstate 5 didn't exist when we lived there. All the houses in Ebe Slough were on stilts because the water backed up every few years from Puget Sound and flooded the entire marsh. I liked living on stilts, and I liked Ebe Slough. Homes on stilts were giant tree houses, and that's how I thought of ours. I could look out the windows into the slough in all four directions, and at the big water pipe that came down from the mountains to our south. Dad didn't like living on stilts and had the house lowered to the ground, an act that forced me outside and into new adventures. Soon afterwards, other neighbors began taking their houses' stilts off too.

Ebe Slough still floods periodically, and most of the remaining homes partially go underwater, but some people were smart and simply enclosed the stilts with wooden walls. This made one story stilt houses look like two story homes, and the buildings remained elevated above the periodic floods. I noticed this construction choice when my siblings and I visited there in 1994, but by then our old house had burnt to the ground, and all that remained was our collective memories.

My brother Bud played with a neighbor boy by the name of Little Everett. I would beg them to take me along on their adventures exploring the slough, but my legs were too short to keep up. I got to know a small part of the slough near our house, mostly swampland where water overflowed inland from the Sound, or spring rains created a forest of tall grasses. A big water pipe came down from the mountains, passed through Ebe Slough, and continued on into Everett. Bud and Little Everett often explored the area under the pipe as they could follow it for miles in either direction toward the mountains or the city. It was only a few blocks away from our house and I could walk there by myself. I was afraid to follow the pipe very far, and stayed close enough to see our house when I was by myself.

I was now four years old and spent most of my days alone. Madge would leave with June and Vonna most mornings and come back in the late afternoon or evening, depending on Dad's work schedule. She only took June with her when Vonna was in school. She never took me, because Madge said that boys could take care of themselves. Dad was far away driving truck, and came home on weekends. He was supporting the war effort by working construction on Whidbey Island. Bud would help me find food when he was home during the day, and sometimes Madge would leave bread on the cupboard after breakfast. Usually Bud spent his days either playing or exploring with Little Everett, or was at school.

MOUNTAIN LION

Bud and Little Everett were bursting with excitement one spring afternoon. A mountain lion had been sighted in the slough, and they were full of talk about lion hunting. People said winter had been hard that year with deep crippling snow in the mountains, and thought the lion probably came down because he was hungry. I knew Bud and Little Everett were going out to find him and I wanted to be taken along. They laughed and ran away; I was too little for lion hunting. The boys headed in the direction of the water pipe at a running pace, quickly outdistancing me. I followed far to the rear even though they had disappeared under the big pipe and out of sight. But finding a mountain lion was a big adventure, and I wasn't going to be left out.

When I got near, the boys were just standing side-by-side looking in the direction of the mountain. I yelled at them to wait, but they didn't answer and they didn't move. Delighted to find them, I ran to catch up, stepped between them, and looked a crouching cougar square in its eyes. The lion was so close that he could jump on me without even taking a step. I felt I could reach out and put my hand in its mouth. I knew then why Bud and Little Everett were standing motionless without talking. I didn't know what to do. I was a half-step closer to the lion then they were and staring directly into the huge cat's eyes while out-of-control tension in my body continued to grow. The slits in the beast's saucer-like yellow eyes held me motionless, eyes that were as big as baseballs seemed to be hungrily focused only on me. I stood staring and unmoving. Time stopped, held me motionless, and left me in this locked gaze with the feline monster. It might have been seconds or minutes but it was a forever memory.

Finally, I turned my head just enough to look for Bud and he was gone. I looked the other way and Little Everett was gone. I was staring down the mountain lion by myself. Now fear took control of my entire body. I remember thinking that if I run he will jump on me. If I keep staring into his eyes, and he is really big, he will jump on me. Either way I am going to be eaten. In panic I turned and ran faster than I had ever remembered my legs moving. My spine surged with strange sensations as I ran. I expected to feel the lion's teeth sinking into my back with every step and my skin began to crawl on its own volition.

As I turned and fled from the lion, I saw the boys watching at a safe distance far down the path. I had stared down the lion long enough for them to reach the intersection to our house a block or two away. My little legs stroked the wind like wings, and my body soared. I caught up with them and then turned to look for the lion, but he was gone. They walked me home, one on either side, talking excitedly, and didn't even try to ditch me. They went from neighbor to neighbor telling their story about the lion with tones of lion hunter bravery and salvation for little brother.

The neighbors called the police who came with guns and searched the area. The officers looked for hours but the lion was nowhere to be found. We were all to stay in after dark in case the hungry animal was still nearby. All the boys in the neighborhood were told not to look for the lion any more, and everyone was to stay out of the slough for the next few days.

The neighbors excitedly talked about how Bud and Little Everett had stared down the lion. A cougar coming into our little settlement created as much talk as the Japanese bombing Pearl Harbor. I tried to add my story, but no one listened to me. I was only four years old, and Bud and Little Everett were big. Bud was ten and Little Everett was 12 or 13. The crouching mountain lion's image became permanently burned into my brain, and I still see him clearly whenever I tell this story to my grandchildren. Many times I've thought about why the lion hadn't eaten me. Was it because Bud and Little Everett stopped to watch as the cat's gaze held me motionless? I wondered as I got older, did they save me, or did I save them?

MOTHER'S BEATINGS - BOWS AND ARROWS

Ebe Slough was the first house in which I remember mother screaming. Men were always coming to the house, or Madge would walk a few blocks and disappear into their cars. When men came to our back door, we children were sent out to play. Mother would stay inside with the men and lock all the doors.

Dad came home early one weekend when a man was still in bed with mother. He banged on the door with his hands and feet until she opened it. Her lover climbed out of the window, shimmied down the two story drain pipe into the dirty water from the kitchen, and ran. Dad locked the doors, and mother screamed as though she were being murdered. The neighbors even came out to listen, but not interfere. Her face was red and puffy days afterwards and she wouldn't leave the house until her bruises disappeared. When the marks were gone, she once again left in the morning and returned later in the afternoon.

Dad was a cruel person according to mother, and deserved to be beaten silly, maybe even more. She in turn was an innocent, helpless woman who did not deserve this beast for a husband. As children, we were told these facts repeatedly, often with murderous overtones added in.

My older sister and brother were both in school when I was four. Mother took June along during her almost daily trips, leaving me at home. June was still too little to take care of herself, although by the next year when June was five, she was left to help one of our neighbors baby sit.

From Ebe Slough there is a big hill that goes up to Lake Stevens to the east of Everett. Dad bought 20 acres of an old run-down fruit farm on top of this hill, about half a mile from the west side of the lake itself. The property had a two story wooden frame house, a huge bolder from the last glacier on its front lawn, and a small building where fruit could be processed and stored. This farm was a great place to live. There were no houses between ours and the top of the hill that overlooked the slough, a wooded area of about a mile or so in depth. I found endless places to explore, trees to climb, and freedom to do whatever I wanted. I was five years old now and able to make my own toys.

My favorite toy was a bow with arrows. I could find plentiful materials for both in the woods, and I had a pocketknife that dad gave me. This was a special gift for a five year old. It was a real knife with two blades, and dad showed me how to keep the blades sharp with a whetstone. Most boys who had pocketknives were already in school. I used the knife to make any toy I wanted. Good string came with flour sacks and I used it for my bow. Arrows were harder to make as green branches were heavy and not straight. One day I discovered old wooden shingles which made perfect arrows. I could whittle the thick end of the shingle to a point and this extra weight at the front made the arrows fly far and straight. I practiced making bows until I got the arrows to fly much higher than the tree tops. I would lose them if I shot toward the woods, so I started shooting them in the direction of our back yard. One day I hit my sister Vonna and she went to mother crying. I didn't mean to hurt her, it was an accident. Madge took my bow and arrows away, broke them up, and forcefully forbid me from making any more.

I had spent many days making bow and arrows, and was lost without them. Outside of climbing trees and exploring the nearby woods, this had been my major source of entertainment. I needed something new to play with and saw pictures of soldiers coming down with parachutes. I liked the idea. It seemed to me that parachutes and umbrellas were just about the same thing. I found an old umbrella and experimented to see if it would work like a parachute. I climbed on a nearby fence with the open umbrella and jumped. It caught the wind and let me float down. I climbed on other things around the yard and gently drifted to the ground, but everything I jumped from was low and I couldn't glide the way soldiers did when they dived out of airplanes. I decided to try jumping from the roof of the house, visualizing flying with the umbrella the way paratroopers drifted from airplanes. Using an umbrella would give my body a chance to fly too. I climbed out of the upstairs window onto the roof, opened the umbrella, and jumped. The umbrella held momentarily and then all the spines gave way. I hit the ground hard, broken umbrella still in hand. I was sore but able to stand and walk. I decided that flying the way the angels did was safer and never tried jumping with another umbrella; besides, there weren't any other umbrellas.

Mother had many men friends with Dad being absent throughout the week, and most days went to visit them. I was gradually able to identify some of the different cars parked down our street and would watch mother get into them and disappear for the day, with or without my sisters. However, I specifically recall one large black car because it was uncommon looking, expensive, and the driver dressed in fancier clothes than other people I knew. Sometimes sister Vonna would go with Madge when she was not in school, or would be sent to help neighbors with their younger children. June almost always went with mother until she was about five years old, and old enough to help one of our neighbors with their diapered baby. Our neighbor bragged about June's ability to change diapers, and Dad expressed surprise that June was left alone for short periods with the baby. I can see the neighbor woman laughing at Dad's concern while she extolled June's babysitting ability.

Brother Bud was almost 12 years old and breaking horses on a nearby farm. Bud knew how to talk to horses. Sometimes he would ride a newly broken horse over to our house and show me. I thought unbroken horses bucked people off, but Bud told me they only did that to people who were mean and ignorant about breaking them. The horses seemed to understand Bud when he talked. He was a horse whisperer, but I didn't know what a horse whisperer was in those days.

Bud was either in school or at the farm, generally coming home in the evening just to sleep. He even ate most of his evening meals there. When I got hungry, I could sometimes find bread and butter or jam. Dry cereals were much too expensive and milk was not always available anyway. I would have eaten cereals by the handful if they had been available, and washed them down with well water. If I couldn't find anything to eat at home, I explored the neighborhood.

The neighbor on the south side of our property raised strawberries. I ate some almost every day for a long time, but finally got a rash over my entire body including my scalp and the bottoms of my feet. All I had eaten that day was strawberries, and I had stuffed myself. Strawberries didn't seem to stick to my ribs the way potatoes or corn did. The rash covered every inch of me and I itched unbearably.

This particular day must have been a Friday, and mother got home well before Dad but wasn't concerned about the itching and hurried off to prepare supper. I was still scratching when he arrived later that evening. Dad wanted to know what I had been doing, and I showed him the strawberry patch. He made me apologize to the neighbor for eating his berries without asking.

The neighbor was a kind man and showed me trees with Bing cherries and apples on another part of his property. He said I could eat as many apples and cherries I wanted, but strawberries were special because he sold them for money. I was happy, because Bing cherries and apples were delicious and didn't give me a rash.

JAPANESE SUBMARINE

Mother practiced covering the windows at night for what everyone called "blackouts." Watch people came around the neighborhood and checked to see if any light was getting out through the covered windows. This was necessary because the radio announced that a "Jap" submarine had been spotted in the Sound, and "Jap" was the name everyone used. I didn't know they were Japanese until well after World War II was over. Dad thought this story was made up to scare people so they would practice the blackouts. The Japs had bombed Pearl Harbor, they were bad people, and might bomb Seattle and Everett too.

I had continuous nightmares as I thought about the Japs coming to get me. The nightmares were always the same. They would catch me, and I'd be on their submarine being held face down as they started preparations to make me into a flag stand. I never understood why they needed a five year old boy for a flag stand, but it didn't matter. They would start drilling a hole in my lower back, the pressure would become intense, and just at the point of my spine snapping I would escape. This dream continued nightly, and the pain was always in my lower back. Before the Japs could make me into a flag stand, I would escape by flying. I wouldn't fly off the ship because I was afraid of drowning, and besides, I didn't know in which direction land was located.

There was an opening in the middle of their submarine that went all the way down to the water. This hole didn't seem strange to my five year old brain, but later I knew I was interpreting it as being the hold of a ship. I would escape by jumping into the hole, and as I fell, I would concentrate hard and begin to fly. Actually, it was more like floating in the air; intense concentration felt like braking one's car. Mentally focusing brought my body to a stalled position as my fall came to an end, and the effect of gravity was neutralized by my mind. I could always get away, but the Japs would come back the next night, capture me, and start drilling in my lower back again. Nightly the whole scenario kept repeating. Flying and nightmares went together with my ability to fly being the source of my rescue or salvation. However, flying before going to sleep was never accompanied by trauma that I can remember. This difference never seemed strange to my child's mind.

I told mother about the "Japs" capturing me and taking me to their submarine. She said that if I ever hit bottom in the submarine's hole I would die. This frightened me as I didn't want to die. I would concentrate hard in order to keep myself suspended; I never hit the water, and the Japs always failed to get me out of the hole. It was a safe place, except I couldn't leave the submarine's hollow interior without them catching me. As I floated in the middle of their submarine, I would drop off to sleep. I was never able to return to my bed any other way from this entrapment; I just went back to sleep floating in the middle of that Japanese submarine.

Some nights I would go flying when I first went to bed. Flying made me feel good. I liked the feeling of levitating my body, and I did this consciously, skimming over the countryside and being free. I'd focus hard, float upward, slip through the roof of the house, and fly low over the ground. I never figured out how I could pass through the roof without making a hole. Sometimes I would even practice repeatedly passing back and forth through the ceiling, but never understood how this worked.

In these early childhood days, the sensation of flying always included my physical body and not just my spirit. I actually flew. There was only one reality. Flying helped me relax, and some nights I could avoid having nightmares by flying when I first went to bed. This specific nightmare stopped after we moved back to Wisconsin.

STUTTERING AND BED WETTING

During the time I had nightmares about the Japanese, I began to have a problem with stuttering. The more I tried not to stutter the more I stut-stut-stuttered. Rather quickly, half of my speech was made up of repeating words and this amount was increasing steadily.

Dad was still away from home most of the time, and only came back on weekends. He was angry at my stuttering and told me to stop. I asked him how, and he always said the same thing, that I should "use my mind." Dad believed that people could just think unwanted behavior away. He told me that he could use his mind this way, and I could too if I just tried harder.

For Dad, keeping bad habits was another form of laziness. On the other hand, getting drunk, smoking cigarettes, having girl friends, and chewing tobacco weren't bad habits. I tried thinking about not stuttering, but it didn't work. Dad talked to me again, and told me to think about not stuttering before I began talking. I practiced this idea, and it worked; I stopped stuttering after a few days. I thought Dad was smart about how we could use our minds to control our bodies. Unconsciously, I was becoming a believer.

The stuttering stopped and bed wetting started. This made Madge angry because she had to wash my bedding every day. It also made my brother Bud angry as we shared the same bed, and nightly he was getting soaked in urine. Mother told me to stop, saying that I should get up at night and go to the bathroom. This house had an indoor bathroom, but I couldn't wake up by myself. Madge didn't tell me how either. She just insisted that I stop. Finally, she got violently angry. Her face became twisted and she looked like another person. Her eyes bugged out, I could see the veins in her neck, and her mouth looked like a witch's. She grabbed me, and pushed my face hard across the urine soaked sheets. I could feel the urine burn into my face as the skin came off, and I fought hard. The more I fought, the harder she rubbed the foul smelling urine and salt into my raw skin. Suddenly my body went completely limp. I didn't consciously try to relax; my body just took control as though it were disconnected from my mind. My arms and legs flipped about like a rag doll. Mother was now free to thoroughly thrash me, and thrash me she did.

Abruptly she stopped, and a funny look came over the evil mask she was wearing. Her eyes went back into her head, the twisted mouth relaxed, and she acted confused. She looked at me as though it were the first time we had ever met. Her hands dropped and she let me go. I got up off the wet bed leaving Madge totally engrossed in her hands; a strange sight as she seemed to be examining each and every line. I went into the small room by the back door that was next to my bedroom, knelt down on the floor, and began banging my head on the wooden boards. The harder I banged the better I felt. The pain from my skinned face was forgotten as I pounded harder and harder. I felt like breaking my head open and letting the useless parts of my brain go free.

Mother appeared and pulled me up. She told me to stop. I didn't want to stop and began banging my head on the wall; head banging felt good and harder head banging felt even better. Madge then wrapped her arms and legs around me until I settled down. Head banging miraculously helped me stop bedwetting, and I never wet the bed again. After that episode of beating my head silly, I could wake up in the middle of the night by myself and use the bathroom. It was a miraculous learning experience, such a simple way to stop bedwetting. It was an experience I didn't understand then.

Mother and Brother Bud were both happy. I felt like I had grown up. I only banged my head when no one was around after that, and whenever my body refused to comply with adult demands. Madge said she thought I was ready for school, and it would be starting in a few weeks. I was excited about going to school. Bud and Vonna attended school, and had wonderful stories about friends, games, and everything that went on there. The one thing I remember most about going to school the first day was having new shoes, and they came with an unfamiliar item – socks. I still wasn't old enough to have underwear like Dad and my older brother, but I had new shoes and socks just like the other kids.

SCHOOL

School started and I was in first grade. We didn't have kindergarten in Ebe Slough, so this was my first experience in the classroom. I had been waiting for weeks to go, and couldn't have been more excited. My first grade teacher was young and looked like my Aunt Arline – small, pretty, gentle, and with a soft voice. She had books, a whole box full of chalk, and toys. She had a separate room full of toys. Teacher told us that when we finished our lessons we could play in this magical toy room. I had never seen so many toys, and they were all store-bought. Our first lesson, at least the one I remember, was to memorize our ABCs. Teacher went over the capital letters, and then the small letters with all of us repeating after her. Then she drew the big letters and the small letters one at a time, and we got to draw each one after her. It was easy because she had a big chart on the wall with arrows that we could follow when drawing our own letters.

"When you learn all your letters," she said, "you can go next door and play." I asked if I could play with any toy I wanted to and she said yes. I could hardly believe that any and all toys in that room were available. All I had to do was remember letters. I wrote all the letters again just to make sure I knew each one, and went to the toy room. Teacher called me back and told me to practice my ABCs. I told her I had and was done. She came and gently took me by the arm. I had to show her that I knew all my letters. After I wrote them for her, she had a strange smile on her face and told me that I could go back and play. I liked first grade a lot, and I liked teacher even more.

Teacher read us stories daily. She had a bookshelf full of exciting stories. She started reading a book called *Old Yeller,* and I immediately fell in love with him. He was a wonderful dog, a fearless dog, and the boy in the story's best friend. Every day we begged teacher to read more about Old Yeller, but Old Yeller was killed protecting his boy from a mean bear.

I couldn't stand the thought of Old Yeller being killed. I felt like crying, but tears were not available. I had safely hidden them all away by the age of three. Teacher explained that he was a brave dog and had fought the bear with all his strength. But he was no match for the bear, and gave his life so the boy could live.

I didn't have any books at home, so teacher let me borrow *Old Yeller* over Christmas vacation. I had grey paper with big lines from school, and I asked my brother and sister for more of their school paper, and copied *Old Yeller* with my newly acquired ability to print. I wanted to keep the story forever, and I read it many times over the holiday.

When I went back to school, my handwritten copy of Old Yeller disappeared. I had already given the book back to teacher, and felt very sad about losing the story, but by then I had it memorized. Teacher read many new stories, and I gradually accepted Old Yeller's death.

Teacher came and visited my family one afternoon after school and stayed for supper. I remember her telling Madge and Dad that I was a very good student, and encouraged them to let me read books. Teacher made me feel very proud and special the way she talked to my parents. I finished eating and Dad told me to go outside and play while he and Madge finished talking to Teacher. A little while later, Teacher left without saying goodbye to me and never talked to Dad or Madge again, and I never got to bring any more books home. It felt like Teacher had stopped being my friend and I didn't understand why. I was no longer an individual with my own name. I had become my father's son, as in, "Your dad …"

There was a large boy in my class who had been retained in first grade. He was a whole head taller than me, and he was mean. He kept hitting me before and after school and during recess. I couldn't wrestle with him either – he was huge and would just knock me to the ground and hit me more. I got the idea that I could use the steps leading into the front door of the school to my advantage. I maneuvered him to stand on one step lower than me so we were the same height. This took away his size advantage, and I could hit him as often as he could hit me. I was taking a beating, but I was also giving him one. After that he decided to be my friend and we often played together on the school grounds. I learned that being the biggest kid in class was not as important as being able to inflict pain. Kids respected pain, not size.

CHAPTER 4
RETURN TO WISCONSIN
LOGGING TRUCKS

After finishing the first grade in the summer of 1943, we moved to a farm near Comstock Wisconsin. We took the northern route from Washington, US Highway 2, through Stevens Pass to Superior. This was a great highway for a seven year old boy! Two lanes, hairpin turns, and just enough space for two carefully driven vehicles to pass each other. I was thrilled by the expanse of the mountains, the sense of driving up through the clouds, and floating down again into the dark green sculpted line of trees. Looking out the side window of the car, I could see deep into the valleys. Huge pine trees shrank to strands of grass and became a dark, blurred green mass at the bottom of this majestic yet mysterious world. There were shimmering lakes, an occasional moose or bear, and trains hugging their chiseled rocky paths below, while trucks struggled to deliver heavy loads of logs to lands less inviting.

My sister and brother were often happy to let me have the outside window seat because it visually projected over the road's edge. Sitting in the outside seat I floated above the edge of this narrow two lane highway. I loved that feeling. I moved with the clouds, swept across the mountainsides with the wind, and glided effortlessly down into the distant valleys. I was flying above the clouds, not just levitating over houses and trees. I was conquering new dimensions of space while being out-of-body, a fearless dimension that let me rise to new heights as I soared above the Rockies. I was learning to master the skies of Earth in my mind, and the space for altered realities grew larger.

By the time it was dark that first day, we had driven through Washington, the neck of Idaho, and into Western Montana. Montana was half the trip from Washington to Wisconsin, or at least it seemed that way. Western Montana's mountains are equally beautiful to those further west, but the sameness of hills and rangeland along Eastern Montana's Highway 2 only prepares one for more of the same when North Dakota finally comes into view. I would repeatedly ask if we were out of Montana, and endlessly the answer was no. Eastern Montana looms dreary and monotonous as it becomes part of North America's Great Plains, plains that stretch from boastful Texas into rugged Canada.

Stevens Pass had trucks piled high with logs, and these metal giants would squeeze our little car tight against the mountain as they passed. Approaching logging trucks appeared to take up the entire road, and some were larger than our rented houses. Their approaching image covered the entire highway and left me with the feeling that our little car would be crushed against the mountainside or thrown into the deep valleys below. The monsters would roar past just inches away. Dad would hug the side of the road so tightly that the passenger-side wheels would kick up gravel on the mountain itself. Gravel pinged and banged against the car's steel fenders like shotgun pellets as white knuckled Dad gripped the steering wheel.

The most exciting part of our entire trip happened the first day, sometime in the afternoon. A logging truck came screaming down the steep mountain road behind us, horn blasting, and logs rocking precariously. We could see smoke coming from its wheels and Dad said the truck's brakes were going out.

There were "turnouts" on the mountain. Turnouts were that part of the road that kept going straight instead of curving downward around hairpin turns. Turnouts steeply climbed the mountainside, allowing gravity to bring these out-of-control death-traps to a stop. Sometimes, that is! Trucks were supposed to go up turnouts instead of becoming flying coffins for the hapless drivers trapped inside. If a truck didn't find a turnout in time, it would gain too much speed and sail off the highway into the valley below.

Dad had stopped driving logging trucks because one of his friends had been killed that way. The next hairpin turn didn't have a turnout and he talked excitedly about the trucker not making it. Dad was agitated and alarmed for the driver as he verbally began to relive his own experiences. The next hairpin turn had a turnout and the truck was stopped near the top, with smoke still wafting from its overheated wheels. Dad was visibly shaken. He kept jabbering randomly about the logging companies not caring about drivers, how brakes often failed, and what a dangerous driving job it was. I tried to ask more questions about driving logging trucks, but the emotional intensity of his thoughts swept my questions away. Dad was afraid of death.

We never stopped at motels as we traveled back and forth from Washington and Wisconsin. Motels were too expensive. Dad would infrequently stop for breakfast at a restaurant he knew, and almost never for lunch or dinner. He only stopped at restaurants he remembered, and would leave known restaurants without eating if ownership had changed hands and he didn't recognize anyone still working there. Dad never forgot a name, never forgot a place he had previously visited, and never forgot the number of a traveled highway. He didn't need or use maps unless he was driving in unknown territory. When he stopped, he wanted to talk to people he knew and reminisce about old times. But mostly we didn't stop, except for gas.

We ate sandwiches in the car made with baloney, cheese, or peanut butter and jelly. Madge made sandwiches while Dad drove, and passed them around the car into the hands of her hungry, eager children. Dad traveled with a big jug of black coffee and sipped on it day and night throughout the drive. He would make coffee stops to refill the jug, or grocery stops to buy more bread and fixings.

Mother had another jug full of Kool Aide or water for us kids. Kool Aide was special. A single pack doled out each day quickly disappeared down dry throats, throats that were accustomed to water without the sweet flavored candy added in. We always had our fill of sandwiches during these marathons. I was especially fond of baloney and peanut butter, the rare exception to butter and homemade jelly.

Somewhere in the endless miles of Montana, Dad decided that he wanted something besides sandwiches, and we stopped for pie. This is the only time I remember having such a special treat in all of our trips back and forth between Washington and Wisconsin. Each one of us was permitted to order our own slice of pie. I ordered apple pie, ate my crust and asked for my parents' uneaten crusts. Other customers began to remark about my eating crusts made without all their normal ingredients. Baking powder was not always available during the war, so customers often ate the fillings and left the crusts.

A family with a little girl that was younger then June struck up a conversation with Dad. Their daughter was admiring June's doll and asked to hold it. Dad in a gesture of sympathy reached over and plucked June's doll from her lap and handed it to the little girl. Acting as if he could afford to buy dolls whenever he wanted to, he told the stranger's daughter that she could keep it. June was choking back tears, but Dad told her not to worry, he would buy her another one. He never did, and June became a collector of dolls during her adult years.

If Dad was unable to keep his eyes open and began to drift off the road, he would stop for a couple hours, parking the car in a quiet place by a river or shaded woods. This was a welcome break from the endless ride, and we would excitedly pile out of the car to explore and play while he, and usually Madge, slept. Mother's responsibility during our marathon trips was to keep Dad awake. This meant forced conversation, and when he began to nod off, she passed coffee and the ubiquitous sandwiches.

I stayed at Grandma and Grandpa's for a few days when we got back to Wisconsin while dad looked for a piece of affordable land. The farm near Comstock was a few miles south of Island City and a couple miles east of Comstock. It needed work, endless work, as weeds had overgrown the pasture, rocks littered the fields, and new cement floors begged to be poured in the milk house and machine shed. Many broken items demanded fixing in all the neglected buildings, but especially in need of immediate repair were the fences. I liked the quiet mystery of thick woods full of animals and hidden adventure. The farm was surrounded by trees with the back pasture ending at the edge of Turtle Lake.

There was a big pond on the farm with turtles, frogs, and occasional water birds. Along with the large nearby woods, there were endless places for a seven year old to explore. Best of all, a boy my age lived about a mile down the road and I could sometimes get free time to play with him. We built a tree fort in the woods that summer, but by the time school started in the fall, my new friend had moved away. His parents moved the same way Dad did; he didn't even say goodbye, just disappeared one day.

HORSES

It was not possible to buy tractors or most other kinds of mechanized farm equipment as the war still demanded most of what the nation's factories produced. Dad bought a team of horses, big sweaty horses, and some old horse machinery. I couldn't harness them by myself. I could hardly lift the harnesses let alone throw them over the animals' backs. I couldn't even reach the middle of their backs without standing on something.

Dad tried to teach me how to control and guide the team, but they would respond only the second or third time I gave them commands. I had to use all my strength pulling on their reins. They would jerk their heads forward, and I would fly into the air. My flight amused them as they turned their heads and curled their lips as if saying, "See who's boss?" I couldn't stop them quickly enough when told to. Dad would yell a few cuss words and demand that I pull harder on the reins. I would strain to make them obey, but the horses treated me more like a colt in training than their boss.

I never liked horses after that except as pets. They would stand quietly and listen when I talked to them the way my brother Bud had taught me when we lived by Lake Stevens. But once in their harnesses, they knew who was in control. Dad would stop whatever he was doing, take the reins and make them obey, and then have to come back repeatedly to help me regain control. Each interruption increased his anger, cuss words, and derisive comments.

The next year when I was eight we got a small tractor, an Allis Chalmers A. A beautiful old rust bucket needing paint – that was

Allis. I liked Allis A; she stopped when I pushed in the clutch, and I could turn her exactly the way Dad asked me to. I could work like a man driving that tractor, staying in the fields until mealtime and only taking breaks when the adults did. I was eight years old that second summer, and had a lot more stamina. Dad would send me to the gravel pit alone for sand while he was tending bar in town. The gravel pit was a few miles away and other farm people were the only traffic on our quiet country road. No one paid attention to an eight year old tractor driver hugging the side of the road at ten miles per hour.

Madge would milk the cows at night while Dad was working in town, and I would help carry milk, get the cows from the field, help clean the barn, and feed them too. My brother Bud was 14 now and had been "placed out" permanently with a farmer near my Grandpa's. Vonna was ten and stayed home to help mother, along with my younger sister June.

Dad and I used the sand I brought home to make cement for milk house and machine shed floors and to fix part of the barn's gutters. Sometimes Bud would help when he was home for a weekend, but his visits were becoming less frequent. I liked mixing cement because it was a man's job. Dad and I made a wooden box and I used a large garden hoe to combine cement, sand, and water. The water was carried from our well where all water was pumped by hand. Dad had to push the wheelbarrow full of cement though, because I wasn't tall enough to lift it off the ground. I could mix cement as fast as he could push it, dump it, and smooth it out. Dad always told the neighbors, when they stopped by, that I never got tired. This was as close to a compliment as he could muster. He would look at me out of the corner of his eye while being extra careful not to make direct eye contact.

Nevertheless, I was developing a man's identity through work, and learning that my place in the world was one of labor, and hard labor meant that I got to spend time with Dad and other adults. I enjoyed being entertained with their endless stories. We didn't have a radio or other things run by electricity on the Comstock farm. I worked all day mixing cement and only took breaks when Dad did. I worked all day that first year, and when the mobile thrashing crew servicing our area came by, I threw oat bundles and fed the lumbering old machine with a thousand belts that separated oats from stocks. We'd get so dirty feeding the thrashing machine that it took a separate, not shared, pan of fresh well water to clean our faces and hands before meals. This we took from a large bucket of sun warmed well water that stood by the front door.

THE BEEKEEPER

Another fun part of the Comstock farm was the Beekeeper. He had many boxes of bees in our pasture back near the woods, and I got to go and watch while he took honey from the bees. He would put on his beekeeper suit with a net that covered his face and neck, as well as a long sleeved shirt and gloves. I liked to watch the bees swarm over his body in protest as he took their winter's food away. I had to stand back so the bees wouldn't swarm me too. The Beekeeper taught me not to hit them but to stand quietly when they landed on me. I was never afraid of bees after that. He also taught me that honey bee stings were only a nuisance similar to mosquito bites, not really painful. Real men could handle them without complaining, so I didn't complain. I would get a big piece of honeycomb when the Beekeeper was finished. This was like having both candy and gum at the same time. I would chew each piece of wax until all the honey was gone, and repeat this until I had consumed the large chunk he had given me. The Beekeeper seemed to know just how much honey a boy my age could eat without getting sick.

Every time he came to the farm, my sisters and I were sent outside to play while he and Madge talked. I didn't mind waiting, for when they finished, I got to accompany him to the hives. He would leave more honey in the house for mother, both in processed jars and in its wax. This was payment for keeping bees on our farm. He always made it clear that he was a generous man and left a little more payment than what was due. Mother liked the Beekeeper even more than I did, and they remained occasional lovers over most of her married life to Dad. However, in Madge's last years of life his children refused to let him marry her, even though he did eventually propose.

Madge's reputation for being a loose woman was widely known. Her reputation raised snickers in groups, and sly glances by individuals when we explained who our mother was. Failure to marry the Beekeeper didn't seem to particularly bother Madge. She often said "he was no good anymore," meaning that he was sexually impotent. She made these comments to his face and in front of me and others to his obvious embarrassment. But he could still be used for transportation, free meals, and non-sexual entertainment, and use him she did.

A Fuller Brush salesman came to our house every few weeks. He was better educated than we were and could play the old out-of-tune piano that had been left by the previous owners. Madge was excited when she discovered how talented he was. She rubbed his shoulders, and stroked his hair while the salesman excitedly beat away on the old yellowed ivories. Then my sisters and I went outside to play while Madge looked at the salesman's wares. The last time he came, I got my first toothbrush. I had always wanted a toothbrush and repeatedly begged her for one. Madge and Dad used salt and baking soda mixed together for toothpaste and always had toothbrushes, and now I brushed my teeth just like the grownups. I felt very mature and wore that toothbrush down to the nub. I felt like I had lost a friend when it was totally worn out, but I didn't buy another one until I was fourteen and earning real money.

THE AXEMAN

As the first member of our family to be "placed-out," Brother Bud had been working on a farm near Uncle Bert's for about a year. Dad made it very clear that he planned to place all of us out when we turned 14. Being placed out was our first step into adult maturity; it was the way we would learn to make our future living.

I was nine that summer when he brought Bud back from his job placement. It was unusual for Bud to come home in the middle of the week. This time, Dad's violent temper was totally out-of-control; he was yelling, cussing, gesturing, and shaking his fists at Bud. Dad treated Bud as though he had committed the ultimate sin, and screamed that he was going to chop his head off.

We had a big wooden block in the front yard where wood was split for the stove and furnace, and where we chopped off chicken heads. Dad dragged Bud out of the car in a headlock, over to the chopping block, picked up the axe, and tried to get his head placed just right to cut it off. Bud was fighting hard, but Dad was dragging him from his backside in a firm headlock and Bud couldn't get free. The muscles stood out on Bud's neck and arms as he fought back. Bud almost freed himself when Dad released one arm to grip the axe. Finally, Bud's head was on the chopping block with Dad's knee in his back, one of Dad's hands gripping the axe and the other stretching Bud's neck across the chicken, blood-dried block by the hair. Dad was waving the axe over his head getting Bud positioned just right for the killing blow.

I was frightened, immobile, and watched the spectacle like I was at a horror movie. Finally Bud's neck was flat on the chopping block, and Dad raised the axe high over his head ready to strike. At that exact moment, Mother snatched the axe from his poised hand while a look of amazement and then terror came over Dad. She began chasing him wildly around the yard yelling crazy things. Mother was running, and at the same time, swinging the axe with both hands. The executioner had become the prey. Dad pleaded with her to stop, but she was consumed with rage, and just kept swinging and screaming hysterically.

She stopped swinging the axe after becoming totally exhausted, and dropped it immediately on the ground where she stopped, like a weight she could no longer endure. Dad went over to the axe, picked it up, and my panic returned. I studied every step he took, but he went to the chopping block alone and firmly buried its blade into the wood. A few days later, Bud was taken back to his placement.

Dad displayed his violent temper often when we lived on the Comstock farm. He would swing shovels, two-by-fours, or anything he had in his hands at us during these spells. Unfortunately, except for a few days each year, I was the only boy at home. I had to be on the alert and keep enough distance to avoid his tantrums. The same applied to his throwing objects, but he never played ball games much as a child and had a poor aim. Fortunately, his violent, tantrum-like physical outbursts were short-lived, and only followed by emotional, verbal tirades. Dad worked some days but mostly nights tending bar, and never had enough sleep. Or maybe it was coming down from the alcohol the night before that made him so cranky.

GOING TO TOWN

Occasionally he would take us to town on Saturday night, and generally let us go to a movie. Movies were 15 cents, pop and popcorn were each a nickel. For 25 cents, I could have all three. It cost 75 cents for my two sisters and me to see a movie and have pop and popcorn. This was equivalent to three bottles of beer in the local watering hole, however, Dad drank whiskey and Seven Up, which cost thirty or thirty-five cents a glass and went down twice as fast as beer. He only drank beer if it was a hot summer day and we were sharing work with other farmers during haying or thrashing season. We got to go to town if Dad was satisfied with our work accomplishments during the week. Being in a good mood depended on how much sleep he had, his hangover, or whether he and Madge had been arguing. However, reasons to argue and fight were as plentiful as the rocks on our farm.

Dad usually got angry just before we were ready to get into the car. We would all have our weekly Saturday night bath, put on clean farm clothes, and wait for his signal to leave. After this scenario of preparation, which Dad watched, he would sometimes go into town by himself, deriding our work efforts or simply recalling a list of negative traits we all seemed to possess. It was his way of punishing Madge for her real or imagined sins, and using the vocabulary of modern warfare, we children just happened to be innocent collateral.

Dad would pump himself up with negative comments that berated Madge and his kids, getting angrier and angrier in the process, until there was no hope of him changing his mind. I somehow became aware of this self-reinforcing negative cycle and the timing necessary to interrupt it, and that summer developed a special talent. If I intervened at just the right moment, I could convince him to change his mind and take us along. I would remind him that I did all my chores, how I had done extra work that week, and that I would do even more the next. I didn't know it at the time, but what I was doing was calming him down and getting him to return to the here and now from the angry no-man's-land he visited. Daily Dad was teaching me how to reinforce my own anger and be negative about people and life. His well of self-reinforced negativism could be dug to murderous depths.

These interventions sometimes worked, and he would change his mind and let us all go into town with him. If he didn't give us 25 cents, we would shop with Madge and walk up and down in front of the theatre until the other kids got out of the movie. Mother shopped for basics like salt, sugar, flour, and spices, and then would visit with friends and relatives on the street until Dad finished drinking. We grew our own food on the farm, and butchered home grown animals for meat. Dad would drink with his friends in the bar where he worked, and come out about the time people on the street were heading home.

It was fun to go to town even if we couldn't go to the movies. We could always find other farm kids or cousins to talk to. But when we could, Westerns with Tom Mix, Gene Autry, Roy Rogers, Hop-A-Long Cassidy, and The Lone Ranger were my favorites. Sometimes the main movies were preceded by shorts featuring The Road Runner, The Three Stooges, and other great films from both silent and early talking films. We kids loved everything playing on the Silver Screen; some movies were just a little better than the others, and demanded louder hoots and hollers.

CHRISTMAS AT STEP-GRANDFATHER'S

Our last year on the Comstock farm, we spent Christmas at Grandpa and Grandma's on Madge's side of the family. We went to their farm a few times each year. We picked blackberries there almost every summer, sometimes went at Christmas time or Thanksgiving, and now and then for no special reason. I was excited that particular year as both of my favorite boy cousins were coming.

Bud never came with us on family holidays after he was "placed out" and on his own. He was 15 in 1945 and able to earn his own living. I suspect he was taking care of his farmer boss's milk cows while the farmer enjoyed the holidays. Bud never said anything nice about the farmer, and I knew he was just waiting until he was sixteen and old enough to get a better paying job somewhere else.

Everything got easier at 16. Factories and bigger companies would often hire boys of that age if they were strong enough and seemed responsible. Boys always lied about their age and some got adult jobs at 15 or were even able to get into the armed services. Computer files didn't exist, and lying about age was easy. Bud got a job working for Carnation Dairy near Renton, Washington, after turning 16. Carnation liked young men who were at least 18 years old, but hired Bud on the spot when he told them he was a farm boy from Wisconsin. His job was milking a string of cows by hand three times daily. He lived in housing provided by the company.

Madge's mother was a good cook. We had mashed potatoes, sweet potatoes with brown sugar, three kinds of pies – pumpkin, banana, and apple – turkey, ham, green beans from a can, pickles, candy and nuts, breads, and a lot of other things I don't recall. We ate until we couldn't stuff in another forkful, including seconds on pie, and some people even had thirds. Grandma's specialty was banana cream pie with Graham Cracker crust. Everyone said the Graham Cracker crust was as good as the pie, and I thought so too.

Grandpa had more cows then Dad, and a bigger barn. The barn was fun to play in, and my cousins and I would make tunnels in the haymow. Sometimes these tunnels would be so long they would go all the way through the middle of the barn and around its four sides. Supporting beams that traversed the hay storage area became trails through the haymow itself. We would get under the beams and push the hay far enough to either side to form a passageway. Grandpa's farm also had a big hill that was great for sleds, and toboggans, and he had both. When we finished eating and opening presents we would spend hours enjoying this hill. We would sled and toboggan until totally soaked and half frozen, trudge back into the house, and as we dried out, devour what was left of the pies and much of the leftovers.

My boy cousins each got their own wood burning set from grandpa. After much pleading, one cousin let me burn part of a picture in the wood sample that came with his set.

I got a pair of socks that looked like grandpa's dress socks, but they were a funny color that I couldn't name. I gave them to Dad the next day.

Dad said this grandpa was not my real grandpa, but a step-grandpa. He really wasn't my Grandpa at all.

Step-grandpa had a habit of trying to grab other men's genitals when walking around the farm. At the time, I didn't know this habit carried over into town as I only saw him on the farm. He married my pregnant grandmother years before and immigrated to The States from Canada. My real Grandfather was a Canadian Mounted Policeman who was assigned distant duties, and was frequently absent from home on long-term assignments. Step-grandfather was the neighbor who helped look after Grandma in Grandpa's absence. Supposedly they were neighbors on good terms. Madge and Uncle Wellington were my real Grandpa Lewis's legitimate children. Uncle Wellington didn't like step-grandfather and infrequently visited us when I was growing up.

My step-grandpa had a BB gun that Uncle Earl shot when he was a boy. Uncle Earl had left Wisconsin as soon as he was old enough to be on his own, just like Bud, and was working somewhere on the West Coast. It was a fancy Red Ryder BB gun, the expensive model. I discovered it while playing in the attic and asked if I could shoot it. Step-grandpa said he didn't have any BBs, but offered to sell me the gun for three dollars. New BB guns that weren't fancy cost $2.98, and the fancy kind a dollar more. Dad told Step-grandpa he didn't have enough money right then, but informed me on the way home that the price was too high. He bought a used BB gun for me later that spring for a dollar and some cents.

I could kill sparrows with it, but I had to get very close before I shot. I usually made my own BBs by cutting short sections of nail and inserting this homemade shot into the barrel one at a time. But homemade BBs didn't fly through the air very well as they tumbled end over end. By late summer I sold the BB gun, and my brother helped me get a single shot 22 rifle, giving me some extra money to cover the difference. The 22 could kill black birds and gophers at a distance, and Dad was happy to get rid of anything that ate grain or messed up the haymow. It could also kill turtles, snakes, and rabbits. Initially, I walked the woods and shot anything that was small. I didn't kill much besides unwanted birds and gophers because bullets were expensive and I had to rely on my brother for shells. At eight years of age, I didn't think about taking the lives of wild things like gophers, snakes, turtles, and birds. They weren't significant compared to killing cows and pigs for food, or even chickens, and certainly a lot less significant than chopping off people's heads.

THE FARM

I learned how to make fishhooks after moving to Comstock. I took small nails, put them in our vice, filed the end to a point, and bent the nail over. I would tie flower sack string tight below the head of the nail so it wouldn't slip off, and I was ready to fish. Worms were plentiful on the farm, and I cut young samplings for fishing poles. I lost most of the fish as I had to keep the line very tight or they jumped off before I could get them on shore. Anyway, I had fun fishing for sunnies and crappies, and mother taught me how to clean them. She loved to eat fresh fish, and would encourage me to get more.

One of my jobs on the farm was cutting thistles, and the pasture was full of them; they stood tall, dominating the grazing area like giant cacti in the Arizona desert. Dad had a small sickle that I held in one hand, knocking down small thistles and weeds with a single stroke, but large thistles were another matter. The giant cacti-like thistles required repeated hammering with this small tool, exhausting my arms after an hour or so.

Dad swung a sickle that was bigger across than I was tall. This sickle had been used in the old days to harvest grain, and was made for a man at least five feet tall. Dad swung it hard and knocked down three or four times the amount of thistles that I could, and he could keep the sickle in motion for a good hour or more. Swinging this huge blade for ten minutes, cutting one thistle at a time, made my arms ache. The thistles grew faster than I could cut them, and Dad was increasingly sarcastic about my inability to keep thistles and weeds under control. I came to understand as I grew up that I was the laziest boy he had ever known, except for my brother Bud who was even lazier.

We had an acre of cucumbers that Bud and I were supposed to pick clean every day. Bud came home the first couple weekends after the cucumbers were ready for harvest and then stopped. He didn't like picking cucumbers on his day off, didn't earn any money for picking, and once the patch was overgrown, he no longer came home. This meant that I had sole responsibility to harvest all the cucumbers the rest of that summer. I couldn't pick fast enough; the green pests grew to gigantic sizes, and Dad's anger increased proportionately with their size. I was a good-for-nothing kid, and Bud was even more useless! Dad would stomp into the patch snapping off the largest cucumbers and stomping them into the ground. All I could do was watch and keep my distance.

HALFWAY TO THE MOON

The day Dad decided to chop off Bud's head was the day I decided to find another place to live.

I liked the moon at night. It was a warm, soft orange globe that hung safely beyond our farm. I even envisioned the Man-in-the-Moon as a real person who liked me. Rural skies were always lit up with twinkling stars, constellations, and sometimes Northern Lights.

I decided to visit the Man-in-the-Moon shortly after Dad tried to chop off Bud's head. I flew into outer space and got halfway between the Moon and Earth where each celestial body seemed to be about the same size. Suddenly, I felt entirely alone in the cold, dark grip of space. The void was entirely black except for the shining Moon and Earth, and the Earth was becoming a shrinking ball of rapidly fading colors. Was I lost? Would I be unable to return if I went all the way? I stopped motionless, and the extreme cold made me shiver; I physically shivered. I felt totally alone in that overwhelming dark void that was beginning to feel more like hell then ultimate escape; the ice gods of space were creeping into my bones.

The Moon lost its appeal and quickly turned into nothing more than a lifeless, cold rock. The Man-in-the-Moon was no longer a friend. As I hung, motionless, I remember quite consciously thinking that this would be the right place to leave my soul. I wanted my soul to be safe in case I did something to make Dad really angry. I "parked" my soul, at least that's how I thought of it then, right there halfway between Mother Earth and Father Moon. It was similar to placing a package in a special hiding place just before Christmas. No one else would ever be able to find my secret nook; one small soul, as invisible as a ghost, tucked along the flyway on an unused path to the Moon. I then flew home as fast as I could, slipped through the roof of the house, under the bed covers, and went to sleep. My mind had a natural homing device. I didn't have to worry about getting lost in space, but at that time I didn't know this.

When I tried to talk to mother about my flying experiences, the angels, and their visits, she just said matter-of-factly that everyone had a Guardian Angel that looked after them. I knew when mine was around, but I never talked to him out loud. He would sit on my bed, or I could feel him walking beside me when I was outside. He never sat at our kitchen table or in the same room when other people were present, and I thought that was a little odd. I only talked to him in my mind, and, that's how he talked to me. It's probably more accurate to say that my angel shared his thoughts with me, and I shared mine with him. When I had an especially interesting experience with him and tried to discuss it with mother, she always shushed me up. She would tell me sternly that I wasn't to tell other people about flying or my Guardian Angel talking to me. People would think I was crazy! I thought to myself, how can anything that is so completely real be crazy? Moses, my guardian angel, was as real as Madge and a lot more understanding.

That old farmhouse at Comstock was just like the two story houses I remembered when I was little. The steps were wooden and steep, and there weren't any lights to turn on at the bottom of the stairs. We used candles and kerosene lamps, and weren't allowed to take either up to bed. I would hurry up the stairs at night, usually running. If I walked normally I could feel something evil right behind me. It would breathe on the back of my neck in the dark, and I was afraid it would crawl into bed with me. Mother told me that the ghost could get inside me if it wanted to take possession of my body, so I would scoot far under the covers, pull the blankets over my head, and hide.

This evil spirit never got into bed with me, but I often heard its breathing as it stood over me. Sometimes I would sleep all night completely covered, head-to-toe, especially in the winter. I asked mother about ghosts, and she thought they were real. I told her that a ghost probably lived in this house. Madge said there could be a ghost, the spirit of someone who had died, and didn't want to leave. She said that ghosts were people's souls that couldn't go to Heaven or Hell. They just hung around and bothered the living. But ghosts could hurt people if they got angry. I had to be careful, very careful!

In my eight year old world, the line between the living and the dead could be crossed at any time; good and evil spirits were my companions. I experienced kindness and understanding from my Guardian Angel, but the ghost that followed me to bed was an evil dark spirit. Mother said that evil spirits could possess the bodies and minds of children. There was a dark world all around that could pull me in at any moment. The light and dark forces of my universe mixed like cake batter prepared for baking. I had to walk cautiously between good and evil, and I did so for many years.

CHAPTER 5

CUCUMBERS & HICKS

Germany was under siege, and the war against the Japanese in the Pacific was hot. Dad sold the Comstock farm, cows and equipment, everything we had to raise money. He bragged that he could buy anything, keep it for a few months, and sell it at a profit. He bought a bigger, nicer farm south of Island City, putting every dime he had into the farm itself. The farm was open with few trees and dark black soil; a rich land capable of providing our family with a lot more than basic subsistence. Tending bar in town was how he planned to earn money to buy cows and machinery. The next summer he planted 3.5 acres of our best farmland in cucumbers, and rented-out the rest of the cultivated land. Bud was still placed-out and working just a few miles away, and he begged Dad to keep this beautiful farm. It was a dream come true for Bud; a farm just waiting for hungry cattle and workable equipment to become part of Heartland America's profitable breadbasket, a farm that could provide a future for both father and sons.

I was able to work long days when I was ten years old. Sister Vonna was 12, and June almost nine. The girls weren't very strong, and only lasted in the field some days for a few hours each morning. The rest of the time they helped Madge with the hundreds of chores farm women performed in those days, such as cooking, cleaning, canning, baking, mending, and an endless list from darning socks to gardening. I picked all day, but the cucumbers grew faster than I could keep up. Without daily picking a large portion of the cukes would grow to gigantic sizes. I had my tonsils out during the middle of cucumber season and missed a week of picking. Dad got irate with my puny efforts as small cucumbers fetched top dollar. Every day he loaded his car trunk, backseat, and front passenger seat with sacks of cucumbers. He promised to give me $20 when school started if I picked all day every day, and I wanted the money to get a multi-shot 22 rifle.

Dad was sarcastic about my sisters and repeatedly said they wouldn't get any pay come the end of summer, 'cause they weren't working hard enough.

He had this funny way of thinking about his children. We were adults when it came to work and babies when it came to privileges. He lived in a different world from almost everyone else I knew who had kids my age. Many families in our area of Wisconsin were first generation Americans, Swedes, Norwegians, Russians, Italians, Swiss, Polish, Irish, and odd names I didn't always remember, but mostly couldn't spell. Most of them wanted their children to attend high school, enjoy a settled life, have long-term friends, and a dozen other luxuries that never seemed to pass through Dad's mind.

Dad had socks, wore shoes all year long, always had a toothbrush, and wore a tie, suit and hat home from his laboring jobs when he was absent during the week. His outfit gave him the appearance of a Chicago gangster stopping by for a visit. These were dress habits that I first noticed when I was five while we lived by Lake Stevens. Wisconsin bartending jobs meant that Dad went to work in a white shirt and tie, but I don't remember if he wore a jacket or not. However, the gangster hat was his usual companion when off the farm.

There were two worlds out there. Dad lived in the one with ties and socks, and my siblings and I lived in the other one. When my sister June and I talked over the years, it was common for us to dwell on socks. Other kids had them and we didn't. Underwear was not visible, so we didn't need that either. Birthdays were forgotten except one that I recall for Brother Bud. He had his sixteenth birthday at our house and Dad provided a gallon pail of ice cream. "All you can eat," he said. We were all going to have a birthday party when we turned sixteen, but it didn't happen. I don't recall birthday presents, but mother always seemed to manage a cake, usually without candles. Dad provided the basics for life, and the rest was left to each one of us. It was a schizophrenic world.

Just before school started, Dad gave Madge money for new clothes for my sisters and me. We went to town early on Saturday and shopped at the Company Store, which had good, cheap work clothes. Madge bought me a new pair of bibs, new flannel shirt, a new pair of shoes and some socks, and similar items for my sisters. Everything cost a little over $20, and she put some small item back to keep the total below $20. I later asked Dad for my summer's pay only to be told that I had been paid; he had given the money to Madge. I protested that the money was for school clothes and paid for my sisters' clothes as well as mine. All of the money I thought I had been working for throughout the summer was not to be. Dad was a master at manipulation and I responded to his unfilled promises the way other children waited for Christmas. That was the end of the matter for him. Further questioning would only provoke anger; anger that could quickly turn to physical assault or other punishments if I persisted. Dad's favorite motivators were fear and captivating lies. I responded to both, whereas Madge only responded to fear.

Dad never saved enough money to buy cows and machinery, and sold this beautiful farm the next year. Years later, Bud told me Dad sold the farm at a profit of $1,000 and used the money to buy an almost new, faster car. We moved to a house half-a-mile east of Island City on Highway 48. Compared to the country, Highway 48 was busy with cars, and our dog liked to chase them, a habit he had picked up on the farm. Only chasing slow moving tractors and an occasional car in the country required less skill than running across a busy blacktopped highway. A direct hit left half of Collie's bloodied stomach hanging out. He couldn't make it back to our place, and crawled under a nearby shed. No matter how I tried to coax him to come out, he wouldn't move.

The crawl space under the shed was not high enough for me to pick him up, and I was afraid to drag him out with exposed guts. The first day he cried softly in pain and drank a little water, but by the following morning he refused both fresh water and food, and just lay with sad vacant eyes staring back at me. Collie died three days later, and emotionally I wasn't even able to retrieve his body.

Living near town wasn't any fun. It wasn't a farm, and it wasn't the city; it was a no-man's land. People on the surrounding acreage wouldn't let me explore their property the way country folks would. All I could do during the day was hike into town and walk the streets looking for new friends. No kids my age lived along this strip of lifeless highway. No other no-man's land kids existed. I was a loner, a country nothing, a buffoon.

BEING A HICK

The town kids thought I was a hick with my bib overalls, no shirt, and bare feet. They'd gang up and give chase when they caught me walking through town. I avoided most of the boys by using the side streets, but when sent into town on errands by Madge, I was fair game. I could fight city boys one-on-one, but not in groups. Three boys, who I discovered later were in my class at school, thought that tormenting the hick was great fun and would give chase as soon as they spotted me. Once school started and I was able to learn their routines, I waited until I could catch them alone. I beat up the first one I caught and told him I'd keep beating him up until he and his friends stopped ganging up on me. I never had to beat up the other two boys as number one got the word out. The name-calling stopped and the three boys finally came to totally ignore me. Unhappily, this was the only attention I ever got from town kids. I was a hick loner, a dirtball, a thing that lived in no-man's land.

Most of the kids in town knew each other, and went to the same grades together year after year. I had gone to second grade for a few months in Island City, but I didn't remember any of the kids in my class except a little Indian boy and his sister, and they only lasted two weeks before being pushed out of school. The teacher wouldn't let me or any other "white" children play with them, and they were the only kids who liked me. Teacher would physically come and take me by the arm, lead me back inside the school to my desk, and make me sit through recess whenever I tried. I played alone, and they played alone.

Some of the boys teased me by wrinkling their faces and contorting their bodies with butts in the air and called me names, "Farty Arty," and "Art the Fart" being their favorites. I decided I didn't like town kids, I didn't like town, I didn't like school, and I didn't like teachers. I stayed away from city kids outside of school, but this made me unhappy and lonely. I longed to be back in the country where I felt free and could play with other hicks in bib overalls just like me.

Summer was hot and I didn't know how to make money in town, I didn't even know how to talk to people in town. Townspeople seemed strange, and their kids were mean. One August day, I walked the half mile into town, looked at the corner dairy store, and wished for a nice cold ice cream cone. Just then Moses, that is what I came to call my Guardian Angel, appeared out of nowhere. He guided me to a specific spot beside the sidewalk on the left side of the ice cream store sidewalk entrance, and told me to pull back the grass.

Moses had a magical way of talking to me. It was like his voice, more, his thoughts, were put directly into my mind, but his communication was always as clear as spoken words, and in this case accompanied by a visual aid. When I pulled back the grass in the exact spot where he directed me, I found a dime and a nickel wedged out-of-sight in the yellow clay. Ice cream was ten cents at the corner dairy, but only a nickel at Sam's, a mile through town on the north end. I walked home, got my sisters, and we all went for ice cream. Moses was an incredible person, or angel, or whatever, to me.

Moses came around a lot that summer. I was amazed that he could know so many things such as where to find ice cream money. I could see him in my mind and knew that he was older, closer to my Grandpa's age. He didn't have facial hair and looked like he shaved every day. He didn't have an accent either, but then, I didn't talk to him out loud. I just knew he didn't have an accent. I was curious about what he did most days because he was always there when I needed him. I didn't think his presence was strange or unusual. Madge said every kid had a Guardian Angel and I knew this for a fact. I couldn't believe he spent all of his time just watching me, and thought that he must have a bunch of other kids that he looked after too. Mother still refused to talk to me about Moses, and I came to believe that she thought I just made him up; that he was just a foolish quirk of my overactive imagination.

The bridge across Highway 48 near our house spanned two sections of Beaver Dam Lake. At night bullheads would pool under the bridge and were easy to catch. I found a real cane pole and some fish hooks in the shed by our rented house when I conducted my usual search of new properties. I would dig worms, and go down to the bridge after dark to fish. I used a short dry stick as a bobber and the line would float slowly under the bridge from the upper part of the lake towards the lower end. Bullheads were just waiting to be caught once the sun went down, and I caught as many as I wanted. Madge initially showed me how to skin them, and we would eat our fill. My sisters didn't like bullheads as much as we did, and besides, they were usually in bed by the time the fish came out of the frying pan. Many of the locals thought bullheads were an inferior fish, wrinkled their noses, and refused to eat them. So I didn't have any fishing competition, I didn't have any fishing competition, I didn't have any …

MIND CONTROLLING CRACKS

The more I walked the streets of Island City that summer, the harder it became. The cracks in the sidewalk gradually took control of my mind, and it got to a point where I couldn't step on them. I had to carefully step over each separate crack. Head lowered, and walking gingerly, I slowly made my way down the street. Before the summer was over, I looked like a kid playing hopscotch. Only this game extended as far as the sidewalk. I was stepping over pavement cracks that needed repair from one end of town to the other. I began to notice people watching me, and some even asked what I was doing. I tried to pretend it was a game, but I couldn't think of a game that had such strange movements, or covered the length of the street. The cracks had total control, and no matter how hard I tried, I couldn't get free.

Every time I approached the sidewalk, my gaze would be forced downward searching for the first crack. Each succeeding crack held my undivided attention until I was able to exit on nearby grass or gravel.

I struggled for a long time trying to figure out how to stop the cracks from controlling me. I tried Dad's idea about using the strength of my mind, but the more I thought about the cracks the stronger their control became. Finally one day I got so angry that I stomped on one, than another, and another. The more I stomped the better I felt. Finally, I was running back and forth across the cracks and stomping, stomping, stomping. I went up and down the street this way getting even with every crack that had tormented me and paying absolutely no attention to anyone watching me. I kept stomping until my bare feet began to throb from the pounding they were receiving. Now, I was able to walk freely over the sidewalk without looking down. I walked and ran over the cracks with a sense of new found freedom that made me feel strong; I was finally their master. They were weak puny imperfections – no match for my bare feet. The next couple of days I stomped a few more cracks, and then forgot them. The sidewalk became nothing more than a concrete path through a nondescript town full of mean kids.

UBIQUITOUS GHOST

The house on 48 was two storied and had a stairway to my bedroom just like the farm house by Comstock, and that's where the ghost reappeared! At night when I opened the door to the upstairs, I could feel it behind me. As I started to climb, this creepy sensation would move up my lower spine, and then an eerie feeling would slide into the back of my head creating a sensation like a little mouse was running around in there. In this way, the ghost seemed to be trying to get into both my mind and my body. The feeling would terrify me. I would race up the stairs, jump into bed, and hide every inch of me tightly tucked under the covers, holding the blankets down so the ghost couldn't pull them up and get into bed with me. It left me alone once I was fully covered, but I had to lie entirely motionless, listening carefully until its breathing stopped. I would practice controlling my own breathing by shutting it down and breathing as little as possible in order to make the ghost think I had stopped breathing altogether. Nights when the ghost's presence was especially strong were nights when I hid under the covers until waking in the morning. I couldn't find a way to get rid of it. It waited for me by the stairway door through endless nights. Whoever the ghost was in real life, it must have died on steep wooden steps, because its horrible breath and creepy body was seeking a new home in mine. But why did it always follow me from one old house to another as we moved around the country? I couldn't understand the ghost's behavior, and attempts to talk about him only resulted in being shushed up by Madge. The emptiness of space had returned to earth with me.

FORGOTTEN GRAVES

Near the fishing bridge on Highway 48 is a cemetery called Lakeside, and mother said two of my sisters were buried there. I begged her to show me their graves when we walked into town to buy groceries. She would say some other time, or that she didn't remember where they were buried. But finally she gave in one day that summer when my sisters and I were walking her into Island City. We had incessantly badgered her to show us the babies' graves, and with considerable reluctance she agreed. Madge didn't use their names but referred to them as "the babies." She walked along the shore of the cemetery for what seemed like an endless period of time, back and forth and up and down the hillside until she finally found one gravestone. The stone had Donna's name on it, but she couldn't find the stone with Carol's, and seemed confused.

I realized later that over the years Madge had never visited either girl's grave until that exact moment. Later when I asked, Dad said there was only one marker and that when Carol died, he didn't have enough money for a second gravestone, and the girls were buried side-by-side. Carol was less than six months old and very little anyway. He didn't remember anything about her, and his demeanor made it clear that it was a memory he too didn't care to revisit. Children, I thought, were like machinery: easy to replace when they stopped working and died.

Afterwards, I went back to the cemetery many times and visited my dead sisters, and I still visit them when I go to Island City. Over my childhood years, I would sit and talk to them, wondering if babies grew up in Heaven, or always stayed little. The only angels I had ever met were adults. I decided that God could help Carol and Donna grow up if he wanted to. Anyway, they were angels and were well taken care of. When I realized this I felt extremely bonded with and close to them, the same way I felt when I died and the angels came to take me to Heaven. Angels were real and my sisters unquestionably lived in Heaven. I visited their grave when I was lonely, and talked about whatever was on my mind. I never had to worry about them not listening or shushing me up. Angels always listened.

As I got older, I asked Madge many questions about my sisters and how they died. She never wanted to talk about them or their deaths, and only gave empty answers without substance or feeling. But as I visited their graves year after year, they seemed to grow older with me. Emotional attachment has such a wonderful way of transcending age.

The very old and the very young share this magical world of love. My dead sisters are ageless and beautiful, and I came to feel as close to them as my other sisters, June and Vonna. This is a feeling that I know is shared by my brother Bud. Often when I stop to visit Donna and Carol around Memorial Day, I find fresh flowers on their graves. Bud and I don't talk about the girls, but we each have our own relationship with them.

We moved into Island City before school started that fall. There was a girl who lived next door in my grade by the name of Jane, and her mother was an English teacher. Teachers, with the exception of the first half of first grade, didn't like me, especially English teachers. Jane wouldn't play with my sisters or me. Her mom never greeted me when I met her in the neighborhood, and I wasn't welcomed to play in their yard. I didn't like the teacher's daughter either. In the winter, she would build snow houses and snow forts, and I would go over after dark and kick them down. She played with other girls in the snow, and even took them inside her own home. The girls would look at me and point and laugh. I hated them all. At first, Jane would rebuild her snow houses, and I would smash them again. After a while she stopped these useless efforts. I didn't like living in town, and I didn't like living next to Jane. When Dad said we were moving to the country and that he had bought a farm, I felt like a boy reborn. Farm people knew the joys of rural life; they talked to each other, played together, and even laughed out loud.

CHAPTER 6

HEAVEN ON EARTH

The farm west of Lorraine was my dream come true. It was a half-mile north of Highway 48 and half-way to Luck as we drove west from Island City. The dirt and gravel road from the highway to our farm had woods along its entire eastside with an open field covering the first quarter mile to the west. Going north, the west woods extended for miles. In summer the trees touched above the road providing an umbrella effect as I walked towards the highway. It was an air-conditioned tunnel with shade, soft light, and the musty smell of the woods all around. Thick mixed woods of pines and deciduous trees, kept moist by ample summer rains, offered up their own special perfume during hot summer days. The road felt cool to the bottom of my feet. To the west of the open field was a farmhouse with a small lawn; grass left undisturbed by the turning radius of the farmer's tractor. I could see trees in every direction I looked from both our neighbor's and other sparsely placed open fields.

This plowed patchwork, laboriously taken from the forest, was a common pattern in Northeastern Wisconsin, but in our part of heaven, most of the land was covered with trees and thick undergrowth. In the middle of this natural animal sanctuary we had less than 40 acres of open cropland – good primarily for growing hay and oats. To our north was heavily wooded land with some open pasture. Dad and I were creating more pastureland each winter by logging off some of the trees. The logged off areas would be covered by undergrowth by the next summer, and it was necessary to repeatedly cut and burn the brush in order to keep the new grazing areas open. A generous quantity of stumps did not permit plowing, and we never conquered this tree lot beyond the stump stage.

The nights were beautiful and tranquil, and the stars were bright sparkling jewels in the crystal clear sky. Dad taught me some of the constellations, and I used them to find my way home if I were in the woods after dark. Winter skies were even prettier than those of summer, with Northern Lights being a gift that more than compensated for winter cold. They would spread across the entire expanse of this sheltered land of emotional comfort and demanding labor, and splash streams of color like paints being thrown onto canvas. Only these colors were alive, they danced, raced, pulsed, and blended together holding me in awe. I never saw lights like this in town. They were the most magnificent Northern Lights I remember as a child. It was beautiful in the country; it was magic, it was a land of tranquility and peace. I couldn't imagine any other spot on earth being more inviting. It created a sense of wonder in me; wonder that is shared by all humankind when we let nature speak directly to us.

I would watch the Northern Lights until bed time or winter's cold would drive me indoors. The Lights would pull me upward like a magnet into their magnificent celestial fold; I'd merge with the colors, leaping, twisting, and soaring above the earth. My soul danced in space with a freedom devoid of earthly bondage. On nights when the Northern Lights were absent, I would study the constellations, or simply let myself be swept into the seductive panorama above me. The immensity of our northern universe lifted me beyond the sky, breaking terrestrial ties. I shared the boundless home of the stars the way I sometimes shared the bed with my brother. I felt transported into space, joining the constellations, and moving with them above the Earth. Impossible freedom was mine; infinite space my friend. The chambers of my mind evolved to span the cosmos.

I knew my body was firmly attached to the earth, but it was a body lost to its self. My physical self would melt away as my mind and spirit moved effortlessly in space. I played celestial games still unknown with the best computer animations; my world was a virtual reality come reality. It was rapture watching the Northern Lights, and ecstasy to play amongst the stars. On those nights, the ghost never came to haunt me. I went up the stairs to my bedroom filled with wonder. The brilliance of the night left no room for the shadow of the ghost, as the chemistry of my brain was temporarily distilled by the glory of unbounded nature. Happiness, pure joy, was being one with a cosmos that stopped in Northern Wisconsin skies to play, and laugh, and sing with children.

Sundays, when Dad was busy working in town, or doing whatever he did in town without his family, meant that I could finish my chores and explore the woods and all that lived there. I often took a sandwich lunch and only returned in time for milking. To the north side of our pasture was a trail that went seven miles through heavily wooded second growth; second growth that had naturally regenerated itself after the previous century's mass logging. The woods extended three miles east before connecting with a county road, and as far west as the city of Luck, ten or twelve miles.

My brother brought back my 22 rifle, which I hadn't been permitted to use in town. I killed pine snakes, scared the flying squirrels, and used it to target practice. I would help neighbors cultivate, drive tractor, and do all kinds of farm chores. I made enough money that season to buy bullets, and was also saving to buy a lever action 22 that I had seen at a nearby gunsmith's, a hermit-type guy located in the middle of the woods without any farmland to support him. Like many locals, living by his wits, but a free man.

The gunsmith was one of those occasional disaffected humans who rejects the religious isolation of monks in preference to communion with nature; people of and from the earth, souls not of this world, who find peace where the history of humanity written in our DNA can still find attachment to the land. I would visit the gunsmith during my brother's infrequent trips home; visiting the gunsmith was a lesson in careful listening and meditation. A lesson taught by the gunsmith's simple actions and words. I bought bullets, both long and short 22s from him. I was excited about having saved almost enough money to afford my dream rifle and I must have talked about it in front of Dad. When he discovered that I had saved over $18, he made me use it to buy school clothes and shoes that fall; my year-long savings were reduced to a little over three dollars. I was 13 and almost old enough to be placed-out. I knew Dad expected me to become self-supporting by the next year. And, for the rest of my life, I bought all of my own clothes, shoes, school supplies and personal items.

Bud and his friend Jerry taught me how to chase bears. We didn't chase the baby bears because that would make the mothers mad and they would fight instead of running. We chased the mother bears when they weren't with their cubs, or the father bears. Being afraid of people, bears would climb the nearest tree when confronted. In 1949, bears were commonly shot by locals, and avoided all human contact. Once the bear had been treed, we would go underneath and taunt it, but the bears never came down. Chasing bears made me feel strong as we would chase them without a rifle. We waved our arms or sticks overhead and shouted like primitives gone wild. But I wasn't brave enough to chase them alone; the mountain lion still lived somewhere in my mind.

I explored the woods for miles around our farm and found two families of flying squirrels. One lived northwest of the farm and seemed reddish in color; the other family was grey and lived in the woodlot on the farm to our southeast. I shot a couple flying squirrels with my 22 before I realized they could fly. I picked up the first one I shot, and then the second, and was amazed at their little wings. They were special, unique, something I had never seen before. I felt a loss similar to what I felt when my dogs died. It was more fun just to scare them with near misses, and watch as they glided from tree to tree. I loved to watch them leap into the air, spread their little wing-like arms, and glide to the nearest branch.

It was amazing to me how nature had given these small creatures wings, while denying flight to their bigger cousins. After I made friends with the flying squirrels, I never killed another one. I sat and studied them by the hour, and they studied me just as carefully. The only other time I shot any squirrels after that was at Step-grandfather's farm. Grandma liked to eat squirrel, and knew how to skin and cook them so they tasted like chicken. Next to her mouth watering pies, this is my only lasting, fond memory of Madge's birth mother. The memory of funny colored socks always seemed to get in the way.

Our nearest neighbor lived on our side of Highway 48, across from the open field to the west as I walked in from the highway. They were a young couple expecting their first child. I cultivated corn for them in the summer, and helped them with haying. I was 12 years old our first Lorraine summer, and that winter was the school year of 1948-1949. Snow was heavy, and dad had the contract to drive the small bus that serviced our two room schoolhouse. Some days we were prevented from being bused to school because the deep snow remained unplowed. If Dad couldn't get out, none of the other kids could either. We didn't have a telephone, and I don't remember any phone lines in our entire area. Electric utility lines came through our part of Wisconsin our second year in Lorraine, but not phones. Local people just knew that heavy snow meant no school, and no travel.

We would wait for the milkman's truck to come with its big plow and open up our road. It was usually afternoon, or even the following day, before the milkman could get through. State highways were plowed by large specially equipped trucks after heavy snows and blizzards, but county roads were kept open by milk trucks with snowplows. Our Lorraine milkman was a marine-like stud who assaulted blizzards the way his military counterparts assaulted beaches; he swaggered, grinned, and chased the local farm "girls" with a vengeance. I learned this about him when his speeding car instantly killed our dog on Highway 48, and he drunkenly staggered over to pronounce the death sentence, and tell me how stupid my dog had been for chasing his car. His equally intoxicated girlfriend just sat in the car and stared. I thought: *two peas in the same drunken pod.*

I loved the feeling of being snowed in. The farm was alone in the cosmos, silhouetting dark trees against white snowdrifts, a beautiful sky as far as one could see, and total silence. These were moments of exquisite peace and happiness. A white blanket would cover our land, and spray the trees with jewel-like crystals that even sparkled in the moonlight. The silence was total, and I could hear the slightest sounds. Nature's blanket of snow silenced the dry grass and leaves as if it were preparing a grand performance. Deciduous trees came alive in frozen ballet form, and evergreens would be dressed in dark green gowns, displaying their special winter elegance against a world painted in sparkling diamond white.

The wind as it gradually awakens from silent sleep in the country has gentle caressing fingers. A touch that lightly strokes the pines more gently than that of any accomplished violinist. As the wind's strength is increasingly expressed, it plays pine needle strings with a finesse that mocks, and then puts to shame, onstage performers. The wind's orchestra continues to play celestial harmonies in this land of naked woods and snow – directed by nature's divine hand, but fewer and fewer people there today enjoy its music. Electronic noise has replaced God's orchestra. Gusts of wind provide crescendos of sound, then losing and regaining strength, return the phantom players to another round of soothing melodies.

There is no comparison in all the cultured world of steel and brick and lights and plastic that city people know. One never hears nature sing this way in the concrete jungles, if its voice is heard there at all. I have never heard such melodies in Minneapolis, Chicago, New York, Seattle, London, or Beijing. The city has no equivalent to the quiet that settles over the country after a commanding blizzard. Complete silence is demanded by the wind conductor, and provided by the snow. Then the orchestra begins to perform with gentle gusts blowing at just the right speeds, bringing forth delicate notes of the pine's frozen needles to play nature's own compositions; compositions of endless variety.

During Christmas vacation I decided to visit our neighbor to see their new baby boy. I walked the quarter mile through the trees, cut across the open field and knocked. The neighbor owed me money for cultivating corn, and visiting the baby would give him a chance to pay me; money I needed for simple presents for my brother and sisters. Dad told me in an exceptionally stern voice that I couldn't ask for my pay; they were poor and had a new baby; neighbors helped neighbors and didn't expect money. It was an unwritten code of this land that existed well before

Europeans arrived on the Continent; even though European immigrants thought they had brought the idea.

The house was dark except for one kerosene lamp, and a soft glow from the isinglass face of their wood-burning, pot-bellied stove in the living room, which was their single source of heat once the kitchen stove had cooled after supper. I felt sorry for them as they sat in semi-darkness looking at their sleeping baby; their eyes watching me like tiny mirrors of flickering light from the kerosene lamp. They didn't offer to pay me what I was owed, and I didn't ask. They were truly poor.

We had an electric generator in our house with real lights, but the generator made the wrong kind of electricity, 32 volts; we couldn't use it to operate a normal radio. But we could play pinochle and other card games by its light after chores in the evening. Pinochle was Dad's favorite family card game and I always had to be his partner; a partner who was expected to remember cards the way his perfect memory did. We had real lights while our neighbor only had a kerosene lamp.

Dad didn't let us bring schoolbooks home. We did school work at school, and farm work at home. He never made any exceptions to this rule, and would destroy any books or schoolwork that he found. We were informed that Grandpa had imposed this rule when he was a boy, and Dad never had any problem getting his work done at school. If we needed to do school work at home, we were either lazy or wasting our time playing. Besides, Dad had to learn English on his own when he started school in America, a handicap that his kids didn't have.

On the walk from our house to the neighbor's open field I thought I heard noises in the woods. The snow was unusually deep that winter and the temperatures had been dropping into the 20's and 30's below zero. Snow crystals snapped under my winter boots with every step – rubber outer shells made to protect shoes from rain, not cold; emitting clear cracking sounds that ice crystals make when they shatter. My imagination seemed to be adding a faint echo to my footsteps. A lighter reflection of feet crunching snow seemed to be coming from the woods as I hurried on to the neighbor's.

On the way back, the echoing started again. I would stop and it would stop. When I started walking something in the woods started walking. I thought about how cold it was, how deep the snow was, and how hungry some of the animals were. I was startled when the wires in the roadside fence squeaked. Something had jumped out of the woods and was now walking in the ditch next to me. Imagination became reality.

I had a small inch long pocketknife in my pants, but decided this wouldn't hurt any animal big enough to attack me, and I wouldn't be able to take off my mittens in time to get the knife out anyway. I mustered all of my will power. I didn't want the animal to think I was afraid, and walked on. Animals can read the chemistry of fear in people the way people read books, and my fear was beginning to talk out loud; the fear of my body chemistry speaking to a sensitive animal's nose. As I came close to the opening in the woods by our house, the yard light was just strong enough for me to see my companion's outline. It was following only a few feet away on the side of the road where it could walk on the plowed surface.

A few yards past the edge of the woods, I bolted across our lawn to our front door, legs flying through the deep snow. The animal raced too, and I saw the clear, unmistakable outline of a lynx in the yard light; it was trying to catch me before I could reach the porch. The snow was too deep for the lynx and my legs were longer and faster in the deep snow; the lynx had to jump over the soft breaking snow like a rabbit. The harsh winter had created a desperately hungry animal, but at the same time had saved me from attack with a soft, thick blanket of white that crumbled under its narrow feet.

I ran into the house, yelling that a lynx was chasing me. Dad just laughed and said it was my imagination; animals were afraid of people, and a lynx was not big enough to attack someone my size. Later I felt braver and went back into the yard.

The lynx's tracks came about 30 feet from the house, stopped, then turned and went back into the woods. I asked Dad to come and look at its footprints in order to prove that my imagination wasn't just being overactive. He wasn't interested, and didn't move. Mother came and looked, and so did Vonna.

A week or two later I climbed the ladder from the barn's milking parlor to the hayloft. I typically threw hay down for the cows while Dad finished milking. I got to the top of the ladder, and paused for a moment to let my eyes adjust to the darkness before climbing into the loft.

We had two small lights in the parlor where we milked, but none in the hayloft. As my eyes adjusted to the dark, two other eyes were peering back at me. I saw the outline of the Lynx's ears, and the milking parlor's lights reflected in his eyes. He knew I was afraid, I had run away from him on the road. As I waited for him to jump on me or claw my face, I held the ladder tight, removed my feet, and dropped suddenly to the barn's floor. This startled the cows and Dad yelled a simple profanity. I told him there was a lynx in the hayloft, and I was afraid to go up there. He insisted that I go into the loft and throw down hay, but I kept insisting there was a lynx and refused. Dad finished milking, and disgusted by my timidity, took an extra pitchfork up to the hayloft and completed the task. The lynx didn't bother Dad, who now let me know that it was either my overactive imagination or lack of courage that caused him this extra work, and he didn't appreciate either one.

The next spring I was walking home after visiting the flying squirrels only to discover the lynx sitting directly on my path, waiting for me. It looked half starved, ragged fur, glazed eyes, and it acted sickly. I thought it must be the same lynx because it wasn't afraid of me. It just stared with glassy focused eyes and didn't move, waiting patiently for a meal. I had two 22 short shells and my single shot rifle. Short 22 shells wouldn't kill a lynx, and I thought it must be rabid as it looked as though it had been beaten with a stick. If it bit or scratched me, I could easily die from the infection. I aimed carefully and shot out its right eye. I thought this would blind the animal, and it did. I reloaded my rifle, carefully walked around behind it, kept as much distance as possible from the dazed animal, raised the rifle inches from its head, and fired. The shot knocked it out and it crumpled to the ground. I hurried home, got some long 22 rifle shells and went back to finish it off. The lynx had recovered from my battering, and was safely hiding somewhere in the nearby woods where I was unable to find it.

SNAKES AND OTHER THINGS

It was Sunday afternoon on a warm August day in 1949 – mid-afternoon and about three hours before milking time. I decided to go into the back forty and cool off in the trees shade. The summer sun was at its August peak, and it was just a few weeks before school started. I only wore shoes in the summer when we left the farm; year old shoes that were by summer too tight for comfort; the cool woods were a relief to my hot feet and sweating body. I stopped along a path that went into an open meadow to our back 40, a short distance from our grazing cows. I stepped on a small, firm log and looked around. The log moved, and my first thought was that it was rotten and coming apart. I looked down and my first impression had been correct, the log was firm. I was standing about two feet from its end. I followed the log's outline in the other direction about eight or ten feet south of the path and discovered a pair of creepy snake eyes watching me. The snake's head was arched toward me with an open mouth that was big enough to cover my head, maybe even my shoulders. I didn't like snakes, and this was the biggest one I had ever personally met. I had no intention of becoming its friend.

We only had pine snakes, garter snakes, and little poisonous copperhead snakes on the farm. This was the biggest pine snake I had ever met in all my miles of local exploration, and pine snakes were common in this part of Wisconsin. Pine snakes loved to swallow whole baby chicks, making it necessary for me to guard the chicken coop with my 22. At first I thought, pine snakes aren't poisonous. Then I realized that this one looked big enough to swallow me whole, the same way smaller pine snakes squeezed down baby chicks. Becoming increasingly frightened, I jumped clear with frenzied feet pumping and fanning the air, and ran into the meadow where the cows were grazing.

Now I was stuck. I either had to walk through a swamp to get out while picking off bloodsuckers, or go back on the same path to reach home. I decided that the cows were bigger than the snake, so I herded them together, and drove them down the path in front of me. The snake was nowhere in sight as I walked between the cattle across the section of path where it had lain. It was too early for milking, and Madge didn't believe my snake story and thought I was just being lazy by bringing the cows home early. She told me pine snakes never got that big. Reality for my parents commonly denied the experiences of both my inner and outer worlds; their reality was invented, mine was real.

A few days later, Dad and another farmer who also had kids in our school, and Mister Anderson, my teacher's husband, conducted the annual school inspection. They looked at the main two room building, the two outhouses where we used the Sears Catalog for toilet paper - one outhouse for the boys and one for the girls, and the school grounds. The grass needed mowing, but everything else seemed in order. As we walked along the eastside of the school building in the warm morning sun, a snake came up out of the grass and appeared to be standing on its tail. It had flaps on both sides of its head, and slowly moved back and forth as if it were doing a little dance. I had never seen a snake like this except in pictures.

The adults all got long sticks and after many attempts were able to hit the elegant dancing viper. The snake fell down and they kept beating it on its head to make sure it was dead. We all went inside the school and looked in the encyclopedia. The snake was a cobra common to India. The adults thought it must have fallen off an airplane that had passed overhead. I told them about the big pine snake on our farm, but they said pine snakes couldn't grow that large, and stopped my story before I could go into detail. Authoritarian adults, I was reminded, only hear what they already believe.

When school started I looked in the encyclopedia. The big pine snake was from the jungle and it killed animals by squeezing them to death. I thought it must have fallen off an airplane too. I told Dad later that I found the big snake in the encyclopedia and it looked like a Boa Constrictor. He said that if it was a jungle snake it would freeze when winter came, and not to worry about it. Every time I went into the woods until freezing weather came, I worried about it. I felt safe in the woods. I could chase bears, and the forest was my sanctuary. The forest was my second home, and I didn't like the idea of sharing it with something big enough to squeeze me to death and swallow me for lunch.

Dad got mad if we tried to bring books or work home from school. Sister Vonna went to tenth grade in Luck, and I sometimes helped her write stories for her English class. I wrote a story for her about the lynx and she got an "A". Her teacher read the story aloud to the rest of the class, and this made me feel like an accomplished writer. Vonna could study nights when Dad worked in town or was milking. Other times, I would be her lookout and let her know when he was coming, giving her enough time to hide her studies. She could also do school work on her bus ride home. Kids who were at the end of the bus route like Vonna often rode for 45 minutes to an hour as the countryside was sparsely populated. Our farm was next to the dividing line that determined whether we went to Luck or Island City. I couldn't study on our school bus because Dad was the driver that first year. Anyway, I didn't like school work, it was boring and uninteresting. What I liked to read was the encyclopedias, but Mrs. Anderson wouldn't let me take them out of the classroom.

FINDING TREASURES

I explored the houses and buildings whenever we moved, and I found all kinds of good things. On the Comstock farm there was a vent that let warm air into my upstairs bedroom. I took the vent out, felt around and found a sack full of old Chinese coins with square holes in the middle. This was the beginning of a new hobby – coin collecting. Initially I traded Chinese coins for any other type of foreign coins available. My new hobby also meant asking grandparents, aunts, uncles, and family friends if they had any foreign or unusual coins. The largest migration of Europeans in America's history had occurred about the same time as my Grandparent's immigration from the Ukraine. I got coins from Italy, Poland, Russia, England, Switzerland, Germany, Austria, and all kinds of other coins and paper money from the Pacific war against Japan. I enlarged my coin collection with Indian head pennies, buffalo nickels, and all kinds of silver coins when I had my paper routes years later. I sold some of these coins in my senior year at the University of Minnesota, paying for a half-year's tuition and books.

In our old house just a couple miles south of Island City, I found a violin with two broken strings. I loved violin music and wanted to teach myself to play, but first, I had to find a way to replace the broken strings. Dad found out about my intentions and before I could get the violin repaired it disappeared. Madge later told me that he had smashed it. Real boys didn't play violins, or any other musical instrument for that matter. Real boys learned how to work, and how to become self-supporting. Dad had a phobia about boys being interested in music, especially classical music. Singing was different; he had sung in church years before when he thought he might become a preacher. Real men sang; sissy men played musical instruments.

CREATIVE READING

The Lorraine house had a great book hidden in the far corner of the attic, a place where Dad would never look: Physics by Charles E. Dull, 1908, University of Southern California. It was the only book in the house, and I hid it from him under my mattress. I memorized that book when I was thirteen, and could quote all the particle breakdowns, equations, and principles that it talked about. It was the best book I had ever read with all sorts of drawings, interesting people, and explanations about how things worked in the real world, even things we couldn't see with our own eyes, thereby adding reality to my personal mysteries. Unseen things were my specialty; I loved physics.

Someone had created a dump at the end of the gravel road to our north. It was next to the overgrown fire road that went seven miles north through the woods. People would throw away many things that were still good such as old batteries they had used to make their radios work. The batteries would get warm in the summer sun and come back to life. I used them to keep flashlight bulbs burning for many nights. I would wire up the bulbs, get under the covers at night, and read. That was how I learned physics while escaping the wrath of my father who was determined to keep me placed-out eligible in one more year.

When I got to my senior year in high school my teacher said I knew more physics than he was teaching. Mr. McDonald let me read anything I wanted to about physics instead of going to class. All I had to do was write reports proving that I was not just wasting time in the library. He liked my reports on relativity and special relativity best, but I cheated a little as I had read both books when I was 15 and hospitalized with pneumonia. I had become a fan of Albert Einstein by the time I entered high school, and his thought experiments fascinated me. He taught me that I didn't need equipment; I could experiment as much as I wanted to just by thinking about things in my own mind. Besides, thought experiments were fun.

The other kids in my physics class told me years later that McDonald read my reports to them. Most of the time, I read Scientific American as it was the only real science magazine our school subscribed to. We didn't have any other good books about physics in our school or city library, nothing that went beyond the college introductory level. Discovering Scientific American meant I could read back issues about anything that interested me, and the contemporary world of science between 1908 and 1953 opened up to my hungry mind.

DAD'S SWEAT

The winter when I was about to turn 13, dad taught me how to pull a seven foot crosscut saw. He would notch the trees with an axe to get them to fall in the right direction, and then we sawed from the other side until the tree fell down. My arms would ache after a couple hours, but he insisted that I needed to be toughened up. I never complained openly because I knew in another year and a half I would probably be placed out just like Brother Bud and expected to do a man's work. Sweat would get into my eyes as I strained to pull the saw, but Dad would only take breaks when he was ready, never when I asked. The next winter I had grown stronger, gained stamina, and found I could pull the saw longer than he could. Dad would say, "Let's take a break."

I would say, "Just a little more." I liked to see the sweat get in his eyes.

About half way through the winter, he rented a saw with a gas engine. We annually cut wood for the stove and furnace, wood for lumber, and pulp wood that we sold for money. I liked working in the woods that second winter. I especially enjoyed watching Dad sweat. I was 110 pounds, five feet, one inch tall. One of my summer jobs was to split winter-cut logs into firewood for the stove and furnace. Usually in August, when the wood had more time to dry, we had a neighbor bring his big saw rig to the farm, and we would cut all the logs into firewood lengths in one day. I split all our firewood, and had the job of keeping both the woodstove in the kitchen and the basement furnace supplied.

The second summer when I was 13, I made enough money to buy whole boxes of 22 shells. Usually I would buy 22 shorts as they were cheaper. I could kill unwanted birds and chicken-eating snakes with them, or just practice target shooting. I would take a spent shell, tap it into a tree, and then see how far back I could step and still hit the spent shell while either standing or kneeling. My brother bought a single shot 22 pistol that was three inches long, and shot short 22 shells. He left it at home, as the people where he worked didn't want it around. I would try to shoot birds with it, but they were hard to hit at any distance. The gun's barrel was too short for good marksmanship. It was the type of weapon a woman or gambler carried for close-range protection.

THE OWL

We had an owl in the woods just south of the house, and it hooted at night when it was talking to other owls. I was exploring the woods one day with the 22 pistol in my pocket, and saw the owl sitting high up in a tree. On the spur of the moment, I raised the 22, aimed carefully and shot. I was surprised when the bird came flapping down, and landed on a branch just inches in front of my face. It looked straight into my eyes like a demanding teacher about to reprimand a wayward pupil. I had never seen owl's eyes up this close before and I just stared back. Its gaze held me in a vice-like grip as life drained slowly from its body, its eyelids began to blink, the eyes turned upwards and the lids closed. A moment later it fell to the ground. I picked it up and put it back on a branch, but it just fell off again. I tried to put it on the branch a second time and noticed blood oozing from its chest. The owl's eyes were as mesmerizing as the Washington mountain lion's had been only they were eyes being consumed by death.

I had never watched anything wild slowly die at arm's length before. We routinely butchered chickens, but killing animals for food was a necessity. I shot unwanted birds, gophers and other small animals at a distance – death from a rifle wasn't real for me. Birds like sparrows ate grain on the farm and Dad wanted to get rid of them. The owl was different because it ate mice, rabbits and other things that ate grain and gardens. The picture of the dying owl became permanently burned into my brain. I wished it could fly again, I wished it would hoot once more, but it just lay on the ground. I couldn't bring myself to pick it up, or even bury it. I just walked away.

I kept seeing the owl's eyes pleading with me, as though it too could put thoughts directly into my mind. It kept asking why. "Why did you do this to me?" I had shot so many birds, gophers, snakes, turtles, and other little animals before and never thought about actually taking their lives. Now the owl demanded an answer, and I didn't have one. Owls have beautiful framed yellow eyes, but they are eyes that have trouble seeing in bright light. This owl strained to see my face while it was dying, the way I strained at night to see it hooting in the darkness. I still see its eyes peering directly into my "unforgiven" soul after all these years, and I still mourn having killed it.

PUBERTY

My younger sister had a girlfriend that lived about a mile from our farm. She came to visit that summer when I was thirteen. The girls decided to teach me how to dance, and dancing with the neighbor girl I discovered that puberty was catching up with me. I noticed my mother watching, and I was embarrassed by my lack of self-control. Dad and I had installed a cold-water shower in the basement that we used during warm weather. The water came directly from our well and was too cold to use on winter days; in winter we used a large washtub for bathing and heated water on our kitchen stove. My sisters would wash first, and in true country fashion, as the boy, I would be third. Madge kept insisting that she needed to wash me, but I kept refusing. She would get angry with me, and say it was all right because she was my mother.

Dad started working in town again that fall tending bar, and I was given additional duties around the farm. One afternoon Madge called me into her bedroom rather urgently. I went in to see what the problem was only to find her in bed. She told me to come over to the bed, and I thought she was in some kind of distress. As I approached, she threw back the blanket to reveal her totally naked body. I stood there in shock as she grabbed my arm and tried to pull me over. I was stronger than she was and wrenched my arm free. Horrified, I turned and left. She never tried to bother me again after that. Her sexual boundaries had been totally destroyed by Step-grandfather, or at least that is what I came to believe years later.

DEER HUNTING

The second winter on the Lorraine farm I was old enough to hunt deer. Dad borrowed a 30-30 rifle for me and I was to use his deer tag if I shot one. I knew the woods for miles around and many of the deer paths. There were mixed woods and meadows to the west of our farm with a frequently used deer trail that I had often walked. This was the closest deer trail from our house, and easy to reach after school. I waited, hiding just off the path's side for a long time, sitting quietly and downwind from any deer coming from the west. A deer appeared moving slowly through a small opening in the trees as it followed the path toward me. I waited for it to get closer, gun sights trained on its head. It came fully into view and I was beginning to squeeze the gun's trigger - then I froze. A neighbor was carrying the deer on his shoulders. The deer's head, and two of its feet, were on his left shoulder, with its hind legs on his right shoulder. The body of the deer rested squarely across the back of my neighbor's neck. If I had finished pulling the trigger, I could easily have killed him. I broke into a cold sweat, unloaded the 30-30, and watched the neighbor walk up to me. I knew hunters should never carry dead deer this way. It was a lesson everyone understood who lived in the woods. Yet here was my neighbor with a broad grin on his face that said, "I got mine," walking past me. I got mine, I got mine!

Days later, I went to a clearing a few miles north of our farm. In the summer many deer would come there to feed, and I often watched them. I got lucky the previous spring and saw two bucks fighting at this location during rutting season. They were busy charging each other with horns fully displayed, heads down, and snorting as they went about determining who was dominant. I was consciously walking very quietly as I approached. I walked Indian style in the woods in order to better observe nature's creatures. That day was an exceptional childhood moment! I watched for a long time then tried to see how close I could get before spooking them. I stepped on and broke a twig; they both looked up startled, and bolted further into the woods.

I watched the meadow for a long time, but no deer came. I then circled around the clearing going north, west, and then back east again. I was trying to make the deer move out of hiding so I could get a shot. It was nearing dusk when one came running across the meadow. A shot to the west must have scared the deer, and it was running fast on all four legs. I shot and it stumbled and fell. Getting up, it continued to run on three legs. I knew the deer could not last long running like that, and I ran after its trail of blood. The deer followed the path east, avoiding the more difficult underbrush as its broken leg was carried in flight. The blood marked path was easy to follow. The trail divided many times with branches going north and south. It ran ever deeper into the woods, and when I finally caught up, the deer was lying on its stomach pushing itself along with its hind feet. The sight was pathetic! This beautiful animal was mortally wounded, blood flowing from its open wound and physical exertion; its last ounce of strength was being used to escape its executioner – me.

I walked around in front of the deer, lifted my rifle to its head, and found that I couldn't pull the trigger. Two big liquid brown eyes were pleading – its gaze immobilized me. The blood continued to ooze from the deer, and eventually its eyes flickered and closed. Except for having brown eyes, the deer died just like the owl. The eyes asked the same question: "Why? Why did you do this to me?" I was trying to decide if I should gut this beautiful, graceful animal and try to drag it home, or go for help. The light was rapidly disappearing and the sky was overcast. The onset of night would leave me in the dark without any stars to guide me, and I foolishly hadn't brought even one match along.

A moment later an older man about Dad's age appeared, said that this was his deer, not mine. I told him that his shot had missed, and mine had broken its leg at the hip. I had never met him and he was not a local person. He scowled at me, repeated that it was his deer and partially raised his rifle in my direction. I knew what this meant and stepped aside. I was confused, angry at losing my deer, and relieved to have it gone at the same time. I stood motionless for a long time and watched this strange, determined thief drag my deer away as conflicting thoughts raced through my troubled mind. I also wanted to put distance between myself and anyone who would use a gun the way he did.

It was now dark and I was in an unfamiliar area. I would normally have followed a neighbor out of the woods, and most likely helped him drag the deer as well. More likely, he would have helped me drag my deer. But, I didn't know this man and wasn't comfortable with his intentions. I had covered many branching paths tracking the deer's blood. The sky was overcast and I couldn't see the stars. I looked at the moss on the trees trying to determine which direction was north, but the moss seemed to point over an arc of about 45 degrees. I headed toward what I thought was west and walked for a good hour or more. It was too dark to see the deer's blood, and the cold of the night felt like a shroud had suddenly been dropped over me. I was familiar with the dirt fire road that ran north through seven miles of woods from our farm, and hoped that I was walking in the right direction to intersect it. It was now dark enough that even the moss on the trees was invisible. I thought I might be walking in circles, and if so, I would be totally lost until morning.

I finally got to what looked like the service road that ran north from our farm, but at my point of contact it was more like two overgrown paths running parallel through thick woods. I had come out at a place that I couldn't recognize in the dark. The woods looked strange in the early winter's night. I walked in the direction that I thought was south for a long time, but remained in the woods. If I had gotten turned around and was actually going north, I would still find a country highway after a few miles. I was no longer sure this was the road that extended north from our farm. I thought I might be on a fire road I didn't know that went east and west. If that were the case, I wouldn't be able to walk out of the woods until sometime the next day. I had never been lost in this expanse of trees before, and began to think this might be my first time. My sense of direction without the sky to guide me was beginning to feel scrambled, and I started to doubt which direction was south.

It was well into milking time, and after suppertime, before I came to the corner of our farm road. I had walked northwest from the deer-killing site for a long time before intersecting our forest road. My night direction must have been off about 45 degrees. The lights were on in the barn, and mother had almost finished milking. I told her about the strange man taking my deer, but I never told her or anyone else about how the deer's eyes haunted and saddened me. Hunting people weren't bothered by dying animals, and didn't talk about such things. Now, I had two pairs of dying eyes indelibly imprinted in my memory – the owl and the deer. I never shot another living thing on the farm the rest of my life except snakes. I never bought another gun. I have fed a thousand birds or more from my backyards, and planted flowers by the hundreds for wild rabbits that lived nearby. May the owl, the deer, and all the small creatures I killed in my childhood forgive me! All life on this planet is intertwined by the same DNA and I have come to feel this kinship deeply.

FRIENDS AND COUSINS

I had never been able to save enough money to buy a bike. Anyway, money that I saved always seemed to buy necessities and school clothes. I went with Dad to a farm auction my thirteenth summer, and he bought an old bike for two dollars and some odd cents after observing me looking it over carefully. The front wheel didn't turn well, and I could tell that something was worn out. When I got it home, and took the wheel apart, one of the bearings was broken into small pieces. I took the broken pieces out, greased the bearings, and put it back together minus the broken bearing. I could ride the bike with great effort, but it was easier to walk, and faster to run. Anyway, I had a bike which I partially pushed and rode over to a more distant neighbor's farm where a boy my age lived. He had a bike and rode it everywhere. I tried to ride with him, but I couldn't keep up. I rode and pushed the bike home for the last time. I never got a new bearing, as the bike was an odd make, and we moved the next summer leaving it behind. Farm auction bargains were not always bargains, I learned. But as far as Dad was concerned, I owned a bike.

I had three boy cousins that liked to visit our Lorraine farm. Marvin and Gifford were brothers, one my age, and the other two years older. My third boy cousin, Jerry, was five years younger than me, a city kid and not very strong. Marvin and Gifford would come to the farm all year-round. They were former farm boys who had moved to Island City at a young age and didn't remember much about farms, or woods, or animals. I liked playing with my cousins and there were endless things that excited them: tree bending, cave digging, swimming holes, shooting the 22, making tunnels in the hay, and skating on the frozen ponds. The farm was a daily adventure for all of us. I especially liked teaching my city cousins about the country; country hicks knew many things that even older city slicker cousins didn't.

Tree bending was one of the favorite things that we all liked. Young saplings striving to become trees became part of our everyday playground. My cousins would help me bend them over so they were close enough to the ground for us to jump off. I would climb the tree and bend it over part way to the ground. Then, Marvin and Gifford would take turns climbing hand over hand until they got as close to me as possible. The third person would follow, and the tree would bend down close enough to the ground for us to jump off. We would keep climbing bigger and bigger trees until we couldn't bend them down anymore. I was a better climber than my cousins and always went up the tree first. They would get tired and want to stop, but I invariably wanted to climb one more tree. I physically pushed them the same way I had come to challenge my father.

The last time we bent trees together, I climbed the largest tree of the day and bent it over about as far down as the eves on our second story farmhouse. Marvin and Gifford didn't want to climb any more saying they were tired. They stood below the tree and laughed at the giant daytime bat hanging in the air – to far up to jump. They told me to climb back down by myself. I was on my own. But, I was at the very tip of the tree making it impossible for me to climb backwards and get off; I was at its very tip trying hard to weigh it down close enough to the ground to jump off. I begged my cousins to help, but they just pointed and laughed. I hung there like a helpless child, my arms aching. They finally realized that I was truly stuck and couldn't go forwards or backwards. Now rested, they made the climb one last time and we all jumped off. My city-slicker cousins knew how to take down my superior, in the country, country attitude.

There was a creek that ran along the edge of our farm on the southeast side. It was dry in the summer, and only had water and fish in it when the spring snows melted. I dug a cave big enough for my cousins and me under tree roots that were hanging over the creek. It was fun to play there, and cool in the summer. I was 12 the first summer when I dug the cave, and not familiar with all the animals that lived in the area. There were badgers in this part of Wisconsin, but they never bothered people unless they were disturbed, besides they were night animals, and didn't usually come out during the day. I wasn't personally familiar with badgers and I never thought about them attacking me. They have really long claws, and can rip flesh the way a hot knife cuts warm butter.

My cousins Marvin and Gifford liked the cave as much as I did. The second summer when I was 13 they came to spend a weekend with me. We walked the creek back toward a swimming pond that had water in it year-round and stopped at the cave. I was laughing and talking as I started crawling in. At first I didn't hear the animal warning me not to try sharing its home. I moved forward on my hands and knees when suddenly attention demanding growls filled my ears. My mind snapped to attention, the cave now belonged to a wild animal. I carefully and slowly backed out keeping my face close to the ground in case it attacked. My cousins and I ran down the creek at a safe distance, stopped, and watched to see if the cave's new owner was following. It wasn't. Later, when we went back with the 22, we found footprints of a badger that we had missed in our eagerness to play in the cave's cool interior. The cave no longer belonged to us, and we never entered it again.

My cousin Jerry was too small to bend trees. He couldn't run very fast, and wasn't very strong either. He was a city kid. He did like to climb trees, explore the woods, and enjoyed shooting the 22. Pine snakes used to come to our chicken coop and swallow baby chicks whole. My job was to watch for them and the 22 shorts were most effective if I shot them in the head. I learned that pine snakes were curious. If I held the 22 at just the right angle, they would strain to look down the barrel. The dark hole at the end of the gun was a death focusing magnet making them easy to shoot, but as a city kid Jerry didn't know this.

We had been in the woods scaring the flying squirrels and were walking the cow path back to the house. A large pine snake was in the middle of the path sunning itself, and wasn't moving. It must have just eaten because snakes would normally slither away when I got close to them. I told Jerry the snake was poisonous and he knew that I only had one bullet left in the 22. I said I had to kill the snake with one shot or it would attack us. Being a town kid, he didn't know that I was making the story up just to scare him and create a little excitement. I lowered the gun, the snake looked down the barrel, and I fired. The snake's head exploded, and Jerry thought I was a great hunter. He believed my story until we were both in our 40's and I confessed the truth.

BEING A NO GOOD KID

The summer of 1949 Dad gave me the job of digging a cesspool. I dug a trench next to the house down to the bottom of the basement floor, down the hill about thirty or forty yards, and then dug a large hole in the ground. Dad outlined the hole so I would get the size right, and told me how deep to dig. The ground was hardpan and I had to use a pickaxe to break most of it free. I made slow progress the first few days and Dad was vocally unhappy with my effort. About half way down the ground became softer and I dug without using the pickaxe. The next day I finished the hole, and had just gone into the house to cool off when he came home. Dad wanted to know what I was doing in the house instead of digging. I told him that I was cooling off and that the work was finished. He didn't believe me, made a face like "oh ya," took me outside, inspected the hole, took two or three chops on one wall to make it straighter, and pronounced it done. A week or two later we laid red-brown drainage tiles from the house to the pit, and poured the walls. I mixed all of the cement by hand. I built the forms with Dad from our own used lumber, lumber from which Bud and I had pulled and straightened the nails. This was the first big construction job that I had completed alone, even if it was with Dad's help. I was beginning to feel that I could do a real man's work.

Dad would not let me visit friends on other farms if they had sisters. No matter how hard I begged, he always said no. This meant that there was only one boy my age within walking distance, the boy with the bike. He didn't like to play with me because I was always working, and never invited me into his house; besides, I didn't have a bike that worked. Some weekends when Dad was gone and I finished my chores, I would run to the little nearby town. Lorraine was only three or four miles away and a quick run. I made a little money working for neighbors and would occasionally take a nickel to buy a bottle of pop: I always bought Orange Crush. I thought it tasted like real oranges. If the blacktop was hot I would run in the ditch or on the side of the road where the grass was cool. My feet were tough and I could run on top of newly cut oats stubble. The stubble would break under my weight and this made me feel like I was partially running on air, but I couldn't run on hot tar for very long.

Lorraine had a gas station with attached garage, all purpose grocery and dry goods store, small town hall, a small implement dealer for farm machinery, and a little nondescript store that sold odds-and-ends where I bought the Orange Crush. It sat at a country road intersection about half-a-mile east of our two room school house on Highway 48. Just far enough away from school that kids couldn't get to the store and back during recess. Like thousands of little bergs that were just spots by the roads across Wisconsin and the Midwest, Lorraine has totally disappeared. The grocery and dry goods store has been turned into a country home, and all the other buildings have been demolished or buried. Even the memories of all the kids who lived and went to school there are beginning to die year-by-year.

I got an infection in both eyes the summer that I dug the cesspool. My eyes gradually became glued shut, and I would be unable to open either one of them. Mother washed each one out with clear well water, and a couple hours later they were stuck tightly shut again. After a number of days of this routine, Dad finally took me to the doctor for treatment as I was unable to work. I remember the doctor telling him that I was in Olympic condition. I wanted to know what Olympic was and the doctor said I was in the best physical shape of any boy my age he had ever examined. I didn't understand his compliment and puzzled over it for some time.

COUNTRY BOYS

I was in eighth grade that fall, and the teacher gave everyone tests to see how strong they were. Almost all the kids were from farms and we considered these tests silly. The teacher had us do a small numbers of pull-ups, push-ups, and sit-ups – about 20 each. All the boys smirked at this small number, and we decided to have our own contest. The contest went on for several days. Some of us could do a hundred pull-ups and push-ups, except the city kid that had moved near the school the summer before. He didn't live on a farm, didn't have a farm background, and couldn't physically keep up with farm boys. One of my classmates did over 800 sit-ups, and I got to 1000. The other boy who did 800 sit-ups was the fastest runner in our school, and he was a year younger than me. He was thinner too and could start running like a rabbit that had been scared out of tall grass. I was a slow starter and couldn't ever make up his jackrabbit start to catch him.

The kid from town was a little fat with a small tire around his middle, never dressed in jeans or flannel shirts, and was totally incapable of wrestling. He was a sissy, and must have felt as uncomfortable in the country as I had felt living in town. I had absolutely no sympathy for him. One day when he mocked my worn, patched clothes, I took the liberty to pound him until he cried. He explained to the other kids that he was crying only because I had gotten his clothes dirty and his mother would be upset with him. I laughed!

I had never been in the same school two years in a row, and Lorraine was my twelfth change of school when I started the seventh grade. Mrs. Anderson was older than my mother, and the school was on the corner of their farm. She had been teaching there all her life; that's how she met Mr. Anderson. She came to Lorraine for her first teaching job right out of two years of teacher's college. Her husband would hire me to sack grain and do other chores before school, or over the lunch hour.

He paid me according to the amount of work I did, usually two cents for each sack filled with grain. It took two boys to sack grain, one to hold the sack and the other to shovel; we each made a penny per sack. Teacher doled out these work assignments partially to get control of those of us who were her greatest challenge. I had some idea of her motivation, but was more than happy to make the money, usually ten or fifteen cents as my share.

Mrs. Anderson taught in one of the school's two rooms. She taught fifth through eighth grade with about 15 total students the first year, and I think 13 the following year when I was in eighth grade. She was busy with all four grades and taught every subject herself. She decided that I should be her helper when I started eighth grade. She had me work with younger kids, and made me tutor them in subjects that I didn't know. If I protested saying that the material was new to me, she just said I should read it first. She identified and filled in almost every hole in my brain left empty by years of poor school attendance. I liked to read the encyclopedias, but she wouldn't let me until I finished my own work and tutoring assignments. She wouldn't let me take the encyclopedias home either. They were expensive, and she was afraid they would get lost. I also think she didn't like or trust my Dad.

The State of Wisconsin changed its laws covering school attendance during my eighth grade winter. It became mandatory for children to remain in school until they were sixteen. Dad was unhappy with this law, grumbled, but was forced to comply. This meant that I would be able to enter the ninth grade and not be placed-out. Employers didn't want fourteen year olds who had to remain in school two more years. I would be riding the bus with my sister Vonna, and attending school in Luck. Vonna liked high school and talked about all the interesting things she was doing there. She had many friends and was happy that Dad let her go even if she couldn't bring her studies home. Girls weren't that easy to place-out, especially in Lorraine where rich farmers basically didn't exist, and large families were common. I had two good years with Mrs. Anderson and thought that I might like the ninth grade. Deep down, teacher had done something strange to my psyche – I was even beginning to like school. I even liked stern, demanding Mrs. Anderson who could freeze boys my age in mid-stride with one practiced glance.

CHAPTER 7

ISLAND CITY AND WASHINGTON AGAIN

After school was over in the spring of 1950, Dad moved back to Island City. He bought a house on the north side of Beaver Dam Lake, about a quarter mile west from Sam's Corner. He and mother went to work at a new 3M plant in town. I was given the job of digging a basement; the house he bought was a three bedroom summer cabin that he was changing into a year-round home. Digging was initially hard as there wasn't enough room to swing a pickaxe overhead. The hardpan meant that I had to swing from the side until I got the opening deep enough to bring the axe overhead vertically. The house sat high above the lake with a dirt path wending down through the brush and weeds below. I wheeled the dirt to the edge of the hill and just dumped it. This saved me a lot of work, and I finished the digging early that summer. Dad hired a man to lay cement block walls under the house; thus, I didn't even need to mix the mortar. The floor remained dirt.

By the time I had finished digging the basement, the Company Store was hiring farm workers to thin rutabagas. Island City billed itself as the world's rutabaga capital and held an annual festival honoring the vegetable every August. Some of the boys in town told me about this job, and three of us went the first morning, riding the company bus to the fields. Everyone thinning rutabagas was either Indian from the nearby Reservation, or people who had come up from Mexico or Jamaica. The first row of "bagas" that I thinned went slowly. Indian people hoeing on the rows next to me helped, showing me how to work faster. After that I could keep up and even helped some of them when they got tired. Indians didn't have good food during the winter and got weak. The other two white boys quit after the first row and never came back. I made 35 cents an hour just like the Indian and Mexican adults, and after deductions for riding the bus, took home over $12 weekly. I had never made so much money and was able to buy a new cane pole, fishhooks, real bobbers, clothes and shoes. I was dressed just like the rest of the boys by the time school started. For the first time in my life I owned and bought T shirts and underwear, toothbrushes, jeans without bibs, and even a sweater with a picture of a deer on it.

I liked living by the lake. I could fish off the shore and the nearby bridge and had many new ways to make money. I mowed the neighbors' lawns with our push mower. This was especially good as I didn't have to buy gas for a power mower, and sharpening the blades was simple. There was an old woman who lived on the second floor above a downtown hardware store. She couldn't walk the stairs anymore and hired boys to fetch groceries. I eventually had to give this job up when my paper routes expanded. I started with the Minneapolis Star Tribune Sunday, and then added the St. Paul Pioneer Press Sunday. Finally, I got the Tribune's evening daily as well. I made a lot of money delivering papers and bought everything I needed for school. I got my first radio as a contest prize for getting new customers. It was silver colored, battery operated, and had a speaker that went under my pillow. I used the radio sparingly as batteries were expensive. I kept these paper routes until we moved back to Washington the following spring.

THE CHILD MOLESTER

After I finished thinning rutabagas, and before I got my paper routes, a kid down our lake road named Bud came to my house with his dad. His dad did all the talking, and encouraged me to take a job helping a farmer put up hay; a job that Bud had given up. I always looked for new jobs and was pleased that Bud's father was thoughtful enough to help me make some extra money. I knew farm work better than Bud, and had been haying since I was seven years old; I suspected Bud was having trouble keeping up with the work as he wasn't very athletic; he couldn't compete in sports, wrestling, or even running. A couple days later the farmer picked me up at home early on a Saturday morning, and we cut, raked, and put up hay throughout the day. He had one other friend helping and I was the only kid. We worked hard all day, and that evening four more friends of the farmer's came to eat supper and drink beer. Haying was a good excuse for rural Wisconsin people to get-together, drink beer, and socialize. Dinner guests were a welcomed part of this tradition, and added to the festivities. Often during these times card games, especially poker was enjoyed and a little money usually exchanged hands.

When it was time to end the day, the farmer said I should sleep in his bed. It was common for me to share beds with my uncles – I didn't think this was unusual as the other two beds were full with the farmers friends. I slept on the outside, the farmer in the middle, the other guy that helped during the day slept on his other side. I just started to drift off to sleep when his arm slid under my neck, clasped forward and held me tight. His leg came across my legs, thereby, pinning me to the bed immobilized. I tried to get out of this strange hold, but he was too strong. He then began to molest me. I said no, but he didn't listen. He told me there were many ways to have sex, and kept asking me if I pleasured myself. His questions completely embarrassed me as the farmhouse did not have separate rooms; one could hear a pin drop. After molesting me, he finally let me go. I tried to bury myself in the bed, and curled into a fetal position. The farmer and his friend made all kinds of strange grunting and sucking sounds. I didn't know what to do as similar sounds were coming from the other beds. I was now aware that the friends of the farmer had all been listening in the darkness. I had been a prop for their amusement. I was afraid of everyone, afraid to run, or even get out of bed, and eventually fell into a fitful sleep.

The next morning, the other five guys ate breakfast and left before I got up. I worked alone all day with the farmer in a state of extreme anxiety and agitation. We were on separate tractors cutting and raking hay. He kept studying me with a strange grin on his face every time our tractors passed – trying to get me to smile. This went on throughout the day. I didn't want to stop working at lunch time, but he insisted. I thought about driving the tractor to the edge of the woods and running, but I didn't know how to find my way home. The acreage we were working on was only good for hay, located in a remote wooded area miles northwest of Island City. We finished working in late afternoon, and I refused to eat supper or talk to him. He drove me home in deathly silence, paid me, and left.

A few days later, a deputy from the neighboring county came to our house. I was in the front yard working alone when he arrived. He asked me endless questions about the farmer, told me the farmer had done the same thing to Bud, and that I was the other "witness." He wrote down everything I said, and quizzed me over and over again about the farmer's exact actions and behaviors. He wanted to know every little sordid detail, and repeatedly asked me about my responses. Had I been a willing participant, had I enjoyed the experience, and what exactly did I say to the farmer. He wrote down what I said, made me repeat my answers many times and carefully checked his notes. I was in near panic before he completed my interrogation.

He told me that if the farmer admitted what he had done to Bud and me, we wouldn't have to go to court and testify; if the farmer denied that he had molested us, we would both have to go to court. I was extremely uncomfortable with his questioning at the beginning. The deputy made me feel that I had willingly been involved in something dirty and disgusting; his repeated questioning of my specific actions with the farmer made it seem like I might have enjoyed those pedophilic acts. By the time the officer finished, the thought of going to court, confronting my abuser, and testifying created a sense of extreme panic, but all I could do was wait. I waited for months but never heard a word from the deputy or the court. Getting convictions, that's what police work was all about; victims, we were rather insignificant.

The officer hadn't talked to either of my parents, hadn't asked permission to interview me, and left me shaken to the core at the very idea of going to court and confronting someone I never wanted to see again, especially face-to-face. I didn't like or respect Bud or Bud's father after that. They had encouraged me to help the farmer, and now I knew why. I wouldn't have been molested if it hadn't been for Bud and his dad. They used me as a second witness so Bud wouldn't have to testify alone in court. Bud avoided me the rest of that summer, and refused to talk about the farmer when I tried to discuss the incident with him at school that fall. I have never forgiven him or his pedophile supporting father, and neither one of them ever expressed regret for what they did to me. Two peas in a deviant pod, I thought; or was it two deviants in the same pod? Together they made it possible for the farmer to have another victim.

Mother asked me what the officer wanted and I explained. She had seen him talking to me in our front yard, but didn't come out until after he left. Her concern focused on my having to testify in court, and the story getting out; meaning, my motives and participation would be questioned, and our family's reputation suspect. I knew she had discussed the deputy's visit with Dad, as he later told me not to visit Bud anymore; explaining that his parents were little-minded people. He berated Bud's father saying harsh things that I don't recall; words to the effect that he was a slimy and ignorant man. I don't remember Dad's exact words, but there wasn't any question that he had no time for either slime or ignorance. I wasn't hard to convince.

CLASS PRESIDENT

I was surprised that fall when the city kids elected me to be ninth grade class president. The girls got together every year and picked one classmate that they all voted for. The boys were never that organized and their votes would be split between two or three candidates – the losers. I enjoyed being president of the freshman class, and was no longer treated as a hick. It was a new experience being accepted by town kids, both boys and girls, and I made a lot of new friends. This helped me get over being shy, and I soon found myself involved in a dozen different activities at school. I didn't have all the chores of a farm boy anymore, only three paper routes; I had plenty of time for extracurricular activities and just hanging-out with my new friends. It seemed as though everyone was my friend now; the dark world had turned and the sun was shining.

I thought as the class president that I should study and set an example, and was surprised when I got all "A's." School was easy and my free time permitted me to go out for sports. I joined the football team, but got knocked around by the bigger kids. I was now five feet four inches tall and weighed 124 pounds; the coach made us all weigh in. My cousin Gifford was a whole head taller than me and weighed over 150 pounds. I remember the 150 pound size as coach said anybody that big could hold his own and inflict pain on the football field. Coach was about this size, a little-big man. Most of the boys in ninth grade were much taller than me as well. I was nearly the same height as many of the girls, but a couple inches taller than most of the girls from Italian backgrounds. Dad was shorter than my uncles, and I was afraid that his small size would be my fate too. I made money with my paper routes and odd jobs, bought clothes, a baseball glove, ice skates, and had enough extra to go to movies, and learn the pool game called snooker. I never did buy a bike as they were still too expensive. The poorer town kids, the majority of us, didn't have bikes either. It was only a fifteen minute walk from one end of Island City to the other anyway.

Before my birthday in March of 1951, Dad decided to move back to Washington. He quit his job at Minnesota Mining, picked up his last check, and came home with a used automobile axel. We used the axel to build a travel trailer that weekend. We were moving to Washington on Monday. He sold the house to Uncle Eric who was moving back to Island City from Alaska in a couple years. We left the furniture, and anything else he didn't want to move in the house. Grandpa and Grandma were going to live there until Uncle Eric returned. This was how Dad usually announced that we were moving. He made all the decisions, never worried about where we kids were in the school cycle, or what Madge thought, and moved at will. Sunday afternoon we loaded the trailer with clothes, kitchen items, tools, and other small things, and early Monday morning set off for the coast. I didn't have time to tell my teachers about our moving or get my grades. My friends informed the school for me, and temporarily took over my paper routes.

WASHINGTON AGAIN

We drove to Washington without stopping, only this time Bud and Vonna continued to work in Wisconsin. Vonna had been "placed-out" just like Bud, and worked for a couple who owned a restaurant on Island City's Main Street. Marrying later in life, the couple never had any children of their own and seemed overjoyed at having Vonna live with them and work in their restaurant. They treated her just like a daughter, and she called them Mom and Pop. Unlike Bud's farmer, they let Vonna go to high school during the day, and work in the restaurant at noon, evenings, and weekends. My sister's new Mom and Pop always treated me the same way as my other aunts and uncles – we were family. They would give me treats such as pie and ice cream when I went into the restaurant to visit Vonna, and even brought me to their home a few times for meals. I spent more time with them, enjoying a family atmosphere, than I did with most of my aunts and uncles. They were urban people from the big city of Chicago, but still understood farmers and small town folk. I found this unusual, and will always remember their kindness.

We moved back to Everett Washington and I once more took the bus to school. The school had seventh, eighth and ninth grades together and was called junior high. This was a step down for me as I thought of myself as a high school student. Sister June and I rode the bus together – she was in the eighth grade. I was assigned an independent study class in Washington State History, a course required by ninth grade students in order to pass into senior high. I really enjoyed Washington history, especially the part about Lewis and Clark exploring the West. I finished the book and my report in two weeks. I asked if there was more Washington history that I could read, but the teacher said no. That was all the history she was interested in sharing with me. Dad was working away from home during the week, and this gave me a chance to read daily. I devoured library books. I never liked the adventure or western stories that most of my classmates read, I liked science, history, and magazines like Popular Mechanics that told me how things worked.

The bad part of returning to Washington was the reoccurrence of old nightmares. The Big War was over, we had won, and the Japanese were confined to their American occupied island. It didn't matter; night after night they would return in my dreams, take me to their submarine, and try to make a flag stand out of me. In my dreams, it always seemed real the way the drill was pressed into my spine, preparing a hole for the flag to be inserted.

This was painful emotionally, but I couldn't make the almost nightly dreams stop. In the second nightmare that followed me from Wisconsin, I was being chased through the woods, or along a highway, by a gang of men on different kinds of motorized vehicles. Sometimes the bad guys would be riding motorcycles, and sometimes they would be in cars or trucks. I knew they wanted to hurt me and I would run wildly through the trees and underbrush trying to escape. As they closed in and I was about to be captured, the panic would peak and I would wake up in a cold sweat.

THE STATION

Dad decided that I needed a job. I was old enough to be placed out before the law had been changed that made it mandatory for kids to stay in school until they were 16. Dad didn't like this law as he considered everyone capable of adult work when they reached fourteen; I was fifteen and he wanted all of his kids to be placed out before then. Bud had been placed out at fourteen, three months before he finished the eighth grade. His farmer-employer hadn't permitted him to finish the school year. After age fourteen, I didn't have to ask Dad for permission to stay out late or engage in adult activities. He was absolutely clear! I was responsible for my own behavior and any consequences that behavior brought; nevertheless, he continued to exercise total control and veto power over all of my behavior. But, this power was only exercised if it involved an inconvenience for him.

When school was out, we moved to Marysville – the next town north of Everett on old State Highway 99. Dad leased a Signal Gas Station that had an attached three-bedroom house. I ran the station during the day, opening it at 7 AM and closing it at 10 PM; working hours approximating what was common on Wisconsin dairy farms of the day. Madge, or my sister June, would bring my meals from the house through an attached back door in the station. I liked being my own boss, and felt very grown up with that job. There were manuals about how to fix cars, where the grease fittings were, what kind of spark plugs they needed, and just about everything a person had to know to keep cars running.

Computers didn't exist then and teenagers like me could learn all about cars just by reading manuals. I read them all when I wasn't busy, and memorized the differences between car models. Customers would question me about servicing their vehicles. They quizzed me about my age, and asked me specific questions about how I did repairs. I would show them the manuals, and explain how carefully I followed directions, how I located all of the grease fittings, or how I cleaned and set the gaps on their spark plugs. Often times I found that other stations were performing bad service: other shops would skip hard to reach grease fittings, or set spark plug gaps wrong, and the like. This helped me build regular customers in spite of my age.

The first day that Dad took me with him to look at the station, I was lost. The man who leased it tried to show me how the station operated and where to locate popular items that customers wanted such as white gas; this being the only station in town to carry it. He showed me how to work the cash register, and attempted to take me into the shop area when Dad stopped him. Dad said that if I was going to be responsible enough to run a gas station I had to figure things out for myself. Dad had visited the station before, as well as the house, and was satisfied that it would meet his needs. He took the man downtown all day drinking, and they both returned drunk about six hours later. The other man was visibly drunk, but not Dad; intoxication was an old friend he knew too well.

I had just practiced opening and closing the cash register, which was the old mechanical type, when two cars pulled into the station, one on each side of the pumps. I knew how to get gas from the pumps as I had often filled our cars and tractors, but I didn't know how to reset the gas meters to zero. I memorized the numbers on the pumps and mentally deducted the difference from the meter's final total. The first man looked at the amount on the pump, handed me the exact change requested, and left with a crooked smile on his face. I realized he thought I had given him extra gas and he was happy to cheat the dumb kid out of the difference. This was my first lesson in customer honesty. I figured out how to reset the pumps before any more cars came.

Then, I started surveying the station to see what was there and where everything was located.

I made a lot of money in that station, and our family got rent well below the going rate for comparable houses. My weekly income after expenses, and helping Madge was over $50. Fifty dollars was a good average salary for working men in 1951. I bought a portable typewriter for $169.00. The sales clerk dropped the 95 centers, and made a big deal out of the bargain I was getting. Every week, I gave Madge $20 to help with groceries and household expenses; by today's standards that would be about $200. She said Dad didn't give her enough money to adequately support the family.

I bought myself new clothes, helped my sisters, and always had money in my pocket. I sent my sister Vonna $120 so she could take the bus from Island City to Marysville. She was lonely, had been ill, and wanted to come home. The first time I sent money, she used it for medical expenses. The second time I sent a little more money at her request; and she came by bus to start her senior high year. Vonna, June and I lived in the attached station house until we moved back to Island City about three weeks before Christmas in early December 1951.

I had an understanding with Dad that I would keep up the inventory in the station, or pay him the difference when we left. I made sure that the inventory was increased a little every month in order to meet this agreement. He didn't know I was giving money to Madge, and she was firm about my not telling him. Dad came home one day with an old, but good used car and told me it was mine. The car was in excellent condition, and I drove it around to the back of the station and parked it against the wall. I refused to drive it on the street; I was only 15 years old and didn't have a driver's license. He didn't care about me not having a license and encouraged me to drive it; people back on the farm often drove without one.

Dad wanted me to quit school and just work, and I felt the car was a gift to help me make this decision. I totally rejected the idea that I could drive the car illegally, and was even more determined to remain in school. I was beginning to think about going to college. Some of my classmates talked about going to the University of Washington in Seattle. I thought I could build up enough business in the station in two more years, save money, and afford college. College was gradually becoming a dream of what might be both affordable and possible. I lived on dreams the way young lovers do.

UNCLE EARL

Uncle Earl came back from Korea in late summer. He was emotionally incapable of any productive work. He told me different stories about the war when he was drunk, but never talked about combat when partially sober; I don't remember him ever being completely free of alcohol during his stay. He babbled on about our troops not being well equipped for winter weather, being low on ammunition, and pushing toward the Chinese Border and the Yalu River. Up to this point the war was only being fought with North Korean troops. Chairman Mao had promised the North Koreans Chinese intervention but had delayed Chinese entrance into the conflict.

The Chinese were using an old military tactic of drawing the enemy deep into their territory, letting them become over confident, and then attacking with force. They used human waves in these attacks, and the front became a slaughtering field. Uncle Earl talked about how our forces killed wave after wave of Chinese troops, but more kept coming. Their overwhelming numbers, our lack of equipment, supplies and ammunition at the front resulted in American, United Nations and South Korean forces being overrun and pushed back to Panmunjon where they were to be evacuated by waiting ships.

The Military Museum in Beijing, just west of Tian'anmen Square on Subway Line Number 1, displays captured American weapons from Korea. Like all military museums it talks about the heroics of its soldiers, how many Americans were killed by a single weapon, and proudly presents China's view of the war. It was a strange feeling carefully reading the displays in English as old memories of time with Uncle Earl returned. Signs everywhere in Beijing, and outside this museum, proudly proclaimed the vision of Beijing's 2008 Olympics: "One World, One Dream."

How small the world had become in the 21st Century I thought – may it get even smaller. "One World, One Dream" would have been an even better motto in 1945, well before this godforsaken exercise of youth killing youth on the Korean Peninsula, at the direction of old men in political power – in wars that never end.

Uncle Earl and his army buddy were sitting in a deuce-and-a-half waiting to board an evacuation ship when Chinese forces encircled them. They bayoneted his buddy, threw gas on him and turned one more soldier into a human torch. When Uncle Earl talked about his buddy's screaming, his eyes turned inward, and his face twisted in pain as his internal movie played through one of those moments the mind never forgets. Somehow, Uncle Earl got away and was taken aboard a waiting ship; a physical survivor; an emotional basket-case. He never told me specifics about how he escaped, but appeared to be racked by guilt for not being able to help his best friend.

Every morning he got up, had a small breakfast, and went to a nearby serviceman's bar to drown his memories and nightmares. He kept a case of beer in my bedroom, which was never permitted to become empty. He would return drunk in late afternoon or evening and continue to drink until he passed out, or fell asleep. After about a month of this routine and much encouragement from his anxious parents, he returned to Wisconsin before permanently moving to California. Korea was mostly a forgotten war except for the continued presence of American troops, and a belated national memorial. The Cold War became the new them versus us focus justifying endless amounts of money for military expenditures, and ever new excuses to hate people we didn't know and had never met in another part of the world we had never visited.

My newest nightmare became more frequent when Uncle Earl stayed with us. I would be walking or riding a motor bike in the woods, the mountains, or along a dam, with this strange gang chasing me. I could never get away, and they continued after me on all kinds of vehicles. No matter where I tried to hide or how fast I ran, the gang would find me. This constant pattern of trying to escape, being found, and running again was repeated endlessly in the nightmare until my psyche would become exhausted and I would wake up filled with anxiety. I would wake from one nightmare, and go back to sleep, only to have another version of the hateful scenario take its turn. No matter what I tried, I could not stop this dream sequence. The nightmares lasted for six more years until I learned to control them during my student days at the University of Minnesota.

MOTHER'S BOYFRIENDS

I talked to my sister Vonna about mother having so many boyfriends. We were both upset by her sexual exploits; many kids over the years were never permitted to come to our house because of Madge's reputation. Adult words were never spoken to our face, at least not to mine, just knowing glances and crooked smiles when she was identified as our mother. Vonna and I decided on confrontation, and asked Madge to sit down and discuss something important. Madge denied having any boyfriends, and severely chastised us for thinking such terrible things about her. We insisted that we knew she did and named some of them; one at that time being a vacuum cleaner salesman who returned repeatedly but never demonstrated cleaners after his first visit. She became totally irate, refused to talk about boyfriends any more, and simply got up and walked away. She never had woman friends outside of the family until a few years before she died; a time when she was beyond the age where she could attract new sex partners.

Years later my younger sister, who had just turned fourteen when Vonna and I confronted Madge, recounted how mother would take her to a nearby military bar during the day. June had to pretend she was mother's younger sister, thereby making it easier for Madge to pick up servicemen. She took them to a nearby motel for sex while June waited patiently in the bar. She did this day after day. This was how she used the extra $20 I gave her weekly. What she didn't spend on her hobby, as it turned out, she tucked away for a rainy day. I thought I was helping support the family by giving her money, but in reality only made it possible for Madge to enjoy enhanced erotica. June was so intimidated by mother that she wasn't able to tell me her side of the story until we were well into our adult years.

CHAPTER 8
BACK TO WISCONSIN

I didn't want to leave Washington. I loved the mountains, the year round green, and I even loved the rain in the winter. I thought I could save enough money running the station to attend the University of Washington in a couple of years. To my chagrin, Dad sold the lease to the station without discussing it with me or mother, and we returned to Wisconsin in early December. He had saved enough money to buy another farm, and mother signed the purchase papers with him shortly after our return.

The farm was about a mile north of Aunt Tillie's. I stayed with my cousins Marvin and Gifford, and Vonna stayed with her other Mom and Pop from the restaurant; I don't remember where Dad, Madge, or June stayed. Before we could all move onto the farm, Madge took June and disappeared. She also took two thousand dollars from Dad's pocket, money that he was saving to buy farm equipment. He was livid and looked everywhere for her. Cussing and carrying on about her signing the purchase papers at the same time she was making plans to leave him. I later learned that Madge told some members of the family that she was sick and tired of being isolated on god-forsaken farms, and was going out-of-state where Dad would never find her.

Dad bought cows, moved Vonna and me onto the farm, and took a full-time job tending bar in Island City. Tending bar was his favorite job; he could drink and work at the same time. I was old enough to run the farm, and would be 16 in a few months. Vonna's job was to cook and take care of the house. We could both go to high school as long as we kept the farm running. This lasted for two months and I became immobilized with pneumonia in both lungs. Dad said I was a weakling, and decided to toughen me up. He took me to the oat bin and made me hold grain sacks while he filled them. He dumped the grain in such a way as to make the maximum amount of dust. At such moments, Dad's total disgust for his useless son would be displayed like a cartoon animation by twisting his facial muscles into scorn and contempt. He was a master actor when displaying unfiltered emotions. I had torn strips of an old sheet and was using them for hankies, but these were soon full.

The dust was choking and my coughing became so violent that I couldn't stop. Dad said, "You're no good, get in the house." My coughing continued uncontrollably and I had to be driven to the hospital. The doctor diagnosed pneumonia in both lungs. Dad had to milk the cows and take care of the farm while I was hospitalized, and this imposition peaked his anger. He only spoke to me and my sister when giving orders after that. He didn't discuss any of his plans with Vonna or me, but a couple weeks later announced an auction where he would sell everything. Vonna went back to Mom and Pop's restaurant, and I went to live on Uncle Bert's farm. Uncle Bert was good to me, let me finish school that year, and was considerate about giving me chores that were relatively dust free. Both Uncle Bert and Aunt Ethel treated me like a normal son, except for weekends when they occasionally took short family vacations.

UNCLE BERT'S

Dad spent the summer making the rounds of local bars in a number of the surrounding towns, bought a new car and found a special girlfriend. He would drive by Uncle Bert's in one of the hottest production cars of the year, a Plymouth whose specific model I've forgotten; holding down its horn, and sounding like a passing high speed train. When Dad was excited or angry he cruised at 85 miles an hour; a habit that gave him two broken backs during his life time. I felt like a totally useless person. I couldn't manage a farm without getting sick; yet, was placed-out in the same kind of farm environment that my allergies didn't tolerate. Pneumonia was an affliction that visited me almost every year on the farm. I didn't have any money left from the gas station in Washington, I didn't have a car, and I wasn't sure if I would be able to start school in the fall.

Uncle Bert was interested in creating a home delivery milk service that I would run. He talked at great length about how much money we could make in this type of value added business. All I had to do was get the customers, bottle the milk, and do the deliveries. Existing home delivery services of this kind were already well established in the surrounding towns. I was to become a milkman of sorts and never finish high school. This idea was light years away from my desire to get a college education. Uncle Bert's face showed his displeasure at my resistance. I was sixteen years old and ready for a full-time job; I also had my sixteenth birthday during the month I moved onto his farm. I kept resisting his milk and dairy business ideas and he finally gave up trying to change my mind.

Uncle Bert was very fussy about how his cows got milked. By early summer, I was familiar enough with every cow to do the milking by myself. This meant that I knew how each cow milked-out individually and what was necessary to prevent any of them from becoming infected. Some weekends, he would take my aunt and two cousins on short trips. It was the middle of summer with the crops planted and only the corn needing a little cultivating. Uncle Bert's farm was well kept, and Auntie had a gas stove for cooking; it was the most modern farm I had ever lived on. Imagine, a real gas stove!

I was alone on the farm when Uncle Bert and my cousins were away, with endless time to think. I walked and swam in the creek just below the hill. I had time to read, as Uncle Bert and Aunt Ethel both kept and read books. Aunt Ethel had been a teacher in a local two room schoolhouse before she married Uncle, and supported everyone going to school. Uncle Bert, like Dad, had only finished the eighth grade. He was capable of reading any of the farming journals and applying new farming techniques, and he did. Education beyond the eighth grade was not especially valued by local farmers at that time.

I decided one warm, sunny Sunday morning, after I had finished milking and eating breakfast, that I would commit suicide. I thought the silo was high enough to kill me if I jumped from the top. I started to climb the metal rungs and got about half way up. I stopped, looked out at the countryside, visually followed the river south a mile or more into the distance, studied the green land below, and felt the warm sun on my face. I thought it would be my luck jumping from the silo to just break both legs and be lying there when Uncle Bert came back that evening from his weekend vacation. The thing to do was to dive off head first. This would splatter my brains over the packed dirt road below and kill me instantly.

I began to climb higher. Then, I thought more about my brains splattered like broken eggs all over the yard, became nauseated, and felt like throwing up. I came down the ladder suppressing the urge to lose my breakfast, and decided I would rather live. I talked to my sisters when we were mature adults, and each one of us had come to that moment, the moment when death seems to be a rational decision. We all said no to the Grim Reaper.

The skies were clear at Uncle Bert's and I could see the constellations almost as well as when we lived in Lorraine. The farm's landscape was open and flat permitting me to watch storms coming from miles away. This was a new experience, seeing thunderstorms build far in the distance. The skies would darken, huge billowing clouds would form, and bolts of lightning and sheet lightning would walk across the sky, accompanied by booming thunder. I loved thunderstorms, their power, and ability to transport me directly into nature. I didn't have to use my imagination. I would just merge with the storm, be part of the wind and rain, and experience all its power and majesty. Standing drenched in the downpour, I'd let the storm surge through my veins as my identity merged with the wind, the rain, the lighting, and the thunder. Instead of banging my head on the floor to create reality, all I had to do was stand in the swirling power of the storm to feel whole.

My liberated unbounded soul swirled with the power of the storm as the rain drenched and renewed the landscape. Always, the ability to separate from my physical body was exhilarating, especially when I joined the forces of nature churning around me. Throughout my lifetime, I remain bound to these forces, enthralled by them, and inseparably connected to the energy of the world in which I live. The primitive ancestry of our species never leaves me. I am thunder, lightning, Northern Lights, raging waters, turbulent oceans, I am nature's son. I am just one expression of energy in this lovely cosmos, but one with cognitive awareness. Reality becomes illusion; illusion becomes reality; only will moves between them. Primitive man still lives; I am that person.

I slept in the same bedroom at Uncle Bert's that I once shared with his brothers. Grandma and Grandpa were now living in our former house on Beaver Dam Lake. My farm bedroom was at the far end opposite the top of the second floor stairs, and the outhouse was still in the back yard; although the outhouse's location had moved periodically when a new pit was needed. Dad stopped one day in late summer; it was the first time he had spoken to me since the farm north of Aunt Tillie's was sold. Uncle Eric and Dad bought a combined bar and restaurant north of Island City. I was to move in with Dad and share the living quarters on the second floor; Uncle Eric was still working in Alaska. I was excited - Dad said he would let me enter my junior year in high school as long as I did my work. Uncle Bert's reason for keeping me on his farm no longer existed. I was to become a bartender rather than a milkman.

THE CLUB

I moved in with Dad a few days before school started, and the first day he immediately began teaching me how to tend bar. Mixing drinks was easy, and anything that was odd or different, such as exotic drinks made in Florida or Mexico, I could look up in a book. I was working until 1 PM and closing the bar by myself within a month after school started. The north half of the building was a bar; the south end was designed as an eatery. Dad hired a local chef to run the restaurant. He didn't like restaurants believing they were only good for enhancing alcohol sales; booze was the source of real money. It was also the quintessential route to endless fun, and exciting women, for Dad.

Dad was as clever about bar business as he was dumb about restaurants. He named the establishment the 5 O'Clock Club.

This meant that anyone who was there at five o'clock could get a free drink. He said that two for one drinks didn't have as much appeal as free drinks. Very few people ever left without buying a second drink, and many stayed for hours, got drunk and ate. The code of country people served him well – always return a favor with a favor, a kind deed with a kind deed, a free drink with ... The place was busy, and he was making lots of money. Dad bought his girlfriend a large diamond ring at something rumored over two thousand dollars – today's value $20,000, a big screen television, new appliances, and took her on vacations as far away as New Orleans, as well as paying off her house mortgage.

Dad had become a Big Spender. His girlfriend had been Miss Minnesota years before, and Dad thought she was as special as she thought she was. I didn't like her and didn't respect her. She would try to take money out of the cash register when I was busy. He held me accountable for all money in the register, and made me pay back any shortages out of my salary. It didn't matter how the money was missing; even if he sat and watched her take the money while he was drinking at the bar and I was busy elsewhere with customers. He never said no to Miss Minnesota, just kept giving her everything he could afford, everything his brother partner could afford, and a little more. Uncle Eric must have wondered where the profits were going; that is - what was reported on the books.

After a few months, when he was sure I was able to manage the bar alone at night, Dad hired a full-time bartender to work during the day. I would work the week nights alone from Monday through Thursday, and the chef ran the restaurant. This left Dad free most of the week, and he spent this time with his new girlfriend. She was Catholic and had been married to a bigamist; unfortunately she was the first wife, the legitimate wife in the eyes of the Church. She was still married in The Faith even though she was divorced as far as the State of Wisconsin was concerned. She never bothered to get an official marriage annulment from The Church; hence, was unable to marry Dad even though he repeatedly proposed. Miss Minnesota enjoyed the best of both worlds, proudly and piously remaining a victim of her formerly abusive husband. She wore pride like expensive clothes – conspicuously.

Dad would work Friday and Saturday nights during football season. Friday nights became my night off, which enabled me to play in the scheduled conference games. During the rest of the school year, I was supposed to have the Sunday evening shift free. Dad expected me to work two shifts on Saturday and two on Sunday during football season to make up for Friday night; although I usually came home after the games and worked until 1 pm. I worked 64 plus hours a week, 5 PM to 1 AM, Monday through Thursday and four combined shifts on Saturday and Sunday. Except for holidays and summers when school was out; then I worked from noon through the evening shifts, except the times when I had a second job.

Dad got used to being off all day Sunday and rarely worked them even when football season was over. I was paid $20 per week, and was able to buy cereal and bread for breakfast, a lunch ticket at the restaurant near the school, and had my evening meal provided free by the restaurant. This left me about $12 per week for living expenses and school. This was considerably more money than most of my other classmates had, and additionally, I ate lunch every day at the local restaurant where I could buy six meals for five dollars. My classmates were impressed by my new status and again voted me class president my junior year. This honor automatically made me Junior Class Prom King, and just as automatically, it seemed, gave me the primary male role in the junior class play. The crack-stomping hick in bib overalls had arrived. Only, I didn't know this until years later.

Dad got tired of providing backup for the kitchen as our chef was an alcoholic and not reliable. The chef often failed to show up on time even though he lived just across the lake from the club. Dad had to find some way to cover for him, or pry our chef out of his alcoholic slumber. This unpredictable situation interfered with his love life, and interfered with what had become his number one relationship in all his world of pleasure. He leased the kitchen out, and totally forgot about it. He then informed me that I would have to pay for my own evening meals. The lease owner didn't want to feed me without compensation, and Dad had not negotiated my evening meal as part of the agreement.

I stopped eating in the kitchen and began making myself sandwiches. I informed Dad that I was looking for a job downtown as I couldn't afford to work for him anymore, which meant that I would also find a room downtown. He rather quickly relented, arranged for me to take my evening meal on site, and I stayed with him until after high school graduation. Dad promised that if I worked for him until I entered college he would help me with expenses. This was an extra incentive, and I forgot about getting a different job. I knew many town people by then and was sure I could make $50 weekly on my own. This change would cut my weekly work hours to 40, and take about ten or twelve dollars a week for a rented room; hence, providing both a time and money saving advantage. But, the promised college support would be gone. I lived on dreams and possibilities.

By winter of my senior year, I was having trouble staying awake in the afternoons. The teacher who supervised study hall regularly came to the Club with her fiancé. She would let me sleep all or part of study hall, even waking me up at the end if I didn't hear the bell. This, along with considerable consumption of alcohol while working, got me through my senior year. Dad didn't care about my finishing school, and discouraged me from going regularly. I had to walk home after football practice and games, or other school activities because the bus left earlier. I didn't have and couldn't afford a used car. Dad had an eighth grade education and was making three or four times as much money as my teachers. He also said he had more fun than they did, and generally derided their intelligence and competencies. Only two of my teachers regularly came to the club, and one teacher's wife. The teacher's wife was married to the football coach and bowled on the team sponsored by the Club.

The one benefit of getting five hours sleep nightly was limited nightmares. I would fall into bed exhausted, and occasionally not even hear my alarm clock in the morning. When I remembered dreaming, however, the dreams were patterned and bizarre. I would be in thick woods being chased by men on motorcycles, or some kind of vehicle that I couldn't outrun. I would be filled with panic; and wake up soaking in sweat. Another dream version was walking in Washington State, either up or down the mountain at what seemed like Stevens Pass. Sometimes I would be on the other side of the pass either going east or coming west. The bad guys would be looking for me along the side of the road, and I had to hide whenever vehicles came by. Eventually, the gang would see me and as they closed in I would once again experience terror that was both new and familiar, and wake up. But, if I drank enough alcohol there were no dreams, just oblivion.

A separate version of the nightmare had me on a vehicle being chased by other vehicles. My pursuers could be on motorbikes or in cars and trucks, and I would be on the same kind of machine. The dreams would repeat in a similar pattern; I would lose my means of escape, be surrounded, and wake up terrified. At first I thought these were all different nightmares, but over time I came to experience them as versions of the same scenario.

The nightmare where I am at the west end of a dam had me circling a set of buildings near the edge of town. The largest building was a drinking place that I knew was full of sexual deviants. Sometimes I would be forced to duck into the building in an attempt to escape my pursuers. This part was really scary; once I got in the building it was impossible to get out. A maze of doors let to other doors, which would sometimes open to reveal my pursuers. As the perverts closed in on me, I would become frantic, run from one room to another, and eventually wake up. These scenarios could be mixed together in any combination and went on for years. I had no idea where they came from or how to stop them. My conscious mind totally failed to connect the dots, those maddening, impossible dots.

I forgot about beautiful skies working nights at the 5 O'Clock Club. Life became a blur of people getting drunk, me getting drunk, other people's choking cigarette smoke, and a struggle to stay awake at school. I missed my first class a couple of mornings because I slept through the alarm clock. The principal told me I should use an alarm clock, and I told him I did. Mine was the old mechanical kind of alarm that had a small hammer loud enough to wake the dead. The principle found my explanations unacceptable, and would give me an unexcused absence. My teachers knew by my senior year that I worked long hours, and none of them penalized me in terms of grades for these infrequent absences. Teachers were some of the most humane individuals in my life, and I grew to like them more than other professional people I knew who came to the Club, and the Club was the isolated place where professional people met their lovers.

Shortly after opening the 5 O'Clock Club, Dad bought a new Oldsmobile 88. I didn't have my driver's license but still used the car to go into town on errands, or stopping to mow Grandma's lawn on Saturday mornings. I had initially refused to drive the Olds until Dad bought insurance that covered me. He finally said I could drive, and assured me that I had been added to his policy. One day the Chief stopped me as I was walking past the police station, and asked if I had a driver's license. I said no. He told me to come in the next week on Tuesday, the day he gave exams, and take my written test. I didn't have to take the driving test; Chief said he had been watching me and thought I was already a good driver.

JUNE COMES HOME

Dad received notice from correctional authorities in Missouri that my younger sister had been picked up as a run-away girl. She was being held by the department of corrections in a semi-secure facility, and the authorities wanted to know if Dad would take her back. We drove to Missouri without making prior arrangements, but the people in charge would not release June without proof that Dad could provide a good home. He was irate but had no choice but to leave her at the facility and return. Dad drove back to Wisconsin on the narrow two lane highway with the speedometer on 85 the whole way, talking about taking June from the correctional authorities at gun point. He acted crazy and was almost totally irrational, only his grip on the steering wheel kept him in the here and now. June was later sent by bus to live at the 5 O'Clock Club. Social Services had determined that Dad could provide a fit home for her; in those days home fitness evaluations usually meant that parents had adequate finances. She lived with us in the upstairs apartment above the Club until spring. June was in the tenth grade, and I was in my junior year.

In March of 1953, Dad forced her to marry a drunk who was a regular at the Club. This man had been traumatized in the Korean War and like many recently discharged vets found alcohol the solution to all of his problems. June was taken to a marriage mill across the border in Minnesota at Pine City, given $100 by dad and sent on her way with this admonition: "You forget you have a father and I will forget I have a daughter." I was dumbfounded by his comment, and realized at that moment that June had been a burden: as a female, she was too young to tend bar, and unable to pay her own way. She was also a daily reminder that Madge had escaped his wrath, and June had been her companion. Dad was using one of the local drunks to get rid of her. This was three months before her sixteenth birthday. It was her second marriage, and doomed to fail from the beginning.

June had run away from a forced marriage that Madge had arranged in Chillicothe, Missouri. Madge's new husband repeatedly tried to rape June, and Madge did not believe or respond to her requests for help. Finally, Madge forced her to marry a homosexual who was over sixty years of age. Together they drove June across the Arkansas border where parents could marry their children off the same day, children as young as thirteen. Madge was paid $200 for this "sale" according to June, and the man used her to troll for teenage boys. June was devastated by this abandonment, was afraid to contact her family in Wisconsin, and when she had collected herself, she ran.

Mother and the pedophile testified in court that she was incorrigible. Her forced-marriage pedophile husband brought papers to the correction facility and annulled the marriage. Nevertheless, she was still committed to the system for two years; the law being just - because it was the law. June's correctional counselor couldn't believe what had happened to her, June never saw or spoke to Madge the rest of her life, and subsequently repressed almost all of her childhood memories up to the time of puberty. Madge never asked me once if I knew where June was or what had happened to her. Dead children, lost children – they came and they went. That was life, or maybe it was use 'em or lose 'em!

June and another girl had tried to run from the corrections center's grounds only to be severely cut by barb wire on the periphery. The cuts had become infected and correctional personnel refused her treatment because she had tried to escape. She told me that our visit, prior to her being released to Dad's custody, had probably saved her life. Correctional staff became motivated to provide treatment because June's father was coming on grounds, and discovered that gangrene was already setting into her barbwire infections.

DOC & THE PRIEST

Life as a teenage bartender offered endless learning opportunities for this working-class boy who had spent much of his life in rural isolation. Drunken customers reveal their lives as sober people never do. The seamy side of life at the Club often presented small town America's version of Peyton Place. Married people met lovers, single people pursued new conquests, business deals were imagined and consummated, and a myriad of life's adventures constantly unfolded. I became a listener of stories, a peacekeeper and sometimes a bouncer, a shoulder on which adults cried, and a club manager throughout most of the week. The local drunks became my friends, and informed me that I would be just like my Dad; a person other drunks respected and looked up to. It was a compliment requiring my forced smile and nod. Two peas in a drunken pod!

I came to know customers expectations, their friends, habits, and vices. I knew who was trustworthy, who the freeloaders were, the braggarts, and the fragile souls desperately hanging onto this tenuous life one drink at a time. Because the Club was located a few miles outside of town it offered relative privacy from the multiple watching eyes of small town gossip. I came to know almost every professional person in Island City – doctors, lawyers, undertakers, bankers, businessmen, teachers, and clergy. Almost all except the nuns who didn't drink, get drunk, and never made fools of themselves in public the way the drunken village priest did! He would get intoxicated, take to pinching the waitress' butts, and after eating and drinking his fill, need help walking to his car. This was always on a Saturday night before early Sunday morning mass when he would be forced to drink the extra wine left over after blessing his congregation. Needless to say, I was discovering diversity in both people and religion.

Dad had become alienated from his church as a young man on Grandpa's farm. He was being groomed for the ministry and had become a favorite of the family pastor. But, Grandpa was stingy with money and doled out small sums to Dad who preferred to spend it on booze rather than adding to church coffers. The minister noted this behavior and two weeks in a row left Dad standing by the roadside as he drove past without eye contact. Dad explained to me how he had become angry, then disaffected from the church, and only returned at the promptings of Mother Ruth during the last few years of life.

Never in my lifetime, let alone my growing up years, did I ever attend church with him. My siblings and I would attend whatever church was nearby with neighbors or church members looking for young recruits. Living in twenty different remembered houses by the time I was fifteen brought me into contact with a broad spectrum of Christian churches. In some, people spoke in tongues, rolled on the floor as their eyes turned inward, came forward to witness or confess their sins, sat quietly or wailed in anguish – such was the world of ritual and salvation across the spectrum called Christianity.

I was most impressed by this variety of Christian interpretations and even more confused. Each church was the true church, and each minister held the answers to salvation. As a child I wanted to be saved from eternally burning in Hell and embraced one local congregation after another. The confusing part of Christianity hit home by the time I was about fifteen. Each church with its separate interpretation of salvation had a solution different from all other churches. In some I could not pledge allegiance to the flag as the American flag was a false idol. In others, I had to openly profess the unforgivable sins I had committed as early as five years of age. I never did understand speaking in tongues – that is, until I was much older. I gradually came to believe Dad's cynical view of most ministers; all they wanted was my money, time, and obedience.

Doc had delivered all the children in our family both living and dead. He stopped by regularly two or three times monthly to meet friends, to relax after making nearby house calls, or when he felt like one of the Club's dinners. Doc would sit at the bar behind which I spent most of my working hours, and watch me carefully as I prepared his favorite martini. Top shelf gin, one-eighth jigger of dry vermouth, and one green olive that had to be carefully handled before being gently placed in the martini glass. Doc liked the olive rubbed around the rim of the glass twice. The olive was turned in its transit thereby enabling olive juice to be the first taste Doc's lips met when sipping. He would sip, turn the glass slightly, and sip again savoring every drop. This way he gradually made transit around the rim while draining the glass. He didn't want a new glass for his second or third martini, but the same mixing routine had to be followed.

Doc and I had been engaging in this ritual for over a year. I had quizzed him extensively about life as a country doctor, and his insights about people we both knew. I respected him professionally; Doc never spoke badly about others or revealed their secrets in my presence, or in earshot of less sober minds swirling in alcohol. He always sat at the bar waiting for his call to dinner, seemed to enjoy watching his drink prepared, and I thought genuinely liked me. One day out of the blue I said, "Doc, how did my sisters die?" This question came after Doc's second or third martini, and it was not preceded by any earlier talk about my siblings or my family. Doc's expression changed instantly. The smile left his face, his muscles became rigid, and he looked startled. He paused, looked deeply into my eyes, and uttered one word, "neglect." I tried to follow this word by asking a clarifying question, but I could have saved my breath. Mention of Carol and Donna's deaths hit him as forcefully as if my fist had smacked him in the face.

Doc picked up his glass, moved to a table away from the bar, and sat down to wait for his dinner call. He never sat at the bar after that or talked intimately with me. The frequency of his visits to the Club decreased as well. I had lost a friend with one question. I did not understand the meaning of his actions for many more years. Neglect can be such a subtle way to take a child's life. Donna's umbilical cord was found untied when she was buried. Her body's fluids had oozed into her diaper until her butterfly heart had nothing to pump. One month, one lost watermelon seed, and a double grave with one marker was to be my sister's lonely legacy. The silent grave at Lakeside screams for attention every time I pass by. I thought of myself lying in the crib day after day with urine and feces slowly drying to my body, and realized how easily an umbilical cord could come loose on a three week old baby. Intentional, unintentional, accident, neglect, or murder; it was all the same to Donna.

TORNADO

In May of 1953 I drove Dad's Olds 88 to Eau Claire for a regional high school speech contest. One teacher and two students rode in my car, and one of my classmates drove her dad's car with the other students and teacher. About half way back on Highway 59 to Rice Lake the storm turned into a tornado. Driving was nearly impossible, but my speech teacher insisted we continue. She had a dinner date with her fiancé and was determined to keep it. I was following my classmate's car, the largest, heaviest Buick available that year. The storm intensified and the Buick stopped on the highway next to a parked car. This was at a Y-junction north of Eau Claire; my classmate was asking which fork in the road she should take. Visibility was extremely poor as we were driving in the middle of a torrential downpour.

As I approached the two cars, a lightning strike outlined them sitting side-by-side; they were completely blocking the narrow two lane highway. The lighting flash also outlined the Y intersection with a utility pole immediately to the left of the two cars, and even further to the left oncoming headlights. The choice was a head-on collision, a utility pole, or attempting to stop before rear-ending the Buick. I braked hard, but hydroplaned on the highway's drenched surface into the back end of her car.

The Buick's trunk flew open revealing packages that had been purchased by the teachers during the day. The Olds' front end caved in pushing the radiator into the motor, making it un-drivable. My speech teacher was in the back seat of my car and started screaming that her new coat was in the trunk of the Buick and would be ruined. She just sat in the car out of the rain screaming semi-hysterically about her coat. I first checked my classmate in the passenger seat of the Olds. He had a bruise over one eye, but was alert and coherent. I checked the occupants of the Buick, and they were all OK. I then closed the trunk of the Buick and informed my teacher that her coat was dry and untouched.

I lost respect for my speech teacher at that moment, and also partially blamed her for the accident. That fall, she refused to grant me permission to take her journalism class. My initial polite requests to stop her screaming after the accident turned into visible disgust. The rest of that school term I questioned her understanding of English literature repeatedly and was amused as she would carefully peek at a copy of Cliff's Notes that she kept hidden under her lectern. Cliff was never wrong and she never seemed to know why. I loved this game as much as she hated it; she evened the score by giving me a final grade of B. I thought her pettiness was even funnier than her lack of intelligence. Detest was mutual.

Police officers came and took notes about the accident. They told me I had made the right decision, had the car towed to a nearby shop and took me back to their station. Neither my classmate nor I received a citation for the accident as it was chalked up to weather conditions. Dad informed me the next day that he had not put me on his insurance policy after all. He took me to the bank the following Monday after school, and I signed an arranged loan that exceeded $1200. The accident was my responsibility. Dad accepted no responsibility.

New 88's were about $2300 in 1953. I worked two jobs all summer. I worked nights tending bar, and the 7 AM shift at the canning factory during the vegetable season. The rest of the summer, my second job as a construction worker was at a new water treatment plant being built for the city. The loan was totally repaid by the time school started. It would have been enough money to pay for my first year of college. Dad told me not to worry; he would help me financially once I started college. He encouraged me to continue working at the Club, which I did throughout my senior year.

I bought a used book on hypnosis for 25 cents at the city library's annual sale that fall, practiced hypnotizing classmates, and became interested in self-hypnosis. However, it wasn't very helpful teaching me self-hypnosis, and the fun of hypnotizing classmates wore off after a couple months. I was surprised at how easy hypnotizing others was, but gave it up by the middle of the school year.

THE COACH

My senior year in high school was mostly one of survival. Our football coach discovered that I tended bar, and told me to stop. Of course I couldn't, and I told him it was my job, that I worked for my father, and I didn't have a choice. The next day he made me run the whole practice period – 40 laps around the field. At his direction, I did the sprints after practice, showered, and walked the three plus miles home then worked until one o'clock. The next week coach made me earn my position on the football team all over again. One member of the team after another lined up to block and tackle me. Then the coach let two or three of them tackle me at the same time. Finally, I was running against the rest of the entire team.

The coach seemed determined to wash me out of the lineup. His facial muscles were set hard, and his demeanor was even harder. I was equally determined not to let him separate me from my classmates and the team. I was bruised and sore by the end of practice, but no one else was able to take my position. The coach left me alone after that. He kept me in the games to play both offense and defense continuously. I knew he was punishing me for being a teenage bartender. I also knew that he didn't like my Dad, or anyone else who was a drunk. He never spoke to me after that unless the school situation forced him to. Our coach-player relationship was as formal as he was stiff.

His wife stopped bowling on the Club's team shortly afterwards as well. After bowling the coach's wife and the bowling team would enjoy a drink together at the Club, a drink that was provided free to members of our team. Coach was a teetotaler. I received punishment that he would happily have given my father. Coach's wife went back to housework and Dad stopped supporting a bowling team after that season. I have never retained the same feelings for sports, or coaches. Coach died shortly after he retired, suffering from a massive stroke. I last spoke to him sitting in a wheelchair on his front lawn during an after dinner walk one warm summer's evening when I was visiting dad. He wasn't pleased to see me. Hard is the crippled heart.

I graduated with honors from high school. A man about fifteen years my senior and I formed a painting partnership that summer of 1954. We did contract painting during the day, and I tended bar at night. I bought a car for $700, and had a similar amount saved for college when school started in the fall. Dad's college help consisted of continuing to pay me $20 weekly for about 32 hours of bartending; one nine or ten hour shift Friday, two shifts on Saturday, and nine to 12 hours on Sunday. I would drive back to college between 9 PM and midnight on Sunday night when Dad returned from his girlfriend's place. Some Sundays I drove back to college after 1 PM because he was too drunk to close the bar; especially those nights when I had to physically help him up the stairs and into bed.

I didn't have enough money to continue college winter quarter, and joined the Army for the GI Bill. I was sworn in three days after finals. I thought that after my army tour, I could come back in time for winter quarter three years later. Dad was mad, had a fit, got red, and chastised me for being so stupid. He wanted me to stay and tend bar full-time – at my old salary. I listened to him, smiled, and left the following Monday for induction. In my absence, hired bartenders stole him blind. Uncle Eric finally insisted on selling the business and recovered his initial investment. Dad had squandered all the profits from the club on his multi-year orgy, and regularly doctored the books to keep his brother from knowing how badly he was being cheated. The same applied to the IRS.

CHAPTER 9

EARLY ADULT YEARS

THE ARMY

I was stationed at Fort Chaffee, Arkansas, waiting to go to officers' school when my life changed radically. My father's naturalization papers said: born in Russia. The Cold War was on, Joseph McCarthy was running a rabid anti-communist campaign, and everyone was afraid of his witch hunts. Legally, the Army could not prevent me from attending officer's school, but everyone with connections to Russia was considered a security risk. Communists seemed to be lurking everywhere and the whole nation was on alert to ferret them out. I was transferred to Fort Chaffee after Basic Training to wait three months for the next officers' training cycle. The army put me in a fire direction control program with 105 howitzers where we played with live ammunition. A couple weeks before completing this training, and about one month before I was supposed to enter officers' school, I was called over to headquarters. I was happy to finally get my orders and be free of the mindless game of lobbying ordinance on imaginary enemies. Instead the officer in charge informed me that I was a security risk. I tried to explain that my father's family had been liquidated in Russia and there wasn't any way I could be blackmailed by the bad guys. The army knew better!

I was given the option of choosing an alternative, or at best accepting a non-commissioned officer rank after successfully completing officer school. I refused to be a second class citizen, and selected an oversea assignment in West Germany as a Fire Direction Control Specialist. For the first time in my life, I was officially a second class American. I was angry, hurt, and stuck in an artillery unit performing a job I hated. If war started, I would be on the front lines directing artillery fire – a good position for Americans whose fathers were born in Russia and who, thereby, were putting the country at risk. Nightmares came back in all their glorious variations. I once again felt like the kid who lived on Highway 48 in no-mans land; I didn't understand why the army put politics above the law; my first real lesson in geopolitics; my initial sensitization to America's journey into globalization.

I found as I went through my first 12 years of education that every time I changed schools I had to fight the "cock" at the top of the pecking order. The kid who thought he was the toughest always wanted to let the newcomer know who was boss. The army was no different. I refused to hide my interests in educational books, music, chess and other things considered uppity by my blue collar peers. Our artillery unit was mostly composed of guys who read comic books or pulp literature, a majority of them coming from public schools in the South with inferior educations compared to Northerners.

There was a small group of college educated personnel specialists who had been drafted and were graduates from Yale, Harvard, University of California Berkley, New York University, and other excellent American schools. Their school deferments had ended with graduation and they were reluctantly but dutifully serving their tours of duty. They readily shared their books with me; we played chess together, and I took college night courses on the base. My new friends also helped me transfer into personnel a few months after arriving in West Germany.

The Sergeant First Class in charge of our barracks happened to be Afro-American. In 1955 everybody was a color: he was black, I was white. When I transferred to personnel, I became one of those smart college types. It took me three months to move out of the forty man squad room designated for artillerymen. For GI duty, the Sergeant ordered me to scrape the cracks in the wood floor of our forty man unit with a nail. That was every crack between every board from one end of the room to the other – every week. I was busy scraping hours after all the other guys had finished. In the Sergeant's mind, this exercise was teaching me that I was no better than anybody else in his unit; how dare I transfer to personnel. In truth, it increased my intolerance of ignorance, and furthered my pursuit of knowledge. He offered a challenge much like the one that Dad had imposed when I was younger: "don't bring any books home from school." Dad taught me to love reading even more than I love ice cream. The Sergeant greatly increased my disdain for bigotry and ignorance.

The Sergeant's dislike for personnel specialists was obvious, even to the point of denying me a simple promotion to Private First Class. I was fair game for any or all of my squad roommates, and with the Sergeant's blessings. I was the only personnel specialist living under his control and he ran with the opportunity. He contrived numerous ways to make my life a living hell; most of them I will spare the poor reader. In addition to the Army Regulations (ARs) and Service Regulations (SRs), I was given the duty of handling all battalion re-enlistments in my new job. I talked the Sergeant into reenlisting for six years; the time needed to complete his twenty year career, bring him a big bonus, thereby, permitting Sergeant to select his last tour of duty. He chose Chicago, a great place for Afro-American duty at the time. I changed his reassignment code one digit through a typographical error, and Sergeant spent his last tour of duty, all six years of it, at Fort Benning, Georgia, attached to a tank unit. He was livid, but I thought our score was now even. I kept score cards in those days.

I was now physically almost six feet two inches tall and a little over 200 pounds. I was confronted by half-a-dozen guys from the squad-room, and one of the biggest guys in our unit, a wrestler from Arkansas. I was used to street fighting and he had been trained according to high school wrestling league rules. I quickly pinned him to his and his buddy's amazement. I repeated the pin two more times to the consternation of all, and that was the end of army wrestling for both of us. My next major encounter was a year later with the unit boxer in Hawaii. I put the guy in the hospital with a pulverized face, one closed eye, and a broken leg. After the wrestling episode in Germany, I was then left alone by other guys in my unit, and continued reading college level books and going to night school.

I was fortunate and moved into the separate twelve man squad room reserved for personnel specialists a few weeks later. The guy in the bunk next to me in my old squad room was not so lucky. He too aspired to a university education, and didn't hide his intellectual interests. One night a number of our pulp magazine buddies pulled his olive drab blanket over his head, and beat him unmercifully with trenching tools. He was hospitalized with one broken arm, numerous fractures, and a face that looked like reassembled hamburger. Three months later, when he left to be discharged, his face was still only partially recognizable. The army didn't provide plastic surgery for guys who got into personal fights. Ignorant leadership, I thought, was rampant in the military!

I explored options that would get me out of artillery altogether; took the flight tests and was told I was eligible for either helicopter or jet school. An Army Air Captain in Ulm, Germany, offered me my first plane ride. He was providing an aerial critique for my dossier. I was permitted to bring my Canon 35-mm camera and take photos. The Captain put his prop reconnaissance plane through its paces, rolls, loops, dives - the works. He kept checking to see how I was doing after each maneuver. I loved it! All my life I had been flying without support. The plane wrapped me in a security blanket of glass and steel and I felt totally at ease. I wanted to take the controls, but army regulations made this impossible. The amazing thing about my first airplane ride was the perspective: everything looked the same from the plane as it had when I flew out-of-body. Playing with the Northern Lights was a lot more convoluted than doing loops and rolls with the Army Air Captain. I was intrigued at how similar the two views were from the air.

Flight school required me to extend my tour of duty more than two years. I planned to transfer to the Air Force in order to fly jets, and this meant an additional four years of service. After much deliberation, I decided that college was a higher priority and withdrew my application. This decision kept me from later bombing innocent civilians during the Vietnam War. Being a merchant of life or death turned out to be a flip-of-a-coin decision. I made the decision to forego flight school because I was beginning seriously to question the military's wisdom, not for humanitarian reasons, but for reasons that I didn't comprehend. In fact, I hadn't even thought about killing people with an airplane. I just wanted to fly.

I responded to the single job opening in our battalion for a personnel specialist. I had taken the three business classes offered by my high school – typing, bookkeeping, and short hand. Island City High only had three math courses, and one each of Biology, Chemistry, and Physics. I took the business classes because I thought they would give me more job options for college. I was the only boy in our high school to take these classes, and that fateful decision rescued me from the mad Sergeant. In my second month as a personnel specialist, the warrant officer in charge asked me to screen all army and service regulations. This was an exceptional opportunity as it taught me how the army worked. I came to know what decisions were made at each level within the military hierarchy. Memorizing the army and service regulations, and all of the changes, seemed to come naturally. I was quoting ARs and SRs like a Philadelphia lawyer within six months.

MOSES

I took leave that January and went to Italy. Seeing the Vatican, and major sights of Rome, brought me into contact with Michelangelo's art for the first time. Next to the Sistine Chapel his statue of Moses had the greatest impact on me. I was unaware that stone eyes could be carved in a manner that made them appear to follow the observer. As I walked in front of this masterpiece it was like meeting my Moses, my childhood Guardian Angel, face to face. I was awestruck, and stared at the statue so long that my buddy came back and nudged me to move on. It was at that moment that my Guardian Angel received his name – Moses. I have called him that until this day.

Moses, my Moses, is a large angel. He is physically impressive, strong looking, and almost as old as my grandfather when I was a small child. At that moment I had a physical body to go with his felt presence and mental picture. This image was both strange to me, and comforting at the same time. When I returned to base after vacation, I felt more relaxed and focused.

My friends told me that the physical agitation that I had expressed when I first came to Germany was gone. Moses new physical presence brought me comfort. Now when he came and sat on my bed, I could see his studied gaze watching me, much the same way that Moses' stone eyes had followed me across Rome's basilica. When he sits on my bed the bed sinks under his weight. I experience him as being about my physical size – at least 200 pounds. I never told any of my friends about him, and I never talked to him out loud. After the experience in Rome and for the rest of my life, Moses would come to my room during troubled times and sit on my bed. Physically he is there with me, but doors never open, and structural barriers never stop him. I am aware when he comes into my room the same way I am aware of any other family member entering. I feel him physically sitting on my bed and have a sense of comfort and companionship with him.

HAWAII

The Pentagon announced that it would be conducting large scale exercises moving whole battalions back and forth from The States to Europe. These exercises were called Gyroscope Operations. Only certain people were eligible – those soldiers who had less than one year of remaining service. All eligible personnel had to be screened onto separate rotation orders. Soldiers with a year or more of remaining service were not eligible for rotation, including me. I cut all the orders for the battalion because I knew the AR's and SR's by heart. I wasn't eligible for rotation, but put myself on the roster to Fort Collins anyway. I was the only non-eligible serviceman on the list, but I didn't have to worry as no one bothered to look. I thought Colorado would be a fun interim place to work for a few months. When I got to Fort Collins I was called into the group commander's office and asked to brief him on the operation. The colonel got excited about all the procedures that hadn't been followed by officers in charge and started talking about a review. I recommended that he just let sleeping dogs lie. He did. Besides, I didn't want my plans to rotate to a new assignment in the Pacific to get squashed.

I had already planned a way to transfer myself to Japan, or some other army base in the Orient. Openings in Japan were all frozen by the time I got to Fort Collins. The only Pacific openings were Korea and Hawaii. I chose Hawaii. This was an easy paper transfer for an enlisted man as our orders were cut at the level of Group, meaning right on the base at Fort Collins, and didn't go through the Pentagon. Officers didn't have assignment flexibility; their order went through Washington. As it turned out, by denying me an officer's commission the army had made it possible for me to see the world in less than three years. At least that's how I thought of it at the time – partial compensation, I thought, for being denied my constitutional rights.

Hawaii was a wonderland for a twenty year old; much like the farm at Lorraine had been for a twelve year old country boy. My life was filled with sea, beach, new friends, and college night classes. Dreams still haunted me at times, but they were not a continuous nightly event. One of the GI's that befriended me on the beach at Waikiki offered to teach me how to use a surfboard. I had taught myself body surfing, but the surfboard looked like a lot more fun.

Weekly duty in Hawaii consisted of four-and-a-half work days with a half-day of one's choice off. I took Wednesday afternoons and usually went to the Waikiki hotel beach strip. The international mix of tourists and locals was an eye opening experience for a boy who had previously cavorted with squirrels and bears. The affluent tourists made up their own rules about love, marriage, and intrigue. Waikiki was an inviting haven for those newly divorced, wanting to but unable to divorce, or for both male and female "haoles" flirting with "local boys, and girls, and each other."

I gradually built up my swimming competency to a point where I would take my lunch in a plastic bag and spend six or more hours out in the ocean. When I got hungry, I would float, eat a sandwich, drink some water, snooze, and then continue to explore. The ships coming around Diamond Head were filled with tourists expecting to see natives diving for coins – instead they saw laughing GI's cavorting in the sun. Hawaii offered tropical nights, golden days, and endless adventure. I began to date regularly, bought a car with my best buddy, and explored the paradise called Oahu. Nightmares became infrequent, and life acquired a balance that was a new life experience for me. I seriously considered staying in Hawaii and attending the University during the day. I was offered my military job as a civilian if I mustered out of service in Hawaii. I also had the GI Bill and a couple thousand dollars saved. It was tempting.

I forgot to forward some critical papers to Pacific Command one Wednesday, and went back to the office after lunch to complete the task before catching the bus to Waikiki. My surfboard friend from the beach was just leaving the office and looked surprised to see me. I was equally surprised to find he was an officer. He hurried on with an embarrassed "hello" as I watched his back stride out of sight. My office mates said he was from DOD, Department of Defense, and was conducting another security check on me. I had never been given even the lowest level security clearance in Germany, Fort Collins, or Hawaii, but also had never been denied work in personnel requiring such clearances. I was acutely aware of being investigated every time I rotated to a new army assignment, and resented repeatedly being treated like a national security risk.

I had been aware of each earlier covert investigation due to my unique position in personnel. My anger returned. I had never accepted being a second-class American, and I found the repeated military investigations without official clearance degrading. I was born in America, was Regular Army as I had enlisted, and had received a number of awards for exemplary service. Second class American, I refused to accept the idea.

It was summer in Honolulu, 1957, and I was making plans to attend the University of Minnesota. I came to the office on time, about five minutes before 8 AM to find my office mates and the officer in charge standing around a table with a large cake. The officer presented a special award letter that offered me a position to an elite Army Officers School on the Mainland. The cake was cut and meant to celebrate my award. As we began to talk, I asked the officer why I was eligible for a commission now, but denied previously. He said I had proven myself worthy of this opportunity, obviously meaning it as a compliment. I thought to myself, I needed a three year hitch to prove I was an American citizen. Aliens joining the American army from overseas, who had been born outside of the USA, did as well. My family had honorably served in WW II and the Korean War, but I was still second-class. I wallowed in this sensitivity, and ground it further into the core of my overly delicate psyche.

The Army took no chances with enlistees whose father's had been born in Russia. The military brass said that family members in the Ukraine could be threatened by the Stalinists, and I would be forced to tell all. Russian Justs and Yeskes had disappeared from the map, along with another 1.75 million German-Ukranians who had been liquidated by Stalin. The 200,000 German-Ukranians who had returned to Germany with Hitler's retreating troops had been sent back from Germany to the Soviet Union with President Dwight Eisenhower's blessings, and worked to death in mines and gruesome gulags. President Eisenhower's reputation regarding this genocide had been as protected from public scrutiny as my future military career had been made problematic; but then, the military and the government both pretended not to know about the German-Ukranian genocide. America remained a morally superior nation.

The award offered by the army was a product of a myopic military mindset that dwelt in the well of human authoritarianism. I knew the service regulations, and I was eligible for any school from West Point to the Air Force Academy. I had prepared entrance papers for my best buddy to enter the Air Force Academy that fall, and he was easily accepted. The strategy I had worked out for him was to spend a few months at the Academy, resign, and apply for European deployment. He executed this scenario, and happily spent the remainder of his tour of duty in Turkey.

I thought a lot about what it meant to be a second-class citizen. I had spent two-and-a-half years proving myself to the army, been denied my constitutional rights, and subjected to multiple investigations like a communist plotter. Would I have to prove myself over and over again once I was commissioned? How often would I be investigated, and how long would I be kept under the looking glass. I didn't trust the military. Political machinations and secret information being kept from the public always had a way of subverting my life goals. With mounting anger, I took the award letter, turned my back, walked to my desk and with much fanfare dropped it into the waste basket. I have no idea what happened to the cake, or the letter. I sat at my desk with my back facing all other office personnel, and worked furiously – totally absorbed and stuck in a pit of seething discontent. I was still angry when I went to lunch four hours later. No one ever mentioned this award again. Knowing the ARs and SRs, I applied for an early release to attend the University of Minnesota and it was granted.

UNIVERSITY OF MINNESOTA

I left for the University of Minnesota in late August 1957; three months before my normal service expiration date. More precisely, I had served two years, nine months, and three days of active service; being released after lunch on that last day; most appropriately, as I had been inducted right after lunch on my first day of enlistment. The nightmares returned with glorious intensity and frequency after I entered the university. The magic of Hawaii deserted me. My attention span shrank in proportion to my increasing level of anxiety; I could absorb new materials well during those twenty minutes, but was unable to sustain longer periods of concentration. My attention span seemed to get shorter as my anxiety increased. I was trying to work 36 hours weekly, and take an accelerated schedule with an additional six hours of lab. Competition at the U was new, and more demanding than my work schedule warranted, especially with all the lab work. I didn't realize at the time how easily my childhood anxiety, with its accompanying nightmares, would come back. Anxiety has a direct way of changing one's brain chemistry, and I was experiencing it intensely.

My second nemesis was test anxiety. Blue books were the common method of testing at the U. As a part-time student during my army days, I had not encountered clinical anxiety. Now it was a big problem! I would sit and stare at the blue book for half an hour, use all my energy to relax enough to write, and then furiously put words on paper for the remaining twenty minutes. Courses containing a lot of detail, such as math and science, became a major problem, even though these had been some of my favorite subjects in years past.

SELF-HYPNOSIS

I made a new friend at the university who went by the name of Doc. Doc was curious about hypnosis, and reawakened my old interest. We got a book on hypnosis and practiced on each other and our friends. At first I used self-hypnosis to improve my concentration. I kept increasing my length of concentration a little each week. By spring quarter, I could focus on textbooks for eight straight hours without a break or interruption. I found these marathons physically exhausting, and began to limit myself to four hours of unbroken concentration. After four hours, I would eat and drink something. Refreshed, I could return to another intense four hours of study. I could generally read and memorize half a semester's work in eight hours in subjects such as psychology, history, sociology, anthropology and the like.

By my second year at the U, I studied from ten at night, after I finished work, until two or six o'clock in the morning, depending of classes and test demands. I did these marathons once or twice during the week and still handled what had become a full-time work schedule. I used self-hypnosis to bring both my anxiety and attention span under control; later I went on to experiment in other areas. It took me somewhere between nine and twelve months to gain this level of mastery, and in the process normalize my MMPI Profile. At the time, however, I didn't realize the changes I was making in my mental health profile. Anxiety was eliminated during hypnotic learning sessions; thereby, stabilizing my brain chemistry as well. This is a pattern not uncommon to many who practice transcendental meditation; only mine was self-directed and learning focused.

I had been raised in an environment where boys physically vied for superiority. I had been tested since age six, and this testing continued through my military service. I was quick to anger, and fought with one intent, win or inflict enough pain to stop the confrontation. Now I was 21 years old, a university student, six feet two inches tall, and 220 pounds with a knockout punch that had become an automatic reflex. This part of my history had to go! Self-hypnosis, practiced meditation and relaxation, and reprogramming fight reflexes all came under the looking glass. Moving quickly to a fight response meant survival throughout my prior life. The reflexes were automatic. My black belt buddy in Hawaii, Peter Choo, had once been the Islands bantam weight boxing champion, and he taught me well on the big bag. I had a bone crunching punch that civilized people didn't appreciate. I made a personal commitment to become non-violent that year. By the time I received my graduation tassel, violent reflexes were a distant memory; I never punched another antagonist the rest of my life.

The eight hour marathons produced unusual physical effects in my brain. I would start each self-hypnotic learning session with something like this: "You will study the text by 'Johnson' from pages one through 300 until 6 AM, you will remember all the materials you read, and you will remain alert with total recall. At 6 AM you will stop reading, sleep until the clock rings at 8 AM, and wake up fully rested." Precisely when I reached the clock time, or had finished the targeted pages of study, I would put the textbook down, look up, and process. These long study sessions usually occurred before I had mid-quarters or final exams.

Text material ranged in complexity and amount of time needed to cover each page, but processing was a moment of exploding neurons. When the study period ended, all the material in the text felt as though it moved from short-term to long-term memory instantly. Thousands of bits of information would transfer simultaneously. My brain was like an ultra-dry sponge being tossed into a pan of super-absorbing water. There was an actual inside-the-brain sound that I could hear. If the reader imagines tens of thousands of liquid molecules moving into this ultra-dry sponge in about three or four seconds, you have an approximation of what I was experiencing. Another way to conceptualize the sensation is to take a bowl of liquid to your lips and slurp as long and hard as you can. This sucking sound, "soooouuuup," exploded inside my head after each eight hour marathon. The sound and effect was incredibly dramatic; I was startled the first time it occurred; I thought a major artery was exploding in my brain. I then realized that my auto-suggestion had been to concentrate without interruption, and recall everything read. For a normal textbook in a literary or prose style, I would be able to recall about 99 percent of the material - including footnotes; a lot of data to transfer from short to long-term memory in a few seconds.

I got married just before starting my second year at the U and used hypnosis with my wife during her first pregnancy and for the delivery of our second son. I used hypnosis when I was driving and tired. I would give myself a suggestion to remain focused and alert until I reached my destination, and it always worked. I could open my clogged sinuses this way. I went on to control pain or discomfort in any part of my body. I could desensitize my hands; stick pins in them without feeling pain, increase or decrease my heart rate, and generally exercised total physical control over my entire body.

I was working for Donaldson Company at the Southdale Shopping Center in Edina that year. Another university student worked in the adjacent department and we often ate dinner together. I told her about using hypnosis to control pain, and its potential use in medicine. She didn't believe in hypnosis, thought it was something akin to witchcraft and very much out of tune with her Catholic Faith. I desensitized my left hand and offered to let her stick a pin in it. She did this without my flinching; she then began to jab my hand repeatedly and with intensity. I had to physically stop her as she was drawing blood.

I now had body and mind control that I associated with Yoga practitioners. Pain, tiredness, and concentration were all subject to my will. I could change my heartbeat and respiration at will, as well as circulation throughout my body. However, the nightmares were still a personal plague. I read all of the classic materials on dreams by Freud, and what I found in the clinical journals at the university's medical school library. Their interpretations of dreams just didn't seem realistic to me. I was determined to stop the nightmares, and the idea that I had to spend years with a therapist, using money I didn't have, was totally out of the question. I needed help with the nightmares now. I was being emotionally exhausted by them and my heavy work and study schedule.

DREAM PROGRAMMING

The answer to my nightmares seemed self-evident. I was taking psychology courses and liked the concept of re-channeling basic drives and needs into more functional options. I thought of nightmares as uncontrolled dreams; dream programming became the solution to my lifelong agonies. I gave myself the suggestion that when one of the nightmares started it would change into something pleasant. I programmed my dreams in great detail, and changed the movie program whenever I wanted. If a nightmare began to creep back, I would just reinforce the preferred movie. I kept this active nightmare repression until I was well into my 55th year. I created any imaginary world I wanted, and revisited this world as many times as I found it interesting or pleasant; I made serial programs that grew and changed over time. I later came to realize how simple it was to plant false memories through suggestion; how easy it was to create an alternate reality; how normal were reincarnation and channeling experiences.

To this day while sleeping and dreaming, I will automatically create a dream sequence that I find pleasant, or a dream story that deals with a past relationship that I still find amusing. My dream controller, or just – Controller – often adds new scenes and episodes automatically; I have taught it well, and some of these sequences have lasted for years. But, as the series goes on, new meaning emerges and I become increasingly comfortable with some part of my history. I could think of these experiences as visiting a former life, being reincarnated – but not so. I am the author, director, producer, and the editor. Nevertheless, in respect to those who experience similar episodes as reincarnation, true memories, or altered states occurring out-of-body, these episodes are totally believable in detail, scope, and their sense of reality. One can return as often as they choose: there are an infinite number of rooms in the mansions of our minds. Reality is such an easy thing to construct; it gets easier with practice; it becomes more real over time; it is a reality that some even die for.

Glen A. Just

Self-hypnosis made it possible for me to control nightmares, and sleep became something I began to fully enjoy for the first time in my life. Deep sleep, uninterrupted sleep - I finally knew what it was like to wake up in the morning fully rested. I no longer had to work myself to the point of exhaustion before I went to bed. I don't remember ever leaving my body after teaching myself this level of total control unless I purposefully wanted to. On the other hand, as a form of meditation, if I had trouble falling asleep I would sometimes use an alternative method; I would pick an object in the room, such as a wallpaper pattern, rotate the pattern in my mind, looking at it from all sides, top and bottom until I relaxed and fell asleep. This relaxation technique cleared my mind as does more formal types of meditation, and deep sleep followed. If I wanted to fall asleep immediately, I would count backward from ten to one, preceded by a suggestion that I would be asleep before I got to one. After a little practice I could fall asleep after counting just three or four numbers.

SCUM

I talked to a university academic counselor about graduate school as I was finishing my bachelor's degree. He looked up my Minnesota Multiphasic Personality Inventory (MMPI) that was on file, and proclaimed that I would never be admitted to any graduate program at the University of Minnesota. I was shocked! I would soon receive my BA, but was scum that the U would now wash away. I had proven myself in the army and had been offered a new opportunity as a second-class citizen. I had proven myself at the University of Minnesota and had become superfluous. My response was now more mature. I rejected the counselor's assessment, and became even more determined not to let the U control my future. The counselor said that the MMPI was a proven instrument, this was my basic personality, and I would be unable to change it the rest of my life. Queried, he said there wasn't any point in my retaking the MMPI. I was what I was. His superior smile and smug attitude stays with me to this day. He loved to squash bugs with his words, and I was one of his undesirable insects.

150

The MMPI was on file because I had beer in my university approved apartment. A university inspector entered my apartment without needing permission, a rule which applied to all students, searched it and discovered beer. The penalty for all such miscreants was to take the MMPI; a contrived method to collect research data. I was 21 years old, honorably discharged from the Army, but not permitted to keep beer in my apartment; an authoritarian approach not especially foreign to the intellectually superior I thought. This profile was from my first year at Minnesota. My profile was dangerously high in three areas with obsessive-compulsive, paranoid schizophrenic, and psychopathic elevations making me unacceptable to any U of M graduate program, according to the patronizing counselor.

When I graduated from the U, I went to work in a human service department in Southern Minnesota. The service used a number of tests including the MMPI. I asked to retake mine, and found that my entire profile was within the normal range. The psychologist in charge of testing taught a course at the local university on the MMPI and had become a friend; he interpreted the trauma and neglect that I had experienced in my childhood as the source of my abnormal MMPI profile and how my profile could change over time. This was a relief, and I became even more interested in psychological testing and its dynamic qualities.

Self-guided therapy, and the use of self-hypnosis, had brought my inner world into balance over the previous three years. I had found an alternative to the costly limitations of contemporary psychoanalysis. I had developed and used dream programming as an efficient way to gain relief from childhood trauma and related nightmares, and developed other techniques that I couldn't find in the clinical literature. However, they were strategies that seemed like logical extensions of the applied psychology I was studying at the university. Most importantly, they worked and were free. They were also treatment techniques that doctors and therapists weren't interested in discussing with me. At that time, hypnosis was unfamiliar to most of the medical community, and Freud was the god of therapy.

Years later, my sister June volunteered to be tested at Washington University Medical School in Seattle. The consulting psychologist informed June that her childhood had been more traumatic than any soldiers he had tested after they had gone through combat. Further, that he had never seen an ex-serviceman with a Post Traumatic Stress Syndrome as severe as hers. She was in her 50s at the time.

I changed jobs when I was 58 years old, replacing a public administrator who had been incompetent. My employer did not want to make another bad hire and put me through a full day of tests. My personality profile was about as normal as they get, and she gave me my evaluation; thereby, permitting me to read it carefully. My boss would sometimes remark in leadership meetings that I was the only person present who could prove that they were normal.

Self-therapy as an undergraduate proved to be of life-long benefit; I had permanently altered my personality and brain functioning. I gradually came to understand, as my clinical insights matured, what had happened to my brain. I had stabilized its chemistry by eliminating childhood anxiety, integrated a fragmented self, and gradually gained control over my "Controller." I am using controller to refer to the brain centers that directs one's conscious functions; the center that can intervene in, or even take control of, automatic (autonomic functions) such as breathing and heart rate. Depth Psychology, as I understood it, did not permit this level of control; hence, I came to reject related therapeutic interventions as being incomplete and obsolete. Dream analysis based on Freud's work was of no lasting value. "Doctor heal thyself" was beyond Freud's abilities.

Every course covering personality development at the University that I had taken from sociology, psychology and anthropology taught Freud's model. I came to realize that Depth Psychology derived from the Vienna School, and practiced by notables such as Freud and Jung, failed because it relied on insight, companionship, and myth. And, so it is with "rent-a-friend." Practitioners of the Vienna School did not offer me insights or a model that was therapeutic; they seemed to be teaching a model of reality that one must first accept or the cure is not forthcoming.

I continued to invent alternatives on my own. Dream programming was simple, cost me nothing, and proved to be an effective way to control nightmares after just two or three weeks of self-directed practice. Anxiety was just as easily brought under control and I was having fun with all the other self-guided experiments at the same time. I thought to myself, Freud couldn't even stop smoking; what little he actually understood of the brain's functions. However, my failed search for answers and self-understanding that started with Freud, the Grand Master of Psychotherapy, eventually came to fruition in contemporary behavioral psychology and neural science. His questioning mind had started a revolution, even though his understanding was limited, and I was one of the beneficiaries.

STATE UNIVERSITY

I started teaching classes at a state university while working as a probation officer for the local county. I taught two-thirds time for one year and then transferred to full-time teaching as an Assistant Instructor. I attended the University of Minnesota at night and during the summer for the next three years, completing all but a couple courses necessary for an MA degree. The U offered me a full-time graduate teaching assistantship in anthropology under the condition that I would teach their introductory TV course. I agreed to a half-time assistantship and the TV course, but this was rejected; full-time as a graduate student or nothing. I was no longer enamored with the U. I left Minnesota with the idea of completing my doctoral work, and never actually getting a master's degree. The University of Minnesota no longer held any special appeal. I rejected the idea of getting a doctorate in anthropology as it required extensive field work, field work that seemed much too expensive with two sons and a spouse. Looking back, my interests had evolved in new directions and anthropology was no longer a priority. Looking back, I was still angry.

CHAPTER 10
STRANGE WORLD OF FEELING
THE GHOST RETURNS

I completed work for my Ph.D. and returned to River City, Minnesota, to work for State University in 1970. I was 34 years old, and now the owner of my first house. I had two sons, a wife from whom I was becoming increasingly alienated, and a mind that felt like a steel trap. Students often remarked at the intensity of my concentration. They would write furiously trying to keep up with the flow of thought pouring from me. I loved this sense of authority and control, the power over all my personal history, and the nightmares.

Except, the ghost returned to the house on Skyline. I had hobbies at the time that required me to go down into the basement. The stairs were wooden and steep: they were stairs much like the ones in the old farmhouses. But, I didn't realize this similarity at the time, only some years later. As I went downstairs, I would experience all the sensations of the ghost's presence. The small of my back would feel it first, than neurons would come to life all the way up to my shoulders, neck, and into the back of my head. The sensation was just as intense and real as it had been during my childhood years. The power and reality of the ghost's unexpected return was shocking and I had to mentally focus and force myself to walk down into the basement.

The first time the Skyline ghost struck, I stopped and retreated back upstairs. This was unacceptable. I had become accustomed to total control over my body, mind and nightmares. The ghost was laughing at Superman and I wanted it out of my life. As long as I lived in the house on Skyline Drive, the ghost periodically followed me down the stairs at night, but never during the day. It didn't bother me once I was in the basement. However, it took some minutes for the effect and sensations of its presence to wear off once I was downstairs and had reached my intended activity. I controlled my nightmares, and the laughing ghost owned the stairs. It became a shared division of labor. My psyche was once again demanding attention.

I was a full, tenured professor by 1978, and had been given a number of awards for my work with American Indians, International and Hispanic students, and for help developing a number of new academic programs. I was active on numerous committees at the university, and was supervising up to a dozen graduate students yearly. I totally believed in science, and rejected everything associated with the supernatural. I read professional literature avidly in psychology, sociology, and a number of subfields in the behavioral sciences. I also continued to read extensively in the natural sciences, as well as history, philosophy, religion, and the emerging literature in gender studies.

MOSES IN PERSON

One day in 1978 I walked into my classroom on the second floor of Armstrong Hall, and Moses, my Moses, my Guardian Angel, was sitting in the far corner opposite the classroom door. I blinked, looked around, and all student attention was focused on me as I started to lecture. There was only one door to the classroom, which held about 30 students, and all seats were occupied. The lone chair, which Moses used, was in the far corner of the room, at the front of the class, and was available for my use when monitoring exams. Moses was a complete physical presence. I was absolutely sure that I could walk over to him and touch a solid object. To observant students, anyone sitting in that chair would be a guest that I would shortly introduce, but no one seemed to notice our guest except me.

If Moses left the classroom he had to walk in front of me as I lectured and continuously wrote on the blackboard immediately to my rear. I looked up a few minutes later, and Moses was still there. I became increasingly nervous and had to force myself to concentrate. A few minutes later I looked again. He was still there. His eyes did not focus on me but on the students as he sat totally still, not a muscle moved, his eyes did not blink, and his face was without expression. I was becoming disoriented and found it difficult to lecture. If Moses had still been there the fourth time I looked, I would have panicked and found it necessary to leave the classroom to regain my composure. With trepidation, I looked once more and he was gone. I breathed deeply, collected myself and finished the fifty minute presentation. Years later, I thought, how perplexing it is that over more than thirty years Moses had not aged. As I write these words, I am aware that I have now grown physically older than he is; he still has a presence that doesn't age.

I was thinking about how overactive my imagination had been that day as I put my lecture notes away. All the students got up and left except one; a young woman who always sat immediately in front of my lectern. Without blinking, she looked at me and asked: "who was that person sitting in the corner chair at the beginning of class?" Now I was really confused. I thought for a moment and asked her to describe him. I didn't want to put any words into her mouth and thought that she might have just noticed my turning repeatedly and looking at the corner chair. But she described Moses exactly as I had seen him. I must have looked startled as she quickly added that she often had these psychic experiences, and she explained it as a psychic experience. I clarified that he was my childhood guardian and said something about being surprised at his visiting my classroom; I don't recall my exact words. I talked to her for a while to confirm what she had seen, and we both left the classroom.

I intended to discuss this experience with her again at greater length and when I was more composed, but never did, and she never brought it up. Moses appeared to be as natural for her as

he was troublesome for me. Moses was a confirmed reality, and I didn't know how to process his physical materialization, and de-materialization. He didn't comply with the laws of physics as I understood them, and still doesn't. His presence was as real as any of the students in my classroom. I was forced to think about time travel, alien anthropologists, and experimental cloaking devices. I can fully appreciate why others with similar visitations insist that these experiences are real.

I had learned in my beginning psychology classes that children often have imaginary friends. This was a great relief to me; I was just a normal kid growing up. Part of the craziness that surrounded my childhood was taken away by developmental psychology. One of my former university professors expressed interest in parapsychology, and talked about people having spiritual visitations similar to mine; however, I never discussed any of my experiences with him. He said that hearing spirit voices was disconcerting, seeing them was even more disorienting, and that most people would freak-out if spirits touched them. I knew what he meant! My interest in parapsychology went up about one thousand percent. Further, if Moses had physically approached me in the classroom, I would not have been able to handle it; touching me – no way!

I didn't want to believe Moses could materialize, make himself known to others, and then disappear into thin air. I didn't want to believe any of this. I had worked hard over the years to rationally explain everything that happened to me as a child. But, then Moses appears in front of me and one of my students and totally destroys my neatly constructed worldview; a worldview which I had painstakingly built from the natural sciences. I could understand my own hallucinations but having him appear and disappear before one of my students exceeded the limits of my scientific mind.

I had explained Moses away with developmental psychology as being part of a normal childhood, a figment of my imagination, something common to millions of children, not fully understood, but common to children; an experience that makes Guardian Angels part of our Western culture. Moses had dramatically informed me that my worldview was incorrect. He still comes around and makes his presence known, or sits on my bed, but he has never again materialized the way he did in Armstrong Hall. At least no one else has ever mentioned that they have seen him with me.

SIX FOOT TWO INCH GIANT

My wife had become an alcoholic during our years of marriage and refused treatment. I moved out of the house and gave her a final ultimatum to seek help or I would file for divorce in six months. We were divorced the next summer. I moved in with a good friend who was also divorced and he spent many long hours nightly providing support. A half- dozen guys who were divorced, or going through divorce, decided to create a support group and I joined them. Our group lasted for about a year and met weekly. I was feeling healthier than ever, running five miles daily, and enrolled in Spanish language classes for extra stimulation. My office was on the first floor of Armstrong Hall with a long hallway extending to the bathrooms at the opposite end of the building. I had walked this hallway daily for eight years. It was a gloomy tunnel with dull grey walls, no artwork of any kind, and a matching featureless, bland grey cement floor. I thought of the building as something the Soviet Union might erect on their Siberian hinterland – bland, featureless cement. There was absolutely nothing in this hallway that would attract attention.

In a fraction of a second my body began to expand as I walked toward the bathroom. I stopped in amazement. My rapid body expansion was a totally new experience. My physical size expanded almost instantly and seemed to fill half of the hallway. I stopped, looked around, but nothing had changed except me. In the deep recesses of my mind I had only been about three feet tall. I had been completely unaware of my psychic size. Now I was a full six feet two inches, 200 plus pounds, or about the size of the Vikings who walked these same halls between chalk talks.

I had the experience of being bigger or smaller throughout my life, but had never gone through such a rapid physical transformation. However, this time I went from being a psychic dwarf to what felt like a giant instantly. I was finally free of the ghost on Skyline, and would shortly be free of a marriage that had become increasingly difficult. I had also gone through a period of months with close support from my friends. Clarity of thought, unburdened emotions, and a new focus on life had all come together in this most astounding way.

THE WORLD OF FEELING

I decided that having total bodily control was not worth trading for the world of feeling. I was close to being a flesh and blood robot as I entered the remaining months before my divorce. Feelings could be totally repressed and pain forgotten. This left me in an isolated cocoon of self. People would remark at department meetings how I never lost control, and remained focused no matter how heated the discussions became. My relationship with my wife had become terminal and mechanical. Sex was an act, not an enjoyment; life was ritual filled with multiple hobbies and extra work distractions.

The sense of living in an emotional milieu with real people had mostly left me. I was losing myself in the bliss of a religious esthetic, and no longer needed the world. This was another special moment when I came face-to-face with what my evolving self was becoming. It was similar to the moment when I decided not to enter Heaven. I stopped all the body and mind controls that I had been exercising. I still do not know if my cocoon existence extended my marriage, or helped bring it to a close. Divorce had become the only answer; it was impossible for me to continue in a relationship that had become a ritual, lifeless, and emotionally draining. Living with a "robot" undoubtedly contributed to my former wife's alcoholism. But at the time, this awareness was completely lacking on my part; I was blind to my own inadequacies. I was also blind to the other parts of me that lived in historical moments of forgotten or suppressed memories of childhood.

GOODBY DREAM PROGRAMMING

I now felt strong enough to unlock my programmed dreams. I wanted to experience all of life as I thought other people must experience it. My nightmares gradually returned but without the psychic pain common in my younger years. I had added twenty years of study, and a modicum of insight, discarded the old Freudian and psychiatric theories of dreams, and was now analyzing them from a developmental psychological perspective. Unlocking my programmed dreams brought an immediate kind of relief; much like removing a band that had been tightly wound around my head. The sense of relief was almost immediate. I finally came to appreciate the amount of energy active repression takes; additionally, it drained my emotional energy the way water passes through a sieve. The energy I had unconsciously used for active repression was now released and I used it to explore new personal relationships, for intense study, running, and giving myself time to experience this new world of feeling.

One of the wonderful changes that occurred was my gradual emotional rebirth. Robotic-like total self-control was gradually disappearing. I found myself getting emotional in department meetings, and extremely irritated by the pettiness of my educated colleagues; a pettiness that my robotic self had kept at arms distance. My university life and colleagues were no longer viewed from a studied distance but now often took on childish forms, and at other times they were simply exasperating. I quickly came to feel that I was wasting my life in what then felt like an academic wasteland which was leading to my intellectual death.

Slowly, I was entering a world common to most of my fellow human beings; a world that my new emerging self did not always like or appreciate. I was a teenager struggling to allow my inner-self to explore the world for the first time. I was embracing life, I was exploring relationships, I was alive, and I loved those aspects of my new world. That is, I loved everything except the nightmares. I remarried, resigned my full professor tenured position at the university, and went out to find the world. More appropriately, I left the university to find myself, to spend time with that segment of humanity that was unsheltered, raw, passionate, less cerebral, and a little more human. The robot that cherished the isolated shelter of academia and pure thought was not permitted to follow.

The movie "Ghost" had been popular. My spouse rented it when it became available and we watched it together at home. Throughout two separate marriages, my wives had been annoyed at my total concentration when I was reading, or watching a movie that I thoroughly enjoyed. I became so engrossed in "Ghost" that she physically nudged me with her elbow and asked what I was doing. I was moving my body with the ghost, jumping from train to train through the train's walls, and moving through physical barriers with him at will. I had projected myself into the animations and moved through every object that the ghost moved through. I became fully aware that I had joined the "Ghost" when she nudged me. After that I enjoyed the experience consciously, and watched the movie a number of times just to repeat the joy of doing something visibly that I normally only experienced psychically.

I could be the Ghost and myself at the same time – what fun! The ability to detach mind from body stays with me as I grow older; however, now I only separate mind and body with deliberate intention and with more conscious effort as my spatial abilities decline, except for audiovisuals like Ghost. I also developed a fuller appreciation for the psychic experience of people who think they are possessed by spirits. Change the object-subject relationship to subject-object and there you have it, or it has you.

HELL

Madge returned to Wisconsin from North Dakota in the late 1970s after her third husband had died of a heart attack. I forced myself to visit her twice yearly. My sense of duty demanded these visits; they were never pleasant, but instead were emotionally demanding. It took me days to make the commitment, only to find during such visits that I had to limit the time I spent with her. Shortly after my second marriage, Madge was taken to the hospital in Eau Claire, Wisconsin. I received a call from my older sister that she was dying and only had a few days to live.

Madge had been seeing two different doctors in two different towns, and getting incompatible drug prescriptions from each one. She had been a clever woman in many ways throughout her lifetime, and frequently her cleverness ended in similar disastrous ways. The drug interactions had leached the potassium from her heart and it was described by her doctor as being mush. Madge had no prospect of recovering and only a few days or hours left to live. Vonna and I took turns sitting up with Madge day and night. Mother knew her moments on Earth were limited and asked not to be left alone. She was as afraid of death as she had been of life during her later years, embracing religion as she approached the end with the fervor of the damned.

I was sitting in her hospital room the second night, it was about two thirty in the morning and I was unable to sleep; Madge's restlessness felt like she was experiencing her final hours. She sighed, drew a deep breath, a pained expression appeared, her face reverted to that of Evil Madge, and she totally stopped moving. I was absolutely sure that she had taken her last breath, and sat staring at her body, and the strange contorted face that appeared. I was about to call the nurse when my attention was drawn under the bed.

From under the bed, and it seemed strange that something should be coming up through the hospital's cement floor from under the bed, came a number of dark grotesque forms. They surrounded Madge on both sides, reaching through the sheet and into her body. I felt the struggle going on inside of her, but after seconds, or minutes, the dark ghoul-like forms wrenched her inner-self free, emitting sounds like wild beasts devouring flesh, and departed downward. I had the overwhelming impression that what was evil in Madge had been taken to Hell, and I didn't think I believed in Hell. I had totally rejected the idea that Hell was anything but a figment of people's imagination. Hell, if it existed, was something we humans experienced here on earth – I thought.

I sat in my chair stunned. I couldn't push the button to ring for the nurse, and I couldn't move. I just kept looking at her body, and tried to make sense out of what had just happened. I had never experienced anything that felt so overwhelmingly evil before. The feeling was similar to totally immersing oneself in water. When mother's evil spirit was taken, the sense of literally being in Hell entirely filled the room and penetrated my entire being. I looked at her corpse for a long time before ringing for the nurse; her usual expression had now returned. I studied what remained of her and thought that at least what had been good in her as a person was now at peace.

In fifteen years I have never been able to visit her grave, even though she is buried in the same cemetery as my infant sisters.

The dreadful feeling that comes with the thought of visiting her grave is accompanied with a sense that the Ghouls of Hell remain in attendance.

Critics who decry the stark realities shared by those of us who live in multiple psychic worlds are like persons who read the flaps on book covers, but are either unwilling or afraid to open and read the whole book. However, these experiential realities are unforgettable to those of us who have them. The dividing line between the cognitive hell of one's intellect and another world known to those of us who experience the damned is incredibly fine. It is so infinitely fine that this line fails to adequately separate the psychic realities that people like me experience, from those that are external. There is only one reality for us and it is a total blending of subjective and objective, internal and external. Do you understand my meaning?

CHAPTER 11

REVELATION

It was 1989, and I was in the middle of a second failing marriage. I married a woman who thought sex was akin to shaking hands, and in retrospect she seemed to be running for a national political office. After divorcing my first wife and undergoing some major growth experiences, I found that sexual intensity had multiplied along with various aspects of my emotional life. Sexual intensity, along with other feelings, had doubled and tripled within the first year of this marriage. I was so blinded by the magnitude of these feelings that I hadn't realized what kind of relationship I was in. It wasn't to last and had no substantive value in terms of a true loving commitment on her part.

I had entered my second marriage as an emotional teenager. My former cognitive-emotional life had been out of balance; life-long my emotional world had been either controlled or repressed. Controlling emotions had been an act of survival that originated in the crib and continued into my adult years. Intellectual development through university days and into my early professional careers was centered around cognitive growth with my emotional world being kept tightly in a small box somewhere in the back of my brain. Permitting myself to experience an enlarged world of feeling, and significantly expanding my emotional capacity, had left me vulnerable to manipulation.

I came to appreciate in a few short months just how out of balance my cognitive and emotional development had become. My world of feeling had followed a jigsaw puzzle's path to maturity; I had grown much faster in some areas of my development while remaining immature in others. My inner self was calling me to finish my work. I wished it had been otherwise;

I wished my puzzle of self-integration to be complete, but no. I didn't want to admit how easily and extensively I had been manipulated in this empty relationship.

I was also re-building a non-profit organization that had been on the brink of bankruptcy. A director on my non-profit board was in partnership with a group of women providing massage therapy, chiropractic services, and a collage of new age training for people in management. I thought I would give the management services a try as I had great respect for her as a humane, caring individual. Her approach to management training was to fully engage her clients as feeling-thinking people, not just the laying on of words, concepts, and models; she had a wonderful way of integrating the two and teaching experientially.

The second training session started with some warm up physical movements that were her interpretations of Yoga. She had studied in India and I found the techniques that she used to be both interesting and helpful. She put her two trainees in a number of different physical positions, and then put me into one that resembled a fetus sitting up. I entered a long-forgotten inner-world, and was transported back to my crib within seconds. A life-long image that had been repressed appeared like magic and gradually came to totally dominate my mind. My trainer became a blur behind the screen of action taking place in my brain. At first my mind was superimposing both the trainer and the internal picture emerging from the depths of childhood; a quirky world in which two scenes and two realities existed at the same time. First, her voice gradually dimmed until her words became inaudible and were totally lost. Next, her visual image faded, and a moment later I lost contact with her, the room, and all its contents. My total reality became a long lost moment from childhood memory.

I was in my crib, sitting up looking through the bars into a room that was only partially lit. Mother was approaching me screaming, totally out of control. Her stomach was distended with my unborn sister June, or maybe it was right after June's birth. She had a pillow in her hands chest high. Her face was distorted and twisted. It was the same mask she wore four years later when my face was forced into the urine soaked sheets in the house by Lake Stevens; it was the mask she wore when her evil soul went to Hell. My right ear, the one that always got earaches, was pounding and I was sobbing.

The pillow came first and then all light disappeared and I momentarily relived her attack in a hole of all consuming pain and darkness. The pressure on the small of my back felt like my spine would snap. I struggled to get my breath, but the force of the pillow made breathing impossible. The sensation of being smothered by mother is still so strong that small enclosed places remain bothersome. I remember waking up in the hospital. I remember refusing to go to Heaven, and I will remember forever the intense pain in the small of my back as it remains permanently damaged. The physical movements of "Yoga" had unlocked long suppressed memories, memories that had been too horrible for my conscious mind to entertain for over fifty years. Now they played out like a Hollywood action movie, totally dominating my senses. The next couple of days I struggled to understand what my unlocked unconscious was trying to tell me. The Japanese flag-stand nightmare returned, and when the bad guys started drilling the hole in my back, the drill turned into Madge's hand, and the pain was identified. I was once again reliving the experience.

One hand ground me into the crib's mattress while the other took my breath away; the re-enactment of the crib attack returned in its entirety. The realization that mother had smothered me, and was the cause of my being hospitalized was painful. Now I understood the hospital scene with Madge standing in the background shadows, and my fear when she approached the bed. The dream distortion that eventually became the Japanese nightmare had permitted me to nurse at her breast, live with nightmares instead of immobilizing fear, and experience the angels.

I knew then that I had had two mothers – a Nurturing Mother, and Evil Madge. I justified the evil mother by thinking about how hard her life had been when she was growing up with an unloving, abusive stepfather. I never fully accepted this justification, it didn't compensate for all the pain she had inflicted. Today as I write this sentence, she is like an actor in a film that I once watched, only, she is a character that arouses absolutely no loving emotions. I do not hate her any longer, and I do not love her. She is like a tree one passes along the freeway – just part of the landscape. The most I can do as she disappears from historical memory is recognize that Madge was a necessary prop for my birth and childhood passage to adulthood.

I can easily comprehend a future where babies are conceived and brought to birth in artificial environments, and then nurtured into adulthood by robots. Madge was an incomplete robot of flesh that never fully became part of the caring, loving world of sentient beings. Mothers that can unconditionally love their children are the true angels of this world; they are just like my Grandmother.

I conquered the ghost when I solved the mystery of my Japanese flag-stand nightmare. The sensation in my back when I encountered steep wooden stairs in low light had been created by long-suppressed fears of Madge's attacks. I never knew who she would be when I heard her footsteps on the stairs. Would she be Evil Madge, or the mother that cared for me? The sensation that started in my lower back, spread up my spine, and into the back of my brain was my lingering unconscious memory of her attacks. The ghost's breath was Madge's as she stood over my crib. Hiding under the covers, and not daring to move was a conditioned reflex.

The steep wooden stairways triggered repressed memories hidden deep in my mind, while my conscious brain repressed them: mind against the stored silicon-like memories in my brain. My unconscious mind had protected me all those years, and at the same time allowed me to grow up with a schizophrenic mother; unfortunately, she had also taught me to internalize some of her dual personality in order to survive. Madge's evil power over my childhood, a power that haunted me for half a century, was finally broken. The steps to Heaven are often slippery, tortuous, and demanding; those that lead to Hell are built by twisted, unfeeling caregivers.

THERAPY

This emergent awareness left me uneasy and troubled. I decided I needed to talk the experience through with a therapist. As I had never previously been in therapy, a trusted friend suggested one, and I was quickly involved in a meaningful therapeutic relationship. I went weekly for a number of months. I discussed the episode of my mother smothering me, the subsequent hospitalization, leaving my soul in space, and the Yoga experience that brought about this new awareness. My therapist asked me numerous times if I thought my mother had loved me. I insisted that she did, and justified her behavior as a damaged, mentally ill person. She would bring up my own comments about Madge and asked me to explain how they reflected behaviors of a loving parent. Increasingly, I began to realize that Madge was incapable of love. This was an extremely difficult realization. I wanted to be loved as a child, and I had held on to the illusion that I had been in order to maintain my own sanity; a necessary illusion that I clung to tenaciously, an illusion that gave my childhood meaning, an illusion that held suicide at bay.

Some sessions later, the therapist quietly, without asking permission, very gently placed a pillow over my head; not enough to make breathing impossible, just slightly restricting. I immediately went into panic, and was transported back to my crib as a small child. I once more relived the attack moment by moment. My back experienced extreme pain from the light touch of the therapist's hand, my lungs ached, and I struggled with every muscle in my body to breathe. The therapist removed the pillow, and after a few minutes I came back to the presence of the moment. Like my two living sisters, I had always been somewhat claustrophobic, and now I was fully aware of its origin. I also became aware over the next few sessions that there had not been one but many such episodes of smothering by Madge; a method of behavior modification that she undoubtedly used on all of her children.

I discussed this experience with my two sisters, and each one had gone through life claustrophobic. Neither sister remembered any of Madge's attacks. One sister had almost totally lost her childhood memories, only being able to recall some of them after about twelve years of age. The other sister remembered almost nothing before she started grade school, with only selected recall until high school. My treatment sessions helped bring forth multiple memories and former dreams as therapy progressed.

I remember learning how to cup my hand over my mouth to prevent the pillow from totally blocking my breathing. I would grow limp from lack of oxygen during Madge's attacks, and at times must have passed out. I had unconsciously produced this memory reflex during the urine thrashing by mother when I was five. On cold winter nights when I pulled the blankets over my head to keep warm, the cupping reflex occurred automatically as well; an act which often puzzled me; a simple act that most likely kept me from joining my two sisters in the cemetery beside Beaver Dam Lake. But it had been close. It was 50:50.

The therapist kept insisting that my mother's behavior was incompatible with love. I argued against this. The mother I knew had been a sick person, but she loved me. She was traumatized in her childhood by a twisted, sexually deviant step-father, but she was otherwise a good person. The therapist asked me to think about her behavior before our next session. I had created a loving, nurturing mother in my mind, one who was troubled, but not evil. It was this fabrication that had allowed me to live with her day-to-day when I was a child. Now I had to confront this blind subjective interpretation too. The realization that my mother was incapable of love left me feeling fragile, and alone. An emotional thread that had helped knit my psyche into whole cloth was gone. For the next few months I eagerly looked forward to weekly therapy; engaging day-to-day reality and my fragile emotions depended on these sessions. I was now experiencing deep emotional dependence on another person; I was light years away from being Superman.

Subjectively, I finally understood therapeutic relationships from the point of transference as I was seriously thinking about when and how I might be able to date my therapist. Within a few weeks of this awareness I realized what had happening and was thankful for the clinical insight that I had kept in its objective, analytical box.

My personal life had been divided schizophrenically much as my mother's life had been. I had an emotional world that took fifty years to develop, fifty years of inch-by-inch struggle to gain emotional integration. My real life existence demanded that I be self-sufficient before I even entered school. I was required to navigate around a drunken father and an abusive mother, and at the same time provide both with adult-like support. I had been trained to be a servant to the world, one who never experienced emotional or physical separation. Not being attached to friends, houses or neighborhoods occurred automatically with Dad's impulsive moves. Emotional development was an elusive state that other people such as my Grandma seemed to care about, not something that was nurtured in our house. Dad and Madge had prepared me to run one-legged races.

I had never been fully attached emotionally to any one person, or any one place. The exceptions had been my Grandmother, my children, and the early years of my marriages. Most of my life I had been a social atom bouncing around physical space, unconsciously searching for a binding force that went beyond sheer intellect. Intellectual forces that became dominant by the time I entered high school, intensified through college, and overwhelmed my other faculties by the time I finished graduate school. I was both saved and sheltered by them; I used the house of intellect to build separate rooms for each part of my segmented emotional world. Politely, I was a complex person. A person whom you probably know if you stop reading this book for a few moments and think about your friends or your colleagues at work.

As I once again contemplated who my mother really was, I was forced to think about my two sisters. Donna and Carol had died within a month and six months of birth. Neither had been strong enough to survive Madge's abuse and neglect. My new awareness brought them more fully into my expanded emotional world. My two dead sisters became a living part of my historical memory as my unconscious mind increasingly gave up its secrets. As this new connection came into focus, I understood more fully why I felt so bonded to the graves in Lakeside Cemetery.

INTERPLANETARY GIANT

About half-way through my treatment series, the therapist asked me if I knew where my child was; she was using the language of Transactional Analysis which she knew I was familiar with. I don't recall the development of our therapeutic exchange that brought this aspect of my childhood into her awareness. Nevertheless, I understood what she meant, and she knew that my child was safely hidden halfway between the Earth and the Moon. She encouraged me to bring it back. She asked me to get it, and I concentrated for a while but was unable to leave my body. I tried to tell her that I couldn't separate my body from my mind and interact with her at the same time. She kept insisting that I could. I tried for a long time, what seemed like half of our one hour session. Flying, leaving my body, was something that I hadn't paid much attention to for a number of years, and now my therapist insisted on it.

I concentrated hard, but instead of flying my body grew at an astronomical rate. In seconds I was tall enough to be halfway to the Moon. My feet were still on the Earth which was smaller than my shoes - more like a big marble in size. I wrapped my giant self around my child, made it safe and quickly returned to the therapist's office. I had left what I thought was my soul in space when I was a child, and brought what I knew was my inner-child back as an adult. This was 1990 and I was 54 years old. My child had been absent for half a century. It had rested secure in the cold of interplanetary space, beyond the possibility of human abuse. The return of my child, who had been tucked away in outer space, to my adult psyche left me with a huge sense of fulfillment; it also reminded me of how empty and fragmented my former shell of self had been emotionally. This empty shell no longer exists, but its memory does ask forgiveness from all who suffered from its insensitive presence.

The following year, I met a man while flying back from Chicago who was writing a book about angels. He was a member of a religious order through which I had developed a major treatment program for adolescents in Central Minnesota. This shared background permitted us to easily fall into conversation. His was a different perspective on angels as he was classifying them by type. I had never thought about different types of angels, and he easily captured my attention. I told him about my experiences and he classified my angels for me. We talked at length all the way from Chicago to the Minneapolis/St. Paul Airport. He had no explanation for my becoming a giant. Being a giant was just an out-of-body experience that didn't fit into his Other World worldview. I have never been able to find examples of this extreme psychic experience in literature. I had been an object of inter-planetary proportion; a size that I later realized could've grown to encompass the universe.

People emotionally grew or shrank as I often did, but to grow to such colossal size was something new; not something discussed in the world literature that I was familiar with. I wondered about history – had preliterate people and their stories of giants shared this mystic experience with me. More appropriately, had I shared something that was part of our collective human capacity? Giants could be a part of one's dreams; giants could be a part of one's conscious waking hours; giants exist where humans exist; however, to become a giant of such size while one's therapist was sitting nearby seemed strange to me. I eventually came to realize that psychically I could be any size I wanted, and had changed sizes both consciously and unconsciously throughout most of my life. As our friendly physicist says, "size is relative." Being whole permits each one of us to fill our universe, really fill our universe; let it be with love.

I stopped seeing the therapist as my work-life, and divorce proceedings were physically and emotionally taking their toll. I planned to renew my contact with the therapist at a later date as she had been of significant help. I never did. Moses returned in the middle of all these changes, and new awareness, and frequently came to sit on my bed. Ben, a psychologist friend of mine at work was a person whom I totally trusted. I had shared my psychic experiences with him and the life-long presence of Moses. He asked me if I ever tried to talk to Moses, and I said no. He encouraged me to do so. Ben was serious.

MOSES TALKS

A few nights later when Moses again came and sat on my bed, I asked, "Moses is that you?"

In a loud audible voice without accent he responded "yes."

Just one word – "yes." I still wanted to believe Moses had been a figment of my imagination. I wanted to believe that somehow his appearance in my university classroom could be explained within my existing scientific world-view. Seeing him in my classroom, having a student share the same experience, and finally having him talk to me was something that I was unable to account for naturally. When Moses said yes in his strong clear voice, I was speechless, and couldn't respond.

No matter how much energy I expended through my university days and adult years trying to explain him away, I always failed. My psychologist friend at work encouraged me to try again. I never did! I simply continue to enjoy his presence. Moses makes his existence known to me less frequently now then he did in previous years. I wonder if or when we will ever talk again. He has been a lifeboat through years of turbulent memories, but also a reminder of how deeply psychic pain can cut; how tenaciously life mysteries remain; how many mysteries we still have left to explain. How wonderful it is!

LOST LOVE

The series of nightmares where I am being pursued through the woods, by the dam, on foot, by motorcycle or car, and in both Washington and Wisconsin persisted. It was the one nightmare that I was unable to conquer. My second divorce was finalized and I found myself filled with intense anger toward her. Once she had moved out of our house, I was the sole recipient of her drunken lovers' middle of the night phone calls. Additionally, she obtained a court order which denied me access to any and all of her family members. I had become as close to her family as I was to my own, and deeply resented the court order. Lastly, the court order made it impossible to obtain related jobs in my field, and I was actively looking. I was stonewalled at least twice from getting wanted jobs because of this court order. People in human service fields don't ask about restraining orders by spouses – they assume.

I had dreams where I physically hit her, and used violent language in them as well. I thought of myself as a pacifist at this point in my life, one who could only hit another human being if they were attacking me or one of my family members with the intent to kill. These dreams were very disturbing as the emotions were intense enough to wake me, and leave me awake for hours. Over a period of months, I consciously gave myself permission to feel this anger. I took time during the day when it was safe to express these near overwhelming feelings in the safety of my home. In order to release such strong emotions, I had to express them verbally at a shouting level.

I eventually came to acknowledge that my feelings were legitimate. Emotionally, the shackles of anger slowly slipped away. It took months, but I finally worked through the pain of losing someone I had initially loved deeply, but came to hate intensely; she had been an integral part of my emotional birth; a partner in my journey to wholeness. But, she had been a lover of love, not someone who had cared unconditionally for me as a special person. She had divorced me for another man who deserted her once she was free. I had become increasingly aware of her infidelities, but had been unable to initiate divorce proceedings even though we had discussed my doing so.

Once her lover deserted, she returned with overtures of reuniting, but by then I had developed a much more objective view of our relationship and she no longer controlled my emotions. Also, I had no desire to follow any further in my father's footsteps with an on-again, off-again marriage. However, acknowledging my emotional reactions toward her, and the legitimacy of being angry, somehow intensified my last series of nightmares. The dream series continued. I was always pursued through the woods, along a dam, in Wisconsin or Washington, by a gang on some type on motorized vehicles. This series of related nightmares stayed with me for the next two years.

FATHER'S DEATH

My father was stricken with esophageal cancer at the age of 90. He refused treatment, and insisted on dying at home. My stepmother, Ruth, and Sister Vonna cared for him over the eight odd months it took him to die. I continued to work in the neighboring state of Minnesota, and visited on weekends. The last month before he died, I was asking questions about his youth. I started by saying, "Dad, when you were growing up...," and he stopped me.

He said, "I don't think I ever did."

I asked him to explain, and he just kept repeating that he had never grown up. I knew what he meant - emotionally, that he had never grown up emotionally as an adult.

I was as happy as he was to drop the subject. Dad just sat there in his easy chair staring into space. We both knew he needed this time to himself. I thought - how awful that he should be ninety years old and have this realization on his deathbed. Alcoholism had taken its toll during his lifetime; he had lived his life as an emotional child. Now in a matter of months, alcohol free, his brain was recovering, and beginning to mature; he was a ninety year old adolescent who would not live long enough to know what it meant to be an emotional adult.

Dad and Mother Ruth had agreed that he would die at home. Their finances were limited and they refused to spend their life savings or mortgage their house for medical services. Dad believed that pain could be controlled with one's mind. He infrequently took any pain medications as the cancer gradually consumed his body. He confided: "I never imagined pain could be this intense." Dad had broken his back twice in car accidents and had fully recovered each time without pain medication. Now he was refusing morphine, except on a few occasions near the end.

One afternoon when Vonna had taken Mother Ruth out for a couple hours, Dad got his single shot 22, managed to climb to the top of the cupboard and take down a box of shells. The first shot went under his chin and up through his left cheek. He had to reload, and the second shot entered his brain. The carpeted floor was covered with blood when Vonna and Mother Ruth returned. Dad lived a few hours longer in the hospital. He was three months shy of being 91 years old. A lifetime of liquid reality had been replaced by the merciless march of cruel cancer cells. Strange that cancer gave him the capacity to mature emotionally after so many years as a child. Strange!

ZEN DRIVING

Dad was dead and Mother Ruth was exhausted. She was not recovering from the months of his demanding care; shortly after Dad's death the doctor's examination revealed she had an advanced case of lymphoma. She began chemotherapy immediately. Eleven months later Mother Ruth died. She had been a nurturing mother to me for more than twenty years, and never forgot one of Dad's children, or my children's birthdays or holidays. During her final months, I drove to her home in Wisconsin on Fridays from Southern Minnesota, and stayed until Sunday night. My sister Vonna was not working at the time and was able to be with her during the week.

It was about a two-and-one-half hour drive between our residences. I got in the habit on my return trips of using a Zen-like state to take my mind off Mother Ruth's condition, and relax before I got home. I would merge my body with the car and let it float along above the highway. This was a simple act of separating body and mind. My cognitive mind would remain focused on the road and driving, while my separated body effortlessly remained suspended, gliding along fused with the car; a state of mind that motorcycle riders and joggers experience as they either run off the road, or in front of oncoming vehicles.

This was a sensation that approximated flying when I was a child. I wasn't riding in the car; I was flying a couple feet above the highway at sixty miles an hour. Driving required almost no mental energy as my detached body directed itself. The same capacity we use to visit the moon, astral travel, or play with ghosts. My tranquil mind stayed totally alert and engaged as it relaxed and enjoyed the comfort of situational freedom, freedom we experience when we separate from our physical bodies. This was Zen driving as I knew it.

This kind of trance state is also reported by astronauts, pilots, and the religious faithful – only for me it was created consciously, controlled and focused. I would stay in this state for about two hours of driving time without fear of falling asleep or losing conscious awareness of the road or other vehicles. I never did Zen driving if the traffic was heavy, and always followed secondary roads home. My monkish mind was withdrawn from the world of troubling thoughts while my sensual self floated in the netherworld of ascetic bliss. How easily we mortals escape from reality; how easily we mortals escape from our bodies; how easily we mortals escape from this world. How easily we create our own realities. What joy when we permit ourselves to be fully human.

Over the years, I increasingly became aware that my physical, emotional, and cognitive selves could be isolated at will in any combination that I desired. Initially I had used self-hypnosis to control my concentration, and then went on to self-experiment – bodily controlling blood pressure, heart rate, sinus congestion, fatigue and other functions that I've discussed throughout Ghost. Self-experiments of these experiential varieties helped me move outside the simple behavioral conditioning that we each experience as we grow from infancy into adulthood. I eventually realized that most of the mystic experiences discussed in world religions, both major and minor, were variations of my own experiments and inner realities. Human capacity is so universal. Over the years, I have wondered why modern universities have left the exploration of such natural human capacities to the mystics; especially since such experiences are so easily studied scientifically.

CHAPTER 12
NIGHTMARES CONQUERED

I was living and working in Southern Minnesota as a multi-county community administrator during the deaths of Dad and Mother Ruth. My work life up to 1994 had been hectic and filled with multiple concurrent jobs that demanded sixty to eighty hours weekly. Moving to Southern Minnesota was my way of settling down and learning how to lead life at a slower tempo. I bought a townhouse that needed considerable remodeling, landscaping, and tender loving care. This setting offered me a chance to engage in flower gardening and remodeling – two of my favorite hobbies, hobbies that in one form or another had followed me from my days on the farm. I was determined to become a domesticated person, and put down roots. I felt that most of my self-analysis was complete except for the one nightmare about being chased through woods by motorized thugs. I was basically content with whom I had become, and able to just focus on one job without having multiple distractions or additional commitments.

I was beginning to heal from the loss of Mother Ruth, as I had with the loss of Grandma, and directed new energy toward my perennial nightmare. The gang pursued me and finally I was captured. I was being restrained so tightly that I couldn't move. I became very angry with my own stupidity for being caught; I was fully aware now that they were sexual deviants, and I was their prey. The restraint tightens, and I am transported back to the desolate hay farm in Northeastern Wisconsin where I had been molested. My pursuer and captor was the sick pedophile who had used me for group entertainment with his equally perverted buddies. The molestation had lasted for forty-four years.

I awoke suddenly as my conscious mind connected with its unconscious counterpart; the wall between the boxes of my mind had collapsed. It was a long awaited, wonderfully welcomed recognition. If neurons could shed sparks, there were fireworks. I was never permitted to speak of my sexual abuse as a child, and left with the impression that my forced participation in the act automatically made my motives suspect. My victimization had been transformed into an imaginative series of nightmares: woods, water, vehicles, chases, sexual deviants, and fear of capture. The nightmares ranged geographically from Wisconsin to the State of Washington.

Some nights I would awake from one version of the nightmare, return to sleep and a second or even a third version would wake me again. The nightmare had grown into multiple scenarios as my unconscious mind sought relief. Relief from other nightmares had been realized and my psyche was free of being tormented by them; unfortunately, my sexual victimization by the pedophile, re-victimization by the county deputy, and compounded victimization by insensitive parents had created a nearly impenetrable box, a box beyond the reach of my conscious mind. What damage is wrought by the abuse of sheltered minds that cannot look beyond the limitations of their own egos; minds without empathy or understanding; living wells of ignorance.

I had variations of this nightmare during the period of time I stopped dream programming, and gave myself permission to develop and explore a full-range of emotions. However, during this time I made myself into a Superman. My pursuers would catch me and I would physically beat them up. I was stronger than any one of them. I was stronger than all of them together. I was invincible. I was unconsciously dream programming. It was a wonderful feeling being invincible. I felt like a martial arts superhero who could single-handedly take on any number of opponents. As I got older and my awareness of ageing emerged, this automatic dream response left me, and I once again succumbed to the nightmare's agonies. My mind imposed its own reality on my dreams as I slept. I had taught my Controller to transcend much of its (my) own unconscious subjectivity. I find this a pleasant thought; a process that can have direct application for the mentally ill who are bothered by out-of-control unconscious illusions and visions.

After connecting this series of dreams with being sexually molested in Wisconsin, I'd identify one version of the dream in the woods, by the dam, on motorcycles, or being chased on foot through the woods, and the traumatic power of each dream version was removed. This took some months as the capture scene was not repeated in the other versions of the dream. However, the Washington versions, either coming down the mountain, or going up the mountain, remained unidentified and continued to haunt me. By this time I had a weird sense that no matter how many nightmares I removed there always seemed to be another one waiting to appear. The layers of onion that were my psyche began to seem endless. Was there something in my infancy or early childhood that I had not identified? I was annoyed, perplexed and highly motivated to remove this last disturbing ghoul of the night.

Most of the nightmares were gone but I was still experiencing almost daily discomfort. I began to seriously question my ability as a self-analyst. Self-analysis had been a necessity when I was younger, and then had become a habit. I continue to wake up from normal dreams, analyze their content and origin, and then go back to sleep. The process has become so automatic that I am sleeping and analyzing dreams at the same time – never fully conscious during most of the process; a habit that stays with me permanently. Where was this daily discomfort coming from? Should I re-enter therapy? Or, were the scars of past years there to haunt me the rest of my life? My sister June continued throughout her adult life to live in this hell of nightmares. Was this to be the collective inheritance for all of Augie and Madge's children?

COSMIC ASTRAL TRAVEL

Moses was very much present the way he had been during much of my life. At times he not only sat on my bed as I was going to sleep, but would be my companion reading in the evening. My favorite reading place was a large easy chair by my front door with an excellent light over my left shoulder. Sometimes when reading I had the feeling that Moses was reading along with me. The dual capacity of my mind permitted me to experience either a real or self-created Moses in this manner; or both, but it was always comforting to have the reality or the illusion by my side. It seemed that Classroom Moses or Child Mentor Moses would always be a permanent part of my life.

Life-long I have seeped my brain in science books of the month, and had been reading some material about The Big Bang, Inflation Theory, and the evolution of the universe. The fine tuning of the universe that makes life possible is so incredibly precise that it arouses endless speculation in both the scientific and religious communities. Inflation Theory means that super-luminary movement, faster than light travel, is possible and occurred with the expansion of space-time microseconds after the Big Bang. This idea intrigued me as it might apply to a Sentient Universe. A universe that stays connected with all its parts instantaneously; a universe that knows no past or present as time flows in both directions, basically meaning that time is an invention of minds that live in only three dimensions; a universe that is finely tuned in such a way as to make the emergence of organic life inevitable.

I found it enjoyable to play with these interconnected ideas. I thought - what the mind can conceive, we humans can experience or even create. What fun is our unbounded imagination as we come to experience this magical, infinite, timeless, bounded and unbounded universe. The only reality you and I have is our own subjective reality, the reality that we create. The distinction between sanity and insanity is our ability to control this reality; especially, being aware of this control. The mansions of my mind were calling for my attention, asking to be combined with the magic of science, using my awareness of space-time.

The speed of light applies to the movement of particles in the universe, but not to the structure of space itself. As we go out further in space, the galaxies recede from each other faster and faster. This means that our little group of galaxies will some day be isolated from the rest of the universe, and the rest of the cosmos will be black because the outermost stars are receding from us faster than light can travel. I combined these ideas with quantum entanglement, and decided to give my mind a chance to explore 14 billion years of cosmic evolution.

I couldn't travel into a future of disconnected galaxies as that future does not yet exist in my frame of reference (what strange limits my mind was imposing.) Subjectively, my Arrow of Time only goes to where the now meets the future, but I could travel to the beginning of time. I was curious to know if entanglement (all particles being initially connected in a micro-point at the time of the Big Bang) could be a phenomenon throughout the universe from the moment of this colossal explosion to the present; if so, Self Awareness would be built into the entire cosmos; Cosmic Awareness being supported by quantum entanglement. The one explanation of cosmic evolution necessary to keep the past, now, and future connected as one; the one explanation that may support an all knowing Sentient Being; an explanation too fuzzy for mainstream physics.

Relativity and most quantum symmetry permits time to flow in both directions, or put simply, time has no meaning to the Universe Itself. Sentient Intelligence is theoretically permitted by physics to move freely across a single landscape of time, or one might say that time is not an experienced dimension to the Universe Itself. The cosmic microwave background explorer

COBE outlines a structural universe that looks like a neural network. I was fascinated by this similarity and the possibility that Cosmic Intelligence might be a byproduct of quantum entanglement; or conversely, quantum entanglement would automatically reflect a Sentient Universe. If so, merging with space-time would permit me to move beyond time that is **now** to any moment in the universe's prior existence. I might be able to experience the birth of the universe, the birth of time, the birth of this universe's Sentient Awareness. The cosmic shaman, I thought, can live. What a pleasant experiment for a cold day in winter.

Many Eastern religious practitioners train adherents to enter their internal void and join with this Cosmic Entity, to experience "nothingness," or "total blackness." I had practiced going to the center of my mind, the center of my being, for many years and experiencing the quietude one finds there. Years later, I discovered that Deepak Chopra gave a quantum twist to meditation, but added layers of mystic interpretation in his quantum integrations. To me, he was keeping the realities of early civilizations while adding on the modern language of physics and quantum mechanics. Was I doing the same?

Centered self-nothingness quiets the chemistry of my brain and brings to rest its many active neural areas; a void of total peace is created, which becomes the place of non-existence. In my readings of world religions, I had never encountered any philosophy which combined the Big Bang and quantum entanglement to experience the reality that would be in the awareness of a Sentient Universe; although the physics of religion flirts with some of these ideas, it tends to incorporate traditional interpretations, along with the physical reincarnation of the body at death.

If atomic particles could remain in contact across space-time at any distance, and quantum entanglement has been proven experimentally, then the Universe can easily be Self-Aware. God becomes the ultimate presence, the Cosmic Mind, the beginning and end of an eternal process of macro-evolution.

The Big Bang had started from a single entangled nano-micro-point. I found these ideas compelling, and thought I would try merging with Einstein's space-time and see where it took me; to psychically experience this microscopic point of the universe and our origin. I shifted my frame of reference and prepared to set off on my journey.

I am aware that in the course of human evolution, application of the mind-body abilities I have been discussing, those that we use to create transcendental realities, were only limited by our understanding of the universe in which we live at any specific period in history. Shamanistic-like experiences are only limited by one's understanding of the cosmos itself. Shaman, priest, cleric, monk, mystic – we all use the same capacities, and engage the world, universe, around us as we know it; same human capacities, different scope of engagement; different interpretations; same brain chemistry and cognitive capacities;

different realities from the same process. The souls of our deceased live in the rafters or attics of our homes, the levels of Heaven are seven or more, the spirits in the Australian Outback live in the sheltering tree, the streets of Heaven are streets and they are paved with gold. The ...

I slipped into the natural cycle of my brain's electrical impulses and left my body. I often thought that the multiple electrical pulses moving through our brains every second must enter space and leave a quantum signature, a unique composite whole of combined quantum fields, an individual thumbprint in space. To my Western mind, how else could any Sentient Intelligence stay in communication with billions of us on this planet, let alone billions of other planets, and whatever else there might be out there. How could any Sentient Intelligence that was part of the evolving universe not be aware of all sentient beings in Its universe. How could my own sentient self not be part of the Universal Whole; how could all sentient beings not be connected in such a finely tuned cosmos? Oh, the joy of playing with the limits of modern physics.

Evolution of the Universe with quantum entanglement is such a compelling thought, especially with the fine tuned equations that make life inevitable; that make intelligence inevitable; that lasts for billions of years; that may last forever; we can only imagine the magnitude of this process. Wholeness is an inherent state that life seeks; children of space-time are never forgotten; communion with and through the particles created at the moment the Universe was born is inherent in our DNA. At least, that was the reality that seemed most compelling as I set off on my Genesis journey.

GENESIS JOURNEY

As I left my body, it felt as though each electrical pulse I was riding was connected to every impulse that preceded it. My out-of-body acceleration was increasing geometrically with each subsequent electrical discharge in my brain. I visually moved away from our pale blue dot, continued to pick up speed as I shot past the Sun, watched the Milky Way fully emerge, multiple galaxies come into view, and then I began to move at ever increasing warp speeds. It was similar to watching Star Trek only the warp speed kept multiplying. It was the most moving psychic experience I have ever had. It was not like watching a science fiction film where the viewer knows they are outside looking in; just the opposite, I was aware that I was on the inside looking out. I experienced the unfolding of the universe in reverse of its evolution; I was inside and part of 14 billion years of Big Bang evolution; totally immersed in a reality as vivid as eating dinner. All but my physical body shared this reality. It was truly wonderful!

Every Shaman or mystic who uses out-of-body experiences to become the bear, sit on the clouds, the moon, to commune with God or the Saints, or explore the world knows this reality. It is a reality of the mind; a natural capacity that many of us activate and come to both know and enjoy. There is little mystery that so many of our ancestors and fellow travelers come to believe this altered reality is other than what it is. Awe of the universe resides within each one of us: it is the sunset, a special flower, a thought beyond the ordinary, a flight of spirit, the soaring of our souls. Quintessentially, it is being fully human; we come to know ourselves in the Gnostic sense. Only fear, or incapacity, keeps us from these most natural altered states of reality. Some of us just seem to have more capacity to experience and create these mystic boxes in our minds.

Subjective experiences like those I am describing are real enough to make the more naive person believe that their physical body is fully involved. The subjective reality becomes a total experience. It is sometimes called astral travel, or reincarnation rather than being interpreted through the insights of dream programming. We subjectively experience visiting a former life before our current reincarnation, or recalling lost memories that are actually false. When the usual neural networks of our mind form new combinations; when the brain's neural network is partitioned and recombined in uncommon ways, the experience leaves one with a sense of still being complete and whole, while the self takes on what it experiences as an altered reality. Thus the body remains in place wherever it may be, but the Other Self soars.

It is impossible for human beings not to subjectively experience this Inner Soul unless the experience is logically blocked through cognitive efforts. Unfortunately, this awareness does not answer the question about souls or lack of souls either. But, it does answer the question why one or more souls are universally assumed by all world peoples historically. After all, the universe is extremely fine tuned, and we are one of its creations.

As I continued to accelerate back in time, the structure of stars and endless galaxies came into focus – voids and walls of galaxies appeared; I was passing through billions of light years of time and space. The mature world of modern galaxies gave way to the primeval cosmos of giant suns and chaotic galactic structures. I lost track of time, while the subjective speed of my movement through the universe achieved incredible cosmic proportions.

The trip itself was very different from letting my mind alone go to the beginning of time. Going back through the evolution of time in this manner is to experience the unfolding of the universe from a first-hand subjective point of view. This means, as is the case with normal out-of-body projections, that the traveler experiences his or her body moving as well. It is being there, it is being part of what was. There is a wholeness of being and connectivity that one comes away with that transcends mere intellect. It also transcends the flesh and blood of biology; we become part of the stuff from which the entire universe is created. A oneness that lets us identify with rocks and trees.

The magic of the mystic, the shaman, the meditating monk is this transcendence of the mortal; transcending what is cognition alone. Only when the complete entity called self is freed from the body, but subjectively experienced as being whole, are we permitted these religious experiences. They are as normal and natural as our breath, and as unbounded as our imaginations. And they take us to the beginning of time. And, they take us to the core of what it means to be human. And, they take us back to the cave, to rhythmic dancing, and to those moments when we humans first developed our modern brain capacities.

My astral projection was experienced as being outward from all points of my body, yet it had direction - I was moving back in time. We humans are bound to the Arrow of Time, for it is only time that gives us direction. It is the direction of our unfolding lives, our moment-to- moment, day-to-day experiences, that separates us from space. It is an imposed reality that permits our physical separation from the cosmic, organic whole. Movement was experienced as I left my current point in time and moved backwards, I followed the time cone of cosmic evolution to its point of origin.

Time flows in both directions, but I could not enter a future time, one that was beyond the time of my personal frame of reference; one that does not yet exist for me. I came to a moment, I thought, that must be only a few hundred thousand years after the Big Bang. I hit a plasma wall that was opaque, and devoid of particles; a time when atoms had not yet formed, a point where time was about to begin - I stopped moving. The telescope of my mind not only permitted me to see thirteen plus billion years of cosmic evolution but to experience it; cosmic history had been condensed into minutes. I didn't like the undifferentiated chaos of the plasma, and the sense of total disorientation that it offered. Its incredibly high temperatures did not yet permit particles to be formed; total chaos reigned; particle quantum entanglement had not yet come into being, Was I experiencing that moment in space-time when this occurs?

The matter of which you and I are made, atomic particles, did not yet exist. It is a strange feeling to experience the plasma that becomes the atoms and molecules of all matter, the stuff out of which you and I emerge, the time before the building blocks of our universe are created. As the hottest part of our early universe, all life, every particle that is living, organic, or subatomic would be shredded beyond recognition in this plasma field. I began to understand what it would mean to burn in hell - to be lost in chaos; to be endlessly shredded into something beyond what constitutes the physical universe as we know it. The plasma field is also the precursor to all matter in the physical universe; it is the mother of Heaven and nothingness does not yet exist. Nothingness only exists when matter and energy as we know it is formed. This was the logic that naturally flowed from my Genesis Journey. Such fun!

I let myself briefly experience the chaos of the plasma, the chaos out of which Everything becomes, and then I moved forward in time, and returned almost instantly to the comfort of my easy chair the way quantum entanglement permits.

Psychically, I had experienced the early birth of the universe, the structure of space-time, quantum entanglement, and Inflation all in a matter of minutes. My subjective awareness transcended time and space. I understood and knew the Arrow of Time the way one comes to know a familiar place; thereby, I came to realize that time is only an arrow for the uninitiated; time is only an arrow for those who live in the present. Subjective reality is oh so real!

Wholeness of being meant total absorption into everything that was and is for the last thirteen plus billion years. I was a separate being, a micro-intelligence sharing all – totally connected to the entire universe of past and present. I had a sense of immense satisfaction and felt like I had entered the essence of what we subjectively feel as the presence of God; a feeling common to millions who are open to the experience. It is a total awareness that the birth of the universe, what we call our world, is a gigantic subjective experience that waits for each one of us. For some of us it calls, for some of us it shouts, for some of us it is beyond denial. It is an awareness that the imperfections of our lives flow from the demand that our universe moves forward in time, from a beginning born from the womb of chaos; a fine tuned universe that understands and creates chaos; the chaos from which life is born.

It left me with a sense that the Universe repeats endlessly in a cyclical renewal of time. Perhaps the Hindu gods do live. Engaging the evolution of time and space connected me to everything "out there" in the most marvelous sense of fulfillment and belonging. You should try it – really! Don't be afraid, it will not hurt you; it will only amaze you.

This mystic experience left me with a magnified feeling of belonging and wholeness to this world, and a new subjective awareness of Heaven and Hell; an awareness that as we reveal the mysteries of our cosmos, we continue to enrich the magnitude of awe in our minds; an awareness that knowing the universe of science leaves as much mystery as that of magical thoughts in ancient minds submerged in ignorance. I experienced a sense of wholeness that went beyond any that I had known before. I had peered into the Looking Glass and saw the face of the entire Cosmos. I thought later about returning to our cosmic origin and entering the plasma of our universe's early birth, but this notion was quickly overwhelmed by the feeling that I would be lost if I did – a psychic experience beyond my capacity, something I did not understand – Chaos itself; the beginning before the beginning.

My Genesis journey left me with an overpowering sense that the universe recycles, and the plasma wall represents the place of forgetting. A sense that Plasma Hell is not a place that a conscious mind would ever choose to enter; or if it did, there would be no returning; a place where Cosmos is undifferentiated before the universe's true birth, but the moment of birth when the Universe is renewed. Hell and Heaven are birth twins, but which one will be our destiny. What fun we have when we let ourselves be fully human.

I had never understood why some religious practitioners wanted to be in a state where all motion stops and they simply experienced the Cosmic Void. Then I realized that what I was experiencing through my mystic journey was the same; what Oneness and being whole was all about. Time has no meaning, and one can travel back and forth through time and space at will. One's inner-self is connected to everything and the Nothing. Two sides of the same coin. I was beginning to understand what "knowing thy self" meant. It is not explained by the ego of Western Man, which stands alone, but the Wholeness of the East, or the world of Gnostic Christianity. Each is a reflection of the other. I credit Western Philosophy of "pure thought" for previously separating my Western mind from what is my basic humanity, from its wholeness and oneness. And, that is not mystical at all. I came to understand why some dualistic minds find Eastern Philosophy unintelligible. I now understand why other searching Western minds find wholeness in "nothingness", the difference being recognition of our basic human capacities; the ability to fully experience who we are.

Ying and Yang had become one. My total being, mentally and emotionally, felt united with the entire cosmos. This psychic experience allowed me to merge with all that is and all that has been. The separation between organic and inorganic no longer has the same meaning. I now have identity with rock, and air, and water too. To experience only the quietude of being, or quantum stillness, to suspend one's connection to a living universe, and not the Universe's Living Self, at first seemed like an unnecessary limitation. Later, I realized that the two experiences are equally subjective, mystic experiences; the same internal process leading to a shared reality. I had only been looking at the same experience from two different perspectives. One was Western physics and religion, and the other Eastern Mysticism.

However, the term mysticism no longer seems relevant; it no longer has the same meaning as my Western mind slowly disappears. This subjective realization of infinite connectedness has been one of my most satisfying personal journeys. One cannot experience swimming in warm salt water off the coast of Hawaii by dipping into a northern Wisconsin lake. I don't know how to describe it properly, and I don't think I can; it must be experienced. May the "Buddhist Monk's" smile once again speak to me, may the quietude of Hindu meditation shine brightly, or, perhaps, the hidden meaning of Mona Lisa's Gnostic smile, along with the special words of the ancients to know thy self.

LAST NIGHTMARE

I had been dating a neighbor woman for about five years, and my relationship with her had become increasingly strained. I gradually found it impossible to watch any movie with her that contained violence, or portrayed traumatizing episodes. I would get a stomach churning reaction within minutes, feel nauseated, and find it necessary to immediately leave her presence. The next stage, and this took about a year to develop, was to feel revolted whenever she attempted to touch me. At first I could consciously restrain myself, but within months, I did not want to be in the same room with her. We ate evening meals together as we had for some years. We would have polite talk for a short time after dinner and then I found it necessary to leave. My reaction was both disturbing and puzzling. I found it highly irritating that old nightmares returned in part or whole during the days I had contact with her. .

The nightmares where I am on the Washington Mountains would not go away. I analyzed them night after night, only to have them reappear and demand endless interpretation. I had become so accustomed to dream analysis that I remained half asleep and half awake as I analyzed their content, but rather unconsciously, I would redirect my dreams and return to sleep. This division between dreaming and being awake had been tenuous for the last year or more in our relationship. Self-analysis of the dreams was as automatic as riding a bicycle. But, I didn't have these irritating nightmares when I was physically absent visiting family, or on professional trips. This awareness gradually emerged and assumed more importance in my self-analysis. The discomfort I was experiencing, along with the dreams, was place specific.

At first I thought there must be another piece of history lurking in my unconscious; one that was struggling mightily to get out, and I tried to interpret my dreams accordingly. I could not find any such trauma, and the dreams continued. I thought about seeing a professional therapist for help. I could easily identify the dream **content**, place it in perspective, and go back to sleep. But, I could not stop the sequence from repeating. During this time, I frequently returned to dreams where I am in the crib by Lake Vermillion. I re-experienced the attacks by Madge, Uncle Gus's death, my death and rebirth, and more, as these snippets of visual irritation and trauma revolved and mixed repeatedly.

A new dream component emerged. I am at the bottom of steep wooden steps, the door opens, and my Dad and uncles are all together drinking. Uncle Gus walks outside in the direction of Lake Vermillion, or it might be Beaver Dam Lake, and sits down. The wind is blowing and leaves on the ground are moving past Uncle Gus as he sits on the grass. A sustained gust of wind suddenly begins to erode his physical body, and magically he blows away with the leaves. I realized at that moment that I must have attended his funeral: "Dust to dust, ashes to ashes."

My neighbor and dating partner broke one of her legs on vacation, and was unable to work, or move about her home. I assumed all duties for her care – cooking, washing her clothes, shopping, everything. She was totally homebound for four months, and returned to work part-time after that for another two months. One day I was startled to realize how closely she resembled my mother. The realization came with a superimposed image of Madge and her together. The vision was similar to placing two colored transparencies on top of each other and holding them to the light. This visual awareness hit me as if I were seeing my multi-year dating partner for the first time. Her physical size, shape, pattern of talking, demeanor, and physical movements were all similar. I could not tell her this as she was aware of my distaste and estrangement from Madge. Perhaps the word loathing is more appropriate when I speak of Madge's emotional impact on me as a child, and its lingering residue.

I broke the relationship, stopped teaching at a local university, sold my house, disposed of most of my possessions, and moved. Breaking physical contact with her stopped the last vestiges of bad dreams. My mind was now free of trauma for the first time in my entire life. The last vestiges of psychic discomfort disappeared with our separation. I was finally free to experience the world. Free at last, free at last, thank God I was free at last. I was seventy years old. I had climbed life's ladder one demanding rung at a time; I saw ever deeper into the land, then the world, then the universe around me. The climb upward is one that we all struggle to undergo, as had been my journey to wholeness and being.

I thought my life was similar to the seasonal bloom of roses. It had not just been a struggle filled with pain, thorns, and endless psychic demands; it had been a lifetime in which I learned to perfect my rose garden by adding endless color and beauty. The angels, when I was two years old, hadn't come to take me to Heaven, they had come to show me how to find Heaven on Earth.

They told me then that I should begin my search. How satisfying is the unity of consciousness. How consciously we seek unity.

The lessons of life never seem to end, and that is a wonderful personal feeling. Each major life experience has brought new understanding and awareness, new insight and a fuller sense of being, and each traumatic experience has offered a lesson necessary to the next step in the creation of who I have become. Life is meant to be a challenge if we are to grow and realize our individual potential; real growth demands that we experience challenges and sometimes trauma and pain.

It is our responsibility, I believe, to engage life from this perspective. It is the unfortunate beings of this world who are never fully challenged; who never know the true meaning of human growth and the expansion of self that comes with our best efforts. Managing and conquering each level of growth requires us to take little steps which sometimes demand all our strength; however, we are never required to have the power to leap tall buildings in a single bound – although we can learn this too. We humans are carried before we crawl, crawl before we walk, walk before we run, but we can fly anytime.

CHAPTER 13

CHINA

I retired at age 65 from a multi-county administrative position in Southern Minnesota. I was teaching adjunct courses at a nearby state university, and serving on two of their advisory boards. I initially agreed to a one year full-time teaching position, but remained for five years. I had become intricately involved trying to help modernize one of their applied behavioral programs, but my wandering spirit was not yet ready to settle down. The campus office next to mine was occupied by three visiting professors from China and Japan. Circumstances gave me an opportunity to tutor one of the Chinese teachers in English, and we talked about my possibly teaching at a sister school in Tianjin. I delayed my visit to The Peoples Republic of China until the fall of 2006.

Since my first retirement at age 65, I had planned to write "Autobiography of a Ghost." For five years I was unable to mentally or emotionally begin, or to even put a storyboard on paper. I wrote the outline in my head an endless number of times and there it remained. I found within two months of arriving in China that I had a nagging and overwhelming urge to write my autobiography of childhood trauma and life of mystic experiences. I was teaching sixteen hours of class, eight in oral English requiring almost no preparation, and eight hours of Business English, which required very little preparation. My teaching schedule went from Tuesday morning to noon on Friday. I was free to write at least half of my leisurely week. To my delight and relief, most of my old mental blocks were gone.

I had become fairly adept over the years at interpreting my own dreams as they were related to childhood trauma and everyday events. But, I had this bothersome dream which started about the time of my first retirement in 2001. I am in a house that I have just put up for sale, or just sold, but I am never able to get everything in order. I discover repairs such as cracked plaster that I hadn't noticed before, rooms needing painting, windows that didn't close properly or were falling out, and an endless number of other items that had to be taken care of before the sale could be finalized. I say the dream was bothersome because it didn't leave me feeling angry, traumatized, or unduly upset. I couldn't discover what the dream meant or where it came from. It was just something that I lived with and found a curiosity within my inner life. Once I put the first draft of "Ghost" on paper the dream stopped. My inner psyche had been telling me to write this story, to put my house in order, and wouldn't leave me alone until I did. The flow of energy in this great universe of ours never ceases to amaze me as it passes through my inner world and creates new moments in time.

I met the divorced mother of a student from the University's International Office, a student who had been assigned to assist my adjustment in China. We were touring Beijing, The Great Wall, and other area sites, and I asked him to invite his local relatives to dinner at Beijing's most famous duck restaurant, Quan Ju De. He had been an invaluable aide to my settling into a new lifestyle, and was kind enough to use his holiday sightseeing with me. My new acquaintance, his mother, soon to become companion, had retired early from one of China's largest banks, ICBC. We both had time to explore China and our new friendship.

This was an entirely unexpected, unlooked for, and generally unanticipated relationship. Two failed marriages, and a five year relationship that had ended with such startling finality, had convinced me that I would never have the energy to sustain another long-term commitment or marriage. Six months later I had completely changed my mind on both accounts.

I wrote a storyboard that had been in my head for a number of years within hours, and typed a rough copy of eleven chapters during two weeks of my spring holiday in February 2007. Thoughts were committed to paper quickly and effortlessly, and I thought to myself that "Ghost" would be an easy task, however, these words were devoid of any feeling, real emotion, or depth. I was still protecting a childhood more fragile than my conscious awareness admitted. I was putting words on paper without connecting them to depth of feelings. Most importantly, they were devoid of insight. These initial sentences had every kind of basic error from spelling, use of the wrong words, dropping words or clauses entirely, and making a jumbled mess of thought sequences. I was free to write, but quickly discovered that I was also cleansing my psyche of whatever painful residue remained when I connected my early years to the present. I had to return to each chapter repeatedly before the flow of words and feeling became halfway readable, and a never to be finished series of pulling psychic taffy ensued!

Snippets of all my past traumatic experiences and nightmares emerged during this time. At first, I was startled to have old nightmares reemerge, even though I could quickly identify their new Chinese environmental content. I soon realized that this was my initial attempt to connect all of my earlier threads of childhood abuse at one time. It was only natural that my mind continued processing thoughts and feelings when I went to sleep. My dreams became increasingly focused and knitted together over an extended number of months as my story gradually became more integrated. Textual integration followed mental and emotional integration with each new cognitive and emotional integration releasing additional hidden memories that required rewriting; each rewriting brought forth new memories and awareness; and in this way, the cycle continued. This psychic integration-rewriting cycle soon became an endless, tiring process; my life's most arduous writing task and my most emotionally rewarding writing effort; a revealing type of self-therapy that the keeper of diaries understands.

At first it was amusing to mix a past filled with trauma and nightmares from Wisconsin and Washington with the landscape of a dynamically changing China. An increasingly uncluttered script emerged in my dreams like the editing of a B-grade

Hollywood movie. However, the writing process now took on a life of its own. I tried various writing tricks to end what my psyche demanded, but nothing worked. Finally, I just gave in and acknowledged that I had to rewrite as long as my inner voice demanded it. I took a break from the story's demands in 2007 and let it sit for half a year, consciously refusing to even look at what I had written.

The child molestation nightmare is a good example of this Oriental-Western dream combination. Instead of woods, lakes, and mechanical chase scenes, I found myself on crowded streets, in packed shopping centers, or at some famous Chinese historical site. The actors were age appropriate and American from my earliest childhood to my last year in Minnesota. My parents were younger than I am currently, my brother and sisters would be five, ten, fifteen or fifty years old. The movie scenes would change nightly as would the actor's ages, and the props. Once I realized what was happening, I looked forward to the next night, and what the free movie would offer. Literally every person in my history appeared and reappeared basically in proportion to their importance in my life. Army episodes, university life, a jumble of houses and farms, cousins, my drunken Dad, schizophrenic Madge – both evil and sometimes nurturing, and the joy of seeing my Grandmother being younger than I am now.

I had periods of limited withdrawal from social life as the most traumatic events unfolded in my dreams, but nothing that was emotionally draining or overly debilitating. This period lasted for about six months from the first words-on-paper to the initial revisions when more feeling and emotion finally began to fall onto the pages. I found, as my history became readable, that I was preoccupied with finishing it. It was the last mile one drives home after a long journey. The drive had been longer than expected and tedious, but I was being drawn relentlessly to its closure. However, the road was full of potholes, slippery, and required more energy than I wanted to give.

Names of old friends, acquaintances, colleagues, neighbors, places, and events came out of the depth of memory. My brain connected box after box of stored items and scripts. I was ready to get on with the remainder of my life and the most rewarding personal relationship I had ever known. I had a short period of resentment toward my childhood tormentors – then a near-total release of negative energy. My mood swung to one of contentment, and sometimes outright joy. I had no future guarantee that this rocky life's journey had ended, but I knew in the depths of my entire being what freedom felt like. I committed myself to being whole, letting myself love and be loved, and engaged each morning with a growing sense of being filled with the wonders of what each day brought, might be – and hope.

MISSING YOU

The silent train begins to wake,

your laughing smile coquettishly

from platform takes this heart away.

Entrancing lips of ruby red

when will they with mine partake,

what quiet moment shall they meet.

A week is longer than my youth.

In seven days the Milky Way

is crossed on hands and knees.

In Beijing Station wait for me,

where I may drown in light

from eyes like jade and pearls.

To my beloved, Li Yihong, October, 2007

CHAPTER 14

CONSILIENCE

My history growing up presented many questions about what was real and what was imaginary. The line between the two realities that lived in my young mind was paper thin. My childhood naturally led me to explore religious explanations for the mystical experiences I was having, but as I matured, the world of science opened up and came to blend with various interpretations of our marvelous universe. I discovered philosophy from my college educated friends while stationed in Germany during part of my army days. I also discovered Freud and psychoanalysis from one of my personnel buddies at that time, and had read most of Freud's major works before I was discharged.

Another one of my good army friends was a Jewish atheist who loved to argue with anyone and everyone the worldview of his faith of non-faith. It was at this time in my life that philosophy, religion, psychology, atheism and the world's diversity of competing ideas began to mix and swirl like rain clouds on a hot summer day. Stimulated by my Jewish friend, I chewed on religious dogma the way a hungry dog attacks soft bones. And for the first time in my life I had leisure time and stimulation to think about the meaning of life, religion, my mystic experiences, and being - what it meant to be conscious, alive, and human. When my university educated army buddies introduced me to philosophy and psychology, a new world of exploration opened up.

By the time I entered the University of Minnesota I was intrigued by the variety of world views that I had been exposed to from my army friends, endless discussions during European travels, and new semi-directed readings from my educated army buddies who mixed Yale, Harvard, New York University, Berkeley, and a number of other learned institutions through my immature brain. I always took courses of interest whether they fit into my four year degree plan or not and these included the Psychology, Sociology, and Anthropology of Religion.

I mixed in social thought courses that helped me watch the Western mind develop from Sumer, Egypt, Greece, Rome, Historical Documents of the Christian Church, and on through the Enlightenment, and eventually into the Modern Era. I was amazed at the old documents of the Christian Church and realized that the many different kinds of Christians I had known generally had little knowledge of their religion's history, which disciples' works were included in the New Testament, and which were left out by the Church of Rome, and almost no knowledge of Christ's Gnosticism. I had always loved history and now the magic of social thought and different worldviews that are sprinkled across humanity became a hobby and a passion.

Sociology, anthropology and psychology began to mix as a single stream through the soft center of my mind, moving me from individual thinkers to macro-social levels of thought and analysis, philosophies and paradigms. As the modern world of science encroached on older philosophies and interpretations of the universe, I discovered by the time I entered graduate school that one can spin word packages endlessly, packages that are called "theories," philosophies, models, world religions, and other less formal names. At first I became skeptical, and then cynical about all religions and prophets - both religious and secular prophets, who proclaimed superior models of how to run or explain the world, and the ability of Homo sapiens to direct their own futures. I rode these currents of thought like a careless cowboy breaking horses – often crashing and frequently lashing out.

The key experiences in my life that forced me to understand what was behind mere words and academic exercises were my early death between two and three years of age; the ongoing presence of Moses and his physical appearance in my classroom; a presence confirmed by one of my students, and my ability to go beyond the intellectual manipulation of words to experience. What I came to know as my own reality, a reality that shapes my current worldview, is that language alone is not sufficient to fully represent the reality that we humans experience and live in.

The experiential realities in our lives can and do go beyond this more limited cognitive realty that is based on language. Thus limited, we are only half of what we can be or can become. Over-dependence on language, especially when it supports a dogmatic vision that interprets our subjective world, serves to limit knowledge and understanding rather than to enlarge it - a type of gnosis destruction or limitation. Experientially going beyond the blinders of language permits us to mix-and-match the capacities (neuro-networks or boxes) of our mind in wonderful new combinations, and to understand those who do.

On the other hand, when trauma, fatigue, thirst, or other special stressors create these unusual combinations and we attempt to explain them with language while lacking insight into how our minds create visions, out-of-body experiences and other altered reality states, we are led to a myriad of mystic explanations; explanations that proliferate across our human history, religions, and charismatic biographies. We thereby fail to grasp a fundamental understanding of our own innate mental capacities and natures. Even a casual reading of mystics, discussions with shamans, or review of Gnostic-type interpretations of who we are as human beings forces us to move beyond our over-dependence on language. Unfortunately, the resulting worldviews and word-packages often continue ignorance of our own natural mental functions. Further, these worldviews have become polarized with atheists at one extreme and a variety of true believers at the other. I believe we are obliged to take the basic mental functions discussed in this book into consideration if we wish to resolve this polarization.

Each religious or mystic interpretation gets packaged with another "other-world" explanation; a crafted world view that is believed to come from beyond ourselves. I have used my auto-biography to demonstrate how we create these mystic experiences, we are their authors; further, we can control and direct them at will. Astral travel, spirit possession, speaking in tongues, reincarnation, and other examples discussed in this book are the products of our minds. In the language of neuro-philosophy, they are grounded in the basic metaphors of our brains as our evolving mind creates our Self. The capacity for these most human creations is given us, it is in our DNA; the mystic products of our own creation come in many forms, but the process is the same.

This analysis does not negate God, nor does it establish God. I believe that we cannot possibly know the Truth unless we remove the blinders that offer so many interpretations of natural brain functions. Further, it becomes impossible to follow blind, mystic interpretations of altered reality states once we learn how to create, direct and control them. Let us look beyond the mirror images we have contrived over the centuries in order to understand the mirror itself.

These word manipulations, I believe, must become much more grounded in experience, experiments, and shared verifiable ways of knowing. I'm not just referring to the knowable world out there, but to the realities created in our minds. Death and traumatic events are very real and have great impact on the course of our lives. Many of the world's historical explanations for these experiences are nothing short of amazing, and some are downright bizarre. Bizarre I have come to understand and embrace in meaningful, life-enhancing ways. Bizarre is often just the other side of everyday, common reality, the other side of the mirror; bizarre often means that we cross-mix the contents in the neuro-networks of our minds in new and wonderful ways. Nevertheless, whether old or new these true to life subjective experiences have origins that are just as natural as other common everyday experiences external to us. They do not, and should not give us license to kill each other, to hate each other, or to remain ignorant of who we are.

SHATTERING DUALISM

Shattering my dualistic mind, which separated intellect and feeling, came initially from Christian mysticism and Eastern philosophies as they bumped against Western ways of thinking; streams of thought from Yoga, Buddha, Hindu and Native

American interpretations of the universe. Influences from the sciences, both hard and soft were thrown into this bubbling cauldron, and gradually merged with my already altered understandings. I continued to have mystical experiences, and sought to explain them by combining traditional religious explanations with formal studies from the academic sciences.

Digging down to bedrock meant leaving the languages of these various schools of philosophy and religion and engaging what they referred to directly: Referential substrate where the essence of our humanity blends with space-time, rocks, trees, animals, and atoms. The universal metaphors we use to create space, time, movement and all the other metaphors of thought that are shared across our species. These common mental capacities and brain functions in our species can create altered experiences that are totally real for those of us who experience them. These experiences become religious facts for our group and magic, witchcraft or superstition for others who do not share our worldview.

I believe that having identified the source of mystic experiences and altered realities, we can no longer claim religious superiority by giving similar shared experiences different names; names that we have inherited from mystic historical personalities. The natural order of the universe, the same DNA, and our shared mental capacities lead us to the same altered worlds; we only see differences as they become colored by the definitions inherent to our respective cultures. Perhaps we should only create inferior-superior rankings of religions in terms of their ability to help us love each other, and, thereby, take responsibility for the destructive acts we so commonly support. When I come to understand these basic, universally shared mental capacities and the visions they create, I can no longer hate you because you initially seemed different; I am only capable of loving you as a brother or a sister.

FINDING MATURITY

As an infant and young child, I embraced my own primitive brain of visual memory and metaphorical creations, and stepping beyond language to direct experience. These were the only realities I possessed. Out-of-body experiences came initially when I had but a handful of words at my command. I explored all the chambers of my mind with a passion as I grew older; it was a wonderful world to travel, it is an incredible world to experience, it is life itself. As I matured, I incrementally committed to experiencing life fully and being whole one level at a time. Living fully and being whole meant that I had to integrate my fragmented mind as it was given to me by my dysfunctional parents. I discovered that living fully meant reordering and integrating the schizophrenic world I inherited as a child. My mental health required both understanding and controlling the altered reality experiences that came from abuse and neglect.

The arrogance of my youth is gone. The fundamental questions of life have new meaning, and I wait anxiously for tomorrow's questions, and the altered directions that come with them. I believe that each of us must travel our own road to find our beginning; it is "the road less traveled."

A huge crack in Western Dualism had gradually opened for me over the years and was shattered when I read Antonio Damasio's seminal work: "Descartes Error." His research makes it impossible to separate feeling and intellect in our rational minds; our minds operate as a whole by combining cognitive processes with feeling continuously. This awareness brought me peace by destroying the divide left by my academic pursuit of "pure reason," or what philosophers like Kant assumed was pure reason. I no longer had to separate intellect and feeling; instead I came to realize the two are not only always combined, but must be combined if we are to fully explain all of our experiences, including altered states of reality.

My dualistic mind had embraced this separation of feeling and intellect in my early years, especially those years in the academic world, in much the same way my schizophrenic mother lived in two separate worlds. I finally came to realize that brain chemistry is always a part of what becomes language, and part of how we create the metaphor from which thought is derived. We humans interact with our external environment while we busily create our own subjective reality, and we creatively blend our external and internal experiences into a whole that we call our worldviews and our religions. I am now happily exploring Neural Philosophy, "Philosophy in the Flesh", of the Lakoff and Johnson variety, and am overjoyed to find that science is inserting unstoppable wedges into the machinations of the superior pure intellect of traditional academic Western Philosophy; thereby calling into question much of the dogma of traditional philosophies, religions, and worldviews that dualism spawns. Simply put, we cannot know the world until we know ourselves. Sound familiar?

I believe that it is the dogma of world religions and word-spun philosophies, philosophies that are not based on how the brain actually functions, philosophies that are not grounded in the substrate of our living, operating minds, that prevent us from a fuller understanding of our universe and ourselves. It is these dogmas that prevent us from knowing our most basic spirituality and they are taught to us by the world's surviving religions; religions with endlessly contrived interpretations. We discover the basic essence of our innate spirituality when we move beyond these dogmas and the twisted metaphors that hold us so tightly in the grip of blindness. Is it not better that we chose to see? Is it true that the blind choose not to see? Is it possible that the mainstream of intellectual thought by world philosophies and religions, views that ignore the actual operations of our brains, is a form of blindness? Dualistic philosophies and religions seem to have been created by aliens without our human capacities. Perhaps we should send them back to Andromeda.

Neural science and developmental psychology, neural philosophy and neural linguistics are teaching us the basics of our brain's structure and chemistry, and how thoughts emerge in our developing minds. The referential metaphor on which all thought is built is universal and only becomes divisive at higher levels of abstraction; the level of abstraction where it becomes possible for us to torture and kill each other. (This process is destructive for the rational mind that has undergone normal development; it is even more destructive for the abnormally developed mind). These levels of abstraction do not exist in the world of shared non-referential experience, unaltered and natural realities that emerge from our psyches; something that I believe every guru, shaman, or Christian or non-Christian mystic knows intuitively – that I know experientially.

Part of my motivation for writing this book is the belief that humanity must come to understand this most essential part of what it means to be human; what every human baby of the world knows when playing with any other infant from around the world. I believe our global metaphorical creations must be fully clarified if we are to achieve a common universal understanding of ourselves as thinking-feeling beings. In my lifetime I have found most of my experiences of death, spirits, and mystical happenings to be commonly shared across cultures and worldviews; however, their interpretations vary tremendously. Similar brain functions, similar experiences, but varied competing explanations.

Touch my heart and you will also touch my mind. To touch my mind you must touch my heart. We can share this journey together. But, we cannot know each other through dogma, and we cannot experience the natural world through philosophies derived from intellectual word games that are not grounded in the actual functions of our brains. I believe we must take this step to a new level of awareness if we are to join each other in this universal quest to sanity; to world peace; to a place where our spirits find harmony. I have tried to remove my mask and reveal my soul, and in this nakedness reach out to our common identity.

CHEMISTRY NOT WORD PACKAGES

Neural Psychology is teaching me, along with other related disciplines, that we are able to practice empathy and sympathy because our brain chemistry duplicates that of the other person by calling forth similar brain chemicals and responses from the depths of our most primitive brains. Our limbic system's shared love and fear responses came thousands of years before the grey lobes tucked behind our foreheads emerged. We know that individuals who are incapable of feeling for others have defects in this system for various reasons; however, we have treatment strategies now that can potentially reverse the horrors of psychopathy and character dysfunction, which are so destructive in the minds of ordinary individuals let alone those of our Hitlers and his kind.

In similar fashion, we can understand most of our mystic experiences through the basic mechanisms I have been discussing in this book; and also in similar fashion, potentially quiet the voices of the faith abusers who carelessly take money and lives of their true believers. The struggle between atheists like Richard Dawkins, as expressed in "The God Delusion," and true believers like Francis Collins, as expressed in "The Language of God" continues, and I believe will continue indefinitely until the basis from which these religious experience come are more fully understood and studied.

Pursuing intellectual pathways to such understanding without developmental and neural psychology is similar to exploring the atom through the ancient Greek's intellect while ignoring modern science. Simply believing that atheists are devious, evil people, or that True Believers are misguided souls fed from the bottle of dogma is to miss the point. I believe the middle ground of understanding emerges from a fuller appreciation for and comprehension of the natural mechanisms in our minds that I have discussed in Ghost. To divide the world into good and evil, or light and dark forces in the name of atheism or religion while ignoring our basic human spiritual capacities and mental functions is a great mistake. Bringing together our growing fields of knowledge and understanding of faith and our basic mental functions, I believe, can help us rise above this level of thought and behavior as we become more compassionate and caring world citizens.

"The God Delusion" by Richard Dawkins attempts to explore actions by the madmen of faith in world history, and does so brilliantly. Nevertheless, he seems quite blind to the historical understandings and messages of the simple shaman or guru in his intellectual shredding of humankinds basic ability to experience the world and the cosmos with unfettered appreciation and wonder, through what we often call religion. Dawkin, I contend, does not distinguish between our innate religious capacity and the dogma of popular religions. This is a great error to blind basic understanding of who we are. "To Know Thyself" is not just a trite intellectual world game, but is a sought after reality driven by the dual relationship between our primitive limbic systems and our sentient minds, brains and souls; however, we may choose to slice and dice these terms.

The evolution of our universe brought forth by exploding supernova, creating the complex organic chemistry of the physical world from which all animal life and our human bodies emerged. What we are is a fundamental creation of this incredible process in a cosmos we are still coming to know. Sometimes explained and sometimes unexplained. However, the bottom line of all life is derived from stellar processes, and appears to be as basic to the universe as stars and planets, and is the fundamental source of our body's atoms and chemistry; the parent of our DNA.

The fine tuned equations of physics that make life possible are a reality we are forced to contemplate. We come to know this reality of origin more fully as our anthropocentric world slowly collapses; but in many ways today, probing the basic realities of our own minds has moved as slowly as integrating the fundamental forces of nature. Our minds are not defined by the dogmas of the ancients, or dualistic thoughts of modern legal or political figures, but by the realities of the universe, or Universe; by the equations of physics, by the fine tuning of these equations, however that may have happened, that makes life and you and me possible.

The questions of other life in the universe; whether our cosmos is sentient or intelligent, and to what degree as discussed by excellent writers such as James Gardner in "The Intelligent Universe;" explanations for action at a distance as demonstrated experimentally in physics; the equations of Einstein that permit time to flow into both the past and the future; coming to understand gravity's relationship to the other main forces, and a potential theory of everything – these are wonders for our minds and our continuous, undeniable quest to know.

Nevertheless, fundamental questions of our inner world are no less compelling: are quantum forces at work in the human brain; how can we develop a common vocabulary and understanding of real life experiences that we call channeling, astral travel, automatic writing, speaking-in-tongues, dream programming and its various world explanations, and the wonderful, if not fun, experiences we humans have when select parts of our brains sleep while other centers become active. The common language of science unites world people by replacing separate dogmas and superstitions with knowledge and understanding; however, this common language has yet to come to the common vocabularies of our major religions.

Personally for many of us, how do we explain our Guardian Angels? I believe it is time to move beyond the visions of our historical shamans, whether they are small or large in stature, religions composed of two people or millions, and use the knowledge that we have so painstakingly wrestled from nature to lay the primitive dogmas of the ancients to rest. Our survival as a species may depend on this. Religious dogmas that fail to understand and use the natural functions of our own psyches have become some of the most divisive forces in our modern world. If we deny the natural functions of our brains and psyches, are we not denying the possibility of an Intelligent Designer? Why are we afraid?

We revere dogmas without understanding the fundamental processes in our brain from which they come; processes that make these expressions universal. To use religious metaphor: The cloak of dogma that keeps us from experiencing – with understanding – the natural functions of our own brains; not using or being afraid of abilities our psyches are designed to engage, separates us from each other; separates our group from their group; separates all of us from the natural design of our universe; separates our spiritual selves from each other. A separation that God or a Universal Conscience would find below the natural abilities with which we have been endowed. I believe it is time for all of us to read more than the book's cover; it is time to read the book of self.

IT'S TIME TO BE

It's time to be, life set me free.
It's time to feel, and laugh, and feel.
It's time to know, it's time to grow.

It's time to see, not blind to be.
It's time to hear; no silence fear.
It's time for you, and you, and me!

CHAPTER 15

UNDERSTANDING MYSTICISM IS EASY

THE MODERN SHAMAN

Let me offer some examples of shaman spirit possession. In my early years of teaching I developed a survey course on North American Indians, and have uppermost in mind my favorite teaching film from this class. The video focuses on a Klingit Indian of the American Northwest Coast; a shaman of the bear clan cloaked in the animal's skin, becoming the animal itself. The shaman moves and dances with the motions of the bear and gradually merges with and takes on its identity. I would join him in this shamanic act of becoming the bear. I am sure the shaman felt the bear's power as he took on its identity. I too would become the bear and loved the feeling of leaving my human body as I merged with that of the bear; thus, enabling my puny flesh and bone to be replaced by the power of the bear.

It was an experience not unlike playing in space with the Northern Lights, or merging with the power of a summer thunderstorm. It is from these early studies, and considerable later work with Native Americans, that I came to understand shamanism and its origin in our most fundamental human capacities, the blend of primitive brain chemistry and modern intellect that enables us to become whatever we wish to become; the ability to be any size we choose to be; or the ability to let our inner spirit roam the cosmos in free flight. We can join the spirit of the tree in the Australian Outback, or feel the power of Neptune as we merge with the power of oceans. It is this capacity that can make us superior to all other living things, or the wickedest creature ever to roam planet Earth. It is not pure intellect that gives us this power. It is the totality of intellect combined with our primitive brain chemistry that creates what becomes our total reality of knowing.

To laugh at or diminish this capacity, these most real innermost experiences we have as human beings, in our fellow creatures, now or historically, is to diminish ourselves. (It reflects our spirituality and is the basis of sacred religions.) More importantly, it closes a window of self understanding. Unfortunately, this limited definition of self, through the perpetuation of ignorance based on sacred or secular dogmas, permits us to so easily kill one another. We kill not in the name of religion in this 21st Century, but in ignorance of the capacity that makes our religious, mystical, transcendental experiences possible.

Leaving our awareness solely at an intellectual level does not permit movement beyond mutual homicide. I believe we must engage and more fully comprehend all that is human in us in order to save ourselves and our planet. I must, without question, truly come to know you as my brothers and sisters. I must know more about you than your intellect; I must know you as you are and who you are becoming; I must experience your intellect entwined with the chemistry of your brain to form what we call mind. I must help you understand more fully who you are, as you help me understand and become more than I have been. I believe we can and must write this book of human futures together.

SHAMANIC BEARS AND ZEN DRIVING

Next, let's bring shamanistic bears and yoga driving, as I earlier discussed them, together and put them in the same experiential box. I left by body when I died in my childhood hospital, and learned that I could leave it whenever I wanted to, and often did. I especially enjoyed yoga driving at the time my step-mother was dying of cancer. The act or sensation of separating mind and body occurs for people riding motorcycles, jogging, meditating, traveling to and sitting on the moon, collectively sitting on icebergs on a hot summer day, and in a multitude of other settings. The experiences feel completely real, although those watching us perform these feats will tell us later that our bodies didn't move. Joining the bear, or wolf, or eagle, as the case may be, involves the same mind-body separation as does yoga driving. When I join the bear, I feel his power and other characteristics that are interpreted within this shamanic journey. I feel like I am the bear, have the power of the bear, and communicate to my human friends this supernatural experience of being the bear, if I am their shaman.

In the preliterate world, I will be a mystical figure. In the modern world, I may be your mystic or guru. For those who have learned to separate mind and body, all of these experiences become possible. And, I can assure you, they are interesting if not downright fun. But, most importantly, these visualizations seem just as real as the chair I sit in as I write these words; it is the basis of true belief; it is a fundamental part of our humanity. Joining normally separated neural networks in our brain in new configurations permits us to experience the other worlds mystically interpreted by our fellow human beings throughout history. However, these simple journeys are no longer mystical to the modern experiential mind. You lose nothing, dear reader, by stepping into the 21st Century.

In my studies of preliterate people, I often put myself mentally in their caves, imagined the dim light of oil lamps or torches, the chanting or emotional vocalizations that occurred and thought to myself – how modern were our ancestors' mental functions; how confusing these experiences were to their minds devoid of modern science. This capacity is not something to be laughed at, to be smug about; instead, something to be understood as normal brain functions that come to us across time and cultures. This metaphorical capacity uses the same brain operations now as it did a thousand years ago, ten thousand years ago, and represents a threshold crossed by humanity probably between 50 and 100,000 years ago; our metaphorical constructs merely vary at different levels of abstraction as we are possessed by spirits, travel to and sit on the moon, or perform automatic writing.

We now have an adequate science to determine specifically how our brains create these realities. Unobtrusively, we can watch through technologies such as MRIs as our neural networks combine and recombine to remove pain from our body, permit astral flight, slow our heart beats, change our respiration, or speak in tongues. Religious experiences of this kind are just as subject to scientific analysis as are plankton. To say with finality that the universe has no larger Intelligence, at this point in history, is to deny the experiences of millions of people such as myself. Shall not the learned person put knowledge and awareness before final premature conclusions? If I read history correctly, we can kill each other as easily in the name of racial inferiority, or being culturally superior, or even oil, as we can in the name of religious ignorance or righteousness. There is a universal underlying condition common to our cognitive-emotional neural networks that is based on metaphor, feeling, brain chemistry and intellect that begs first understanding. It is given to us as part of our DNA, but from where it is ultimately derived is still a question unanswered.

The constants of physics that are so finely tuned still beg the question of how, or by whom, they are derived. Religions still beg the question. Curious minds of every kind still beg the question. It is time for us to become accountable for a real answer – dogma is not sufficient. As science and experiential experiments unlocked the mystery of mysticism for me, I encountered an ever larger, more exciting, mysterious, and fun universe. My personal journey begged a larger question: Why do we not study religious experiences the way we study all other human behavior, perception, and sensation?

COLLECTIVE SHAMANIC BEARS

A friend of mine is Native American and very active in the Christian faith. He believes deeply in God and has spent much of his life trying to be a good person who cares for others. He survived two jungle outposts in the Vietnam War after they were overrun by the Viet Cong and spent months in those jungles alone before he could get back to American lines. He has experienced Hell on Earth and seeks Heaven for the rest of eternity. Treble (not his real name) spent a year living in a teepee in the middle of nowhere. This was his Spirit Quest; a quest that was not to be. Treble and I talk about my unsolicited and at times unwanted visitations, and his attempts to touch the supernatural. He has never been able to enter this mystical world. Many people cannot even though they try, while others of us do so naturally, or even when we wish not to. The capacity to leave our bodies is not universal even though it is common.

In North American traditional native cultures one became a shaman if these experiences occurred unsolicited, often to the person's dismay, and often with considerable resistance. Treble would have been delighted if he had been so appointed! I wish I could share mine with him. People across the world and throughout history have known and shared these visions, and from them they have come to accept their responsibilities as shaman priest, priests of major world religions, or clergy of all faiths. Let us simply acknowledge the commonalities of all such experiences, our fellow kinship, our basic human capacities. One is not larger than the other; one size fits all; the experiences emerge from the common shared capacities of our human psyches. If we believe that God is real, let us remove our blinders experientially with the knowledge of science, and not be afraid. We cannot come to know the Truth by continuing to wear ancient masks that permit only blindness; ancient masks that deny our most fundamental cognitive and emotional capacities.

I will not give you details for reasons of confidentiality; however, I was inducted into the Native American Church (NAC) some years ago during my early days as a college professor. It was an honoring time for a lost brother who had been killed accidentally just as he was entering his young adulthood. NAC ceremonies are usually held in a large tent, have a fire ceremony, start at sundown, and go until sunup. The ceremonies are overseen by an Elder (in days past a shaman) who is respected by the tribe - a person who possesses certain gifts to call forth the spirits of the deceased. Many Western field workers in anthropology and other related study areas have remarked that their experiences in similar settings were totally real. This was true for me as well.

The NAC spiritual setting was warm and felt like my own family gathering even though I was the only white person there. About an hour or so before sunrise the spirit of the young man returned to acknowledge his family, friends, and tribal relatives. I first became aware of his presence while I was half sleeping, half awake but trying to take in all that was happening during my initiation. When the young man returned, I was aware of his presence and outline as he stood by the fire pit. No one spoke, no one, but we all turned collectively in mutual respect to honor his spirit and its visitation.

It is a strange sensation looking at a deceased person's spirit at the same time as a hundred other people and being aware that each one of us is having the same experience; I purposely say same experience because I don't know if it was the same vision. Additionally, I had never met the young man when he was alive. The next day on the powwow grounds where the ceremony had been conducted, I was pleased that other members of the NAC attending the ceremony smiled and nodded at me in recognition of our collective visitation. Some things do not have to be talked about as they seem to retain the most meaning when unspoken. It is similar to the shared experience one has laying a mile off shore in the warm Hawaiian sunshine; one doesn't talk about it as words will simply detract from the wonders of what is. "Pure Intellects" often talk while the rest of us just experience, feel, and come to know. I am not disdaining intellect, but challenging the outdated concept of "pure intellect" – the hypothetical intellect that does not connect the chemistry of our modern brains with its primitive limbic system. Dualists know not the difference, dear friends.

COLLECTIVE TRIPS

I had counseled a young man in his late teens who had been involved with drugs before I started my college teaching career. After I began teaching, the young man, who was very bright took a number of my courses and frequently stopped by to chat. We became close enough friends that I later attended his wedding. "Rave" continued to be involved with drugs on-again, off-again throughout his college career. In the early 1970s in Minnesota marijuana and psychedelics were both popular, and Rave became one of their staunch advocates. I discussed my NAC experience with him and asked for his opinion as peyote is part of the NAC ceremony. He laughed at my not understanding "collective trips" as he called them.

On hot summer days, Rave and his friends would get high and go on out-of-body explorations together. One such story I remember well involved an iceberg: try to think of a hot summer day without air conditioning and psychedelics all coming together. Rave told me how he and his friends would climb the iceberg, sit on it to cool off and explore the surrounding area enjoying its soothing effects. Rave did not believe the iceberg existed any more than I did. It didn't matter; he enjoyed the experience and felt the cooling effects anyway. This is the same reality we use to kill each other; the same reality that permits us to willingly blow ourselves up, or walk into the fires of the Inquisition. It is your reality and mine, and is not strange at all.

I believe we can more fully understand the subjective experiences of Rave and many types of similar experiences by the mentally ill when we come to subjectively comprehend what is going on in our brains; the capacities I have been discussing in this book. There is a compassion that develops on the part of mental health workers who direct therapy for the mentally ill and the chemically muddled mind – minds that are cognitively fragmented – that goes well beyond intellectualization. Our humanity is more fully expressed when feeling and cognition are combined as one.

Call it mysticism if you will; I prefer to call it our basic human capacity, the blending of cognitive and chemical processes that are a part of all mental functions. It is our ability to fully experience humanity; the ability of our brain to duplicate the brain chemistry of our fellow humans in acts of sympathy and empathy; the ability to metaphorically duplicate the images emerging from the depth of our primitive brains and the ability to create on demand the primitive sensations of our limbic systems. It is the ability to identify with others who have the same brain functions that we have. Collectively, it seems, the modern mind has one basic form when it functions in an integrated fashion; when thought and feeling are used together to their full capacity.

I used similar hypnotic suggestions with myself and others to diminish the effects of summer heat before I could afford air conditioning, but hadn't thought of setting out with a group of friends on such a collective journey, a careless reading of religious literature. After this discussion, I connected group hypnotism, group suggestion, and realized that similar collective experiences had been around at least since recorded history. Group experiences of this type have been common religious phenomena at least since the pre-Christian Egyptians and the spread of group hypnotism through the early Christian era and across many cultures that I had some familiarity with, especially through my experiences with native people, as well as formal studies in anthropology.

It is much easier to have these collective experiences if the culture supports the expectation, or your friends who come together seeking common relief from the heat have shared views of this altered reality. When the psychedelic trip wears off or the effects of group hypnotism, we are back with the heat or our crutches. If the illness or disability is psychosomatic, we may experience a permanent cure. What is modern is ancient; what is ancient is modern. We all access the same fundamental human resources, at least this seems to be the case since prehistoric times when we started burying our dead, and honored the afterlife. The cosmos **is** fine tuned.

When I look at primitive art around the world, visit the Chinese caves of Zhoukoutian near Beijing, or think of the primitive art of the Cromagnon some 32,000 years ago at Chauvet-Pont-d'Arc, France, I see shamans dancing by firelight, shadows moving on the walls, chanting figures entering their animistic worlds, and smile. Chanting and rhythmic dancing movements can bring many of us to trance states in a matter of minutes. Modern humankind has similar experiences, but we are often afraid to acknowledge them, but it doesn't stop us from seeking or having these experiences.

We hide our subjective selves in the fine art of modern chanting, or the drug induced sensation of rock music; otherwise, we often sneer with cultured superiority. The smugness of word packages, word games, and intellectual puzzles are so much safer. But, through this foggy looking glass we find practitioners of what we politely call mysticism and struggle for understanding by joining our favorite guru in California or India; when it is so much simpler to understand how we can naturally enjoy our own brain chemistry and intellect coming together in the most wonderful ways that make you and me completely human. We can create and be what we wish to be, but when we do so without understanding our own capacities, we continue to wear the blinders of dogma.

The key to understanding is to give up the fear perpetuated by dogma. We do not need drugs to enter altered states of reality, but world people have often used drugs to generate these naturally produced experiences, experiences that some of us create, direct, and control by combining our emotional and mental capacities in new configurations; altered states that are available on demand. Mysticism understood is no less awe inspiring by giving us a conscious awareness of how to manipulate our brain chemistry and cognitive functions; it simply opens another encyclopedia of questions and additional avenues for exploration.

CHANTING & SPEAKING-IN-TONGUES

The boundary between my inner and outer words was even thinner and more tenuous when I died in the hospital when I was about two years of age. Language was not developed enough to hide the basic primary metaphors from which my world was being constructed, and I simply constructed it from experience. I was not old enough, or sophisticated enough about what the world believed to be true, I was simply a normally endowed human child struggling to survive in a world that seemed not to care whether I did or not. My life flowed into the channels of the shaman; channels that often brought horror or quick rejecting responses of craziness from those around me, or evoked smug comments from poorly trained mental health counselors in settings like the University of Minnesota. I can now smile at the flow of history, and the eyes of science as they combine with my own, bringing light, understanding, and peace. Sometimes – even forgiveness.

I spent a number of years closely involved with Native American people and their struggle for equality and freedom. I was at a powwow in Northeastern South Dakota one July afternoon dancing to the rhythm of the drums. I began to sing and chant softly with the drums and found myself entering a peaceful state similar to meditation, a state bordering on body-mind separation, or trance. As I continued to dance, I increasingly became aware that the rhythm of the drums was resonating with my own brain chemistry, or more precisely, my brain chemistry was responding to the rhythm of the drums. The rhythm was intoxicating, the methodical beat of my dancing feet shared the beat of the drum; the memory in my muscles acted alone; and the joy of mind-body separation began to emerge. I though later that I was finally beginning to understand why chanting is so popular with many different religious groups; it transports us to a most pleasant spot between Earth and the "nether world;" the worldwide universality of drums and rock and roll, and chanting voices; and the world of spirits; to the night before the crucifixion.

I had this same experience with a small group of Native American friends in my house some time later, and decided to explore the effect more fully. I found that chanting rhythmically to recorded drum music and then letting my voice rise to its own natural level was activating both the voice centers in my brain as well as specific brain chemicals that induce a trance-like state. At the same time other centers of my brain were relaxing and slipping away to a meditative state. In the privacy of my home I discovered how to induce speaking-in-tongues. The sensation of being separated from my body, while my vocal cords were still active, left me with the feeling that my voice was being directed from somewhere else. I had set up the process, relaxed other brain centers, but kept my voice engaged by chanting; hence, I was aware of my own control.

The effect I got from speaking-in-tongues was that of my voice being controlled from "out there," by someone or something else. Biblically recorded in the Gnostic texts as (XYZCMQRSTVW); a feeling that comes when one part of our brain disconnects from another part where it is normally associated. The sounds are strange, another language, or gibberish depending upon one's cultural point of view. This is an enjoyable experience and one that activates endorphins, and probably brings other brain chemicals into action as well. I began to understand why certain people love evangelical ceremonies where they can enter these trance states and speak in tongues. It is a natural high, and natural. Of course, the interpretations of the experiences vary, but we are always reluctant to give up pleasure especially when it borders on ecstasy. It is the runner's high, only multiplied.

As a young child and adolescent growing up with physically demanding work, I enjoyed the pleasing effects of singing, chanting, and whistling. I often took sections of popular songs and repeated them over and over as I cultivated corn in the hot sun, picked cucumbers, or performed other physically demanding tasks. I would perfect their harmony through repetition, or improve my opera whistling performances this way. I watched movies of field laborers singing Negro Spirituals and shared the relief that came from their songs; sometimes imitating their rhythm and sometimes making my own. In the army I loved group singing on long marches for the same reason. Our brains have these wonderful endorphins available for our relief and they flow like music, and they flow with music, and they flow with chanting - when we let ourselves enjoy the chemistry of our primitive brains.

CHANNELING & AUTOMATIC WRITING

The world truly has become a small place for me, and human differences insignificant, while the awareness of my mind, soul, and self enjoy primitive instruments such as the reed flute, or voices lost in ancient chanting common to our species. I believe that attempts to explain human experience from any dogmatic interpretation, thinking that excludes the fundamental human capacities that I have experienced and talked about, are doomed to fail. I am referring to natural brain capacities and functions that have been given endless mystical and supernatural explanations from one culture, or one religious group, to another. They are not to be intellectualized away, any more than they should be dogmatized; they are to be understood as gifts freely offered to most of us who have and are walking on this planet.

As human beings we are born with a sense of awe towards the wonders around us, wonders that grow from the cradle, in the home, neighborhood, to the Earth, through the cosmos, and to the beginning of time. It is only the limits of our awareness and knowledge that sets boundaries. Most importantly, we come to understand that religious interpretations, philosophical interpretations, or scientific explanations are always partial within the limits of these boundaries. We know personally that we are driven to find meaning and purpose in our lives, but more than anything else we create meaning.

The search for meaning is universal and quite easily conceptualized as being given to us by the Other. We are brothers and sisters built from the same atoms and chemistry that is shared across our known universe and species. We have the capacity to be as small and ignorant, or gigantic and enlightened as we choose, but the basis for all this beauty, intrigue, and our unanswered questions is universally in our DNA; it is universally in the fine tuned equations of physics that make life and this universe possible. It is the basis of wonder; it is the source of our ability to love or hate.

I have a friend who became interested in automatic writing a good twenty years ago and has practiced it often over these years. She believes that automatic writing has provided her with explanations for the causes of cancer and a number of other serious problems of medicine still waiting for solutions. She is bright with an IQ above 140 on standard tests. She also quite strongly believes that the messages she gets through automatic writing are coming from "beyond," beyond somewhere besides the here and now. She works in the medical community at a well known university center but has never found anyone there who would take her findings seriously. I commiserate with her as my attempts to discuss experiences such as dream programming with professional people in my early years brought me into contact with the same mindset. A few years ago she became a channel for a famous doctor who works on the East Coast of America - fifty years in the future. She knows his name, where he went to university, and communicates with him on and off. This is not a single experience on her part with the doctor from the future that she channels.

The doctor is of Irish-American descent and will help my friend with whatever she requests. I asked her to get the lottery numbers for a specific lottery worth a few million dollars and she did. Unfortunately, the numbers did not work. She was a bit baffled by this. I then asked her to have the doctor friend explain some fairly new hypotheses I was reading about in physics dealing with string theory. The questions were well outside of knowledge areas familiar to her, and the answers coming back had no meaning, it was merely a well constructed word package: an easy experiment I thought to test reality. I also had her check with the doctor as to how he communicated across the huge distance our planet moves in the Milky Way Galaxy over a fifty year period of time; something I thought the doctor must be aware of as he consciously chose her to be his channel to the past. The answer: equally devoid of meaning. She believes in the "truth" of automatic writing and the answers she gets. She is a Channeler, a true believer. She is fully human and inquisitive; one who is searching for answers, and seeking to know. She is not afraid, but she is usually alone.

What do the Channeler, Speaker-of-tongues, and Shaman all have in common? The ability to detach one brain center from consciousness and have the experience of feeling something outside directing and guiding what becomes spirit possession, speaking unknown languages, or channeling. A rather normal human capacity in my experience with wonderfully varied interpretations of reality by various human participants. When we stop taking language literally and think of what it represents, the referential and metaphorical world underlying language, it becomes much easier to find our human commonalities, to study our brain chemistry, its neural development, and how we learn and experience.

Cognitive-emotional capacity means feeling and intellect combined in the way researchers such as Antonio Damasio say it is combined – that is the basis of rational thought, not Kantian or Western Dualism. Human capacity begs understanding that doesn't laugh at the shaman or the guru but acknowledges our common brain functions, our shared capacities, with them, even though we may have learned different ways of organizing and explaining these experiences. Human capacity to know is not the strange stuff of mysticism but awareness that this is just letting ourselves fully use what is in our DNA, and experiencing everything that our brains permit. Often times, as we give ourselves this permission, the walls between our inner self, and the external world just slip away, and we know more fully who we really are. Mysticism has new meaning and clarity when these most fundamental experiences are shared, talked about and researched. We are equally lost in the delusions of mental illness as we are in the superior realm of pure intellect; we are equally lost in the reality of pure intellect as we are in the delusions of mental illness. Did I repeat myself?

Human capacity is not one cleric, one preacher, or one demi-god proclaiming the righteousness of his or her worldview: Perhaps it is time that we no longer grant the demi-gods this permission. Our common humanity (brain functioning) can easily share this capacity to alter realities, and thereby come to explain and use this ability more rationally. When we understand mysticism by being able to create and control its states on demand, understanding that combines modern science and philosophy with our history as a world people, one that can lead to a new awareness of who we are and why we behave the way we do, the power to abuse others is greatly diminished. To know thyself is to know your cousins, is to know those who have walked, are walking, and will walk the face of this planet. It is time to drop the boxes of rubble that each disciple of each religion or mystic enterprise tries to carry to the top of his or her special worldview, and instead, use the primeval stones of self to build a mountain from which we can all see more clearly. The shrinking world is giving us this permission. Consilience!

YOUTH REVISITED

As a child and young man I wanted to talk to adults about my out-of-body and mystic experiences, I needed to talk to adults about these experiences, I needed a rational explanation for what I was experiencing, but was denied this opportunity. I was treated as a strange or crazy child. My initial encounters with Western mental health were through the mysticism of Freudian Psychoanalysis, and the MMPI with its inept and smug interpreter. No one in my early life understood what was happening to me; on the other hand, many strange, incoherent, baffling, and often erroneous explanations were offered – if any were offered at all. As I grew more experienced and compared psychoanalysis to shamanism, my educated friends, and the few psychiatrists that would engage me in these discussions, would immediately put up a defensive wall. The Western mind understood the psyche, not the Eastern mind, or that of the shaman; or, that is what was intimated or argued. I had trouble appreciating these models of reality and various worldviews, until I realized how small the box was into which our Western minds had been shut.

I am eternally thankful for my second life, a life that has brought me to Antonio Damasio, developmental and neural psychology, neural philosophy, and the expanded world of natural science. Self-experiments of the experiential kind can be a wonderful life-long journey as long as each one of us is careful about how we proceed. I engaged in many self-experiments as the reader knows, and found the interface between science and religion was often very tenuous; the distinctions and differences lacking except for our interpretations. Researchers into other cultures and ways of knowing generally either bring their cultural interpretations to the moment of new experiences, or suspend their Western thinking and enter the cultural realities of their new friends, and their new friends' ways of seeing. This, I believe, is a loss to both worldviews, to science and both individuals.

A married couple, who were friends of mine at State University, was actively involved with an East Indian Guru. He came to visit America and their home and they were delighted to introduce me to him; they were also aware of my involvement with native people. He had taken vows of silence and corresponded only through written notes. The Guru sat on his bed, occasionally burping from the excellent alcohol he had drunk the night before, which was also supported by the most expensive steaks available, and with the pomp of sweeping hand movements admitted me into audience. I was informed after a very short exchange that I had been an Indian chief of the Great Plains in a former life. This was a clear invitation to explore my prior existence with him as my mentor. I smiled, thanked him briefly for the information, and having turned down his offer, found it necessary to say goodbye. I am quite sure he would have been happy to take me on a journey into the past, and would have helped me discover my "Indian heritage" as my bank account slowly dwindled, a journey perhaps equivalent to one of my programmed dreams, but one that I preferred to direct myself, one without cost or muddled interpretations of native culture.

Dream programming taught me that reincarnation can be totally real and reliving one's former lives equally real. These journeys can be as complex as any Hollywood movie with multiple characters and serial editions, and provide one with true to life experiences. I could be that Indian chief with or without the Guru, I could enter the "Dream Time" of my ancestors with all the history of my people orchestrating the journey, I could channel with an Irish doctor fifty years in the future; or, I could be whatever I chose to be. When I dream programmed to remove traumatic nightmares, I learned this process well. The process is the same, however, who one experiences as the "controller" may be different.

I bring my story to an end with the poignant words of Coelho's Alchemist:

"Every search begins with beginner's luck. And every search ends with the victor's being severely tested."

"To show you one of life's simple lessons," the Alchemist answered. "When you possess great treasures within you, and try to tell others of them, seldom are you believed."

"You already know about alchemy. It is about pentrating the Soul of the World, and discovering the treasure that has been reserved for you."

And, so it has been my fate to know this treasure.

EPILOGUE

INSIGHTS

Insight 1: Transcendental intra-psychic experiences occur when neural structures are combined in new configurations and process stimuli in unusual ways. As I have demonstrated in **Ghost**, uncommon neural networks lead us to speak in tongues, experience astral travel, ghosts and angels, reincarnation, automatic writing, and spirit possession. Individuals throughout history and across the modern world have these experiences, but they are unusual enough that those who do not experience them come to believe that those of us who do are in contact with God or the supernatural. Most of us, at least initially, come to believe traditional explanations for our own altered reality experiences. We come to accept explanations for our mystic experiences given to us by our own cultures and religions, and we become mystics, prophets or shamans. However, if the experiences disagree with our culture's traditional worldviews or religious philosophies, or are too extreme, we are labeled misfits, agents of the devil, or with other names that are equally uncomplimentary.

As we come to understand the origin of transcendental experiences, it becomes obvious that neural configurations that process input from our senses in culturally normative ways are suspended when new or different configurations emerge and create these true-to-life altered realities. New configurations can emerge due to trauma, which was my own experience, or any extremely stressful condition such as dehydration, starvation, life threatening episodes or unusual physical changes due to tumors, cancer, or drugs. In my own history, smothering attacks by my mother, which led to my death experience around two years of age, along with extreme neglect, brought about my first out-of-body experience, visitation by angels, the appearance of my Guardian Angel and endless visitation by a haunting ghost. These intra-psychic experiences were just as real as eating lunch.

Native Americans vision quests were achieved through fasting, exposure to the physical elements, us of drugs such as peyote, traumatic events such as war, or physical conflict. Related altered reality experiences by various people from around the world, as revealed through historical sources such as the Bible, and numerous ethnographies published by anthropologists, are well known. Typically, supernatural contact was assumed and the shamanic experience was interpreted as putting one in contact with whatever spirit or spirits the culture assumed was out there. When the shaman's experience, the mind of the mystic, becomes part of a major religious movement it is assumed that the visions or messages come directly from that groups' God or gods.

Insight 2: Visions and altered reality states are culturally dependent and come from our own minds or psyches. Understanding our basic human capacities for these experiences, which are interpreted religiously, forces us to confront their varied explanations historically and world-wide. This mystic capacity is so universal that it can only be built into our mind-brain structure, an expression of our DNA, a reality that emerges as we acknowledge the universality of similar religious experiences across history and cultures; most telling, we are able to document their intra-psychic origin. Further, it is not the variety of interpretations for these experiences that is critical, it is the basic human capacity that makes these experiences inevitable that demands explanation. I find interpretations of various experiences of altered realities in pre-literate and pre-modern cultures interesting because they parallel my own. We thus come to understand that experiences of altered reality; experiences that form the basis of both polytheistic and monotheistic religions, are an inevitable expression determined by the structure of our own brains, and how our minds develop from this structure.

Brain chemical changes, which are triggered by stress, can bring about new neural configurations that emerge from anxiety, depression, physical trauma, or unusual physical changes in our brains caused by blood clots, tumors, and cancer. It is now common knowledge that chemical levels within the brain change under extreme conditions as do operating neural configurations.

Brain plasticity permits compensation when one part of the brain is damaged or stops working properly. At a different level, or more specifically in new configurations, brain plasticity using new neural combinations produces altered states of reality and mystic experiences.

Lazy brains, especially for the elderly, are reconditioned by neural scientists like Michael Merzenich at the University of California, San Francisco. Reconditioning that increases memory and probably grows a limited number of new brain cells. In my case, I simply reconditioned my own brain as a university student and continued this process throughout most of my adult years. In 1958 I was unaware of how I was modifying inter-neuronal connections; I just kept creating new effects that I found interesting. I thought brain restructuring was possible from the courses I was taking in psychology and the information I was discovering in world literature related to religion and social thought. It seemed obvious to me at that time that my brain was also producing new cells; however, this contemporary fact was not accepted by the medical community in the 1950s.

As a university undergraduate, I thought of reconditioning my brain as a process of rechanneling basic and secondary drives; only later did I come to think of this process as creating new neural configurations. In contrast to the work being done by Merzenich, I didn't use computer programs or hardware as this technology did not exist. I used self-hypnosis to create expressions within neural pathways I wanted to take control of or reconfigure: pain control, improved concentration, anxiety reduction and control over depression. In today's language I was modifying inter-neuronal networks.

Insight 3: If newly emerged neural patterns create an external reality moment-to-moment, a reality that family and other observers do not experience, but involve everyday events, the person may be considered psychotic or mentally ill; similar to the interpretation of my MMPI Profile when I was an undergraduate. For example, one of my relatives was in an auto accident and began to have hallucinations a few months later. In one hallucination, he was leaving church with his mother and remarked that his deceased grandfather was walking toward him across the parking lot. Later evaluation determined that a blood clot had formed in his brain as the result of this accident and was the source of his hallucinations. For a number of years, he was treated as a psychotic rather than a patient with a life-threatening blood clot in his brain. Failure to understand altered states of reality almost cost this young man his life. Before receiving adequate diagnosis and proper medical intervention, he was inappropriately treated for a number of years by medical personal who assumed that his symptoms were caused by something other than a blood clot.

Insight 4: The brain can act as if it were a movie camera. I do not mean that we just use our eyesight to simply scan the world and record. The brain can scan its own recorded landscape, which includes everything given to us externally, as well as everything created internally by our own mind-brain processes. All of this landscape of the mind, some of which is created whole, is used to create movies in the mind, and can be configured in any combination. If the movie, or movie segment, is experienced during waking hours of normal activity, as was the case with my relative, the episode is considered to be psychotic and the person is diagnosed as being mentally ill. We don't just say that his inter-neuronal connections have been modified. However, in the case of this young man, his blood clot was diagnosed later and additional procedures were implemented to help it dissolve. Gradual shrinking of the clot permitted normal neural processing to reoccur; normal processing that had not occurred with antipsychotic drugs. This young man lost critical years of his youth due to inappropriate diagnosis and treatment, and is fortunate to still be alive.

Dream programming is a good example of our brain's capacity to provide us with nighttime movies as we sleep. Physical smothering attacks by my mother when I was still crib confined, as well as later sexual abuse, each created traumatizing nightmares.

When I entered the University of Minnesota as an undergraduate, I was plagued by these nightmares and brought them under control with dream programming. I learned to substitute my own programmed dreams for nightmares and taught my psyche to switch from nightmare to preferred dream whenever the nightmares emerged during sleep. This switching process occurred while I was still asleep; I did not need to wake to reactivate the dream program. I was simply using my archive of stored sights and sensations to create real-to-life, pleasing and sometimes sensuous night movies. I taught my brain this process and used dream programming to control nightmares into my mid-fifties.

The capacity to automatically control dreams and redirect them while I'm still sleeping stays with me as I age. Dream programming offered me relief from nightmares, but I also found after weeks of viewing a specific dream-movie that I grew tired of the content. Within a few weeks of teaching myself this ability, I learned to alter the movie scripts. I created alternatives similar to movies recorded on CDs where one can change the endings or sequences through various options that are provided. I changed the dream-movies on demand; adding new segments, deleting movie sequences that became tiresome, or substituting a character with whom I had become bored with one that was new and more exciting.

Eventually I came to realize that this same capacity can be activated by a skilled guru, hypnotist, shaman or mental health worker to create experiences of astral travel, reincarnation, or false memory. In effect, the dream programming technique can be used to substitute implanted realities in place of those that exist external to the individual. In my dreams the implanted realities were treated by my mind as being on an equal par with external realities.

Insight 5: Reincarnation, Heaven or Hell and everything in between can be experienced through the recombination of different neural networks in our brains. I recounted earlier an attempt by an Asian Indian to take me back to a former life as a Plains Indian Chief. I refused his offer as I assumed he would use a similar method, but the point I'm making is that many individuals believe they are revisiting their former lives because the experiences are completely real. I suspect that some of the gurus leading people through their former lives are also True Believers. Not true in my case as the gurus' behavior made it very clear that he was searching for a new source of income and had used information from my friends to prepare for my visit.

Insight 6: Dream-movie experiences are just as real as any other experience that the brain encounters as it involves related changes in brain chemistry and activation of any of our senses, and draws upon whatever the brain has recorded from external experiences as well as what it has created whole from a myriad of internal sensory re-combinations. As most comprehensive beginning psychology texts demonstrate, we never experience the external world raw and in the buff, we always experience the external world in terms of our sensory processing; alter the processing and we alter the reality. A good example being the one hundred million light sensitive cells in our eyes that have external images reduced by a factor of one hundred as they enter the brain. This visual reduction process of our brains is functional and efficient; however, the process as it encompasses more extensive operations taking place in our brains permits us to create whatever reality we choose.

An interesting awareness that develops from dream programming is the permanent creation of memories from the dreams themselves. I created characters and scenes for my dreams that later appeared on their own in new un-programmed dreams, and were treated in my normal dreams just as factually as events that had occurred in my real life. My mind was treating self-created materials as being equally representative of my real world. This provided me with additional insight into the reality of reincarnation journeys. It helps me understand the True Believer.

Insight 7: By itself, our brain does not normally become aware of how its own neural networks are operating. The brain is designed to help us make split-second decisions in order to survive and it does this by preparing automatic reflexes to events that are harmful to us. For example, you do not think about closing your eyes when something comes flying towards them – you just blink. If you had to think about closing your eyes, they would still be open when the object hit. This design is built into the evolution of our brains as a species, as it is with other mammals that we observe. Normal to our brains means typical neural processing of the common world the brain lives in. When trauma, tumors, neglect or stress alter these typical neural pathways the mind may treat experiences from these new connections as coming from outside of itself. We experience mystic phenomena, spirits, the supernatural, God, gods, or whatever explanations have been handed down within our own culture. I am arguing that we must go beyond this pre-scientific understanding of how our brains actually work and embrace science before we can begin to address what is out there in The Intelligent Universe.

The mentally ill are unaware of how their brains are altering normal sensory input, as most of us are, and feel a sense of helplessness with their lack of control over these altered states. This loss of control creates panic, anxiety, depression and a sense of helplessness; thereby fostering emotional dependence, degrees of withdrawal from social interaction, even total withdrawal, and a need for pharmaceutical drug intervention to stabilize brain chemistry. In my experience, learning to control altered states of reality returned this control to me, relieved my anxiety and depression, and stabilized my brain chemistry.

As I became aware of this process in the 1950s, I found great difficulty discussing these insights with the mental health community. I was either responded to as a lunatic by individuals like the University of Minnesota counselor reading my MMPI Profile, or a religious mystic. I wasn't comfortable in either camp. Research over the past fifty years generally supports the arguments that I am making; further, research by professionals like Antonio Damasio and Michael Merzenich provide depth of insight for the curious reader. Neural science continues to diminish our previous ignorance in this area. Understanding brain functions from the standpoint of self-control, and redirecting and controlling newly created inter-neuronal connections provides additional insights. It also offers relief. And, it is fun under one's own control. Try the Cosmic Shaman trip and you will understand my point more fully.

Psychological evaluation in the 1950s did not distinguish between individuals like me who were aware of creating their own altered reality states and those who were not. One size fit everyone half a century ago and we were all evaluated according to the same standards. One or two steps up from blood-letting to cure illness, but not yet sufficient enough to create insight. Even worse, fifty years ago psychiatry was dominated by Freudian mysticism and psychoanalysis. Rigorously controlled research hasn't been kind to the level of scientific methodology employed during these earlier times. But, that is the nature of science. The current world of neural science generally supports the kind of brain plasticity that I have presented in Ghost.

Insight 8: Modified inter-neuronal connections and resulting altered states of reality can be brought under individual control through practice by techniques common to various religious practitioners or initiated through hypnosis or self-hypnosis. I discovered this process through self-hypnosis without having contact with traditional shamans, gurus, or prophets or Freudian-based psychoanalysts. Hence, I was free to look for explanations in the natural sciences. My initial discoveries occurred while I was a university undergraduate in psychology, and I looked for scientific explanations for my experiences. At the same time, I was seeping myself in religious history, western social thought and a collection of ethnographic studies in anthropology. Gradually, I came to realize that the neural configurations that I was creating produced phenomena similar to that found in my formal studies.

At first I struggled with the idea that there was some kind of controller in my mind directing these experiences. My initial primitive ideas of a mind controller approximated that of a little man sitting in my brain, what some psychology books referred to as a homunculus. When I read Damasio's **Descartes Error** and discovered his explanation for consciosness, I was greatly relieved. I had been aware that I was teaching my brain to behave in extra-ordinary ways, but I did not have working concepts to express this process in other than religious terms. Terms that I found unacceptable; terms that I now know attempt to explain these natural phenomena as coming from outside, from the supernatural. As I gradually learned that I could control and teach the distributed conscious network in my mind-brain, I further realized that I was able to create and direct any neural network pattern that I wanted to experiment with.

Insight 9: Metaphorical constructs that I parsimoniously associate with Lakoff and Johnson's **Philosophy in the Flesh**

deepened my understanding of how the brain derives and uses concepts of space, time, size and other related constructs to represent its relationship with the external world, our own bodies, and our minds. Universally we use these metaphorical constructs to represent both our external and internal worlds. The capacity is universal and constructs are similar across our species if not the same at their most basic level; however metaphorical constructs become increasingly complex with more sophisticated speech development. Interpretations of our external and internal world gradually emerge as we become social beings, along with different cultural configurations that combine the entire sensations of our individual worlds of experience. Lesson learned: human metaphorical capacity provides a similar base for experiences of altered reality, but images within these altered reality experiences take on forms shaped by our own culture.

Insight 10: The Controller can take control of functions that are normally automatic (autonomic nervous system functions) and direct them during waking hours or in dream programming. This includes all human senses as we teach our Controller to master and direct them: Zen driving, astral travel, dream programming, pain reduction or elimination and other related experiences that I have discussed in earlier chapters. Initially, as a university student, I practiced controlling pain by desensitizing various areas of my body - areas that I could stick pins into without feeling pain; controlling my heartbeat, breathing, and opening closed sinuses. After I gained this level of control I went on to create dream programming to conquer my long-term nightmares.

Insight 11: Our minds become integrated as we experience an increasingly stable environment; interactively, a stable environment is experienced as we integrate our psyches cognitively and emotionally. We know that when we are anxious others tend to mirror our anxiety and to some degree become uncomfortable. We change our interactions with others as we change ourselves. Individuals who cannot control their anxiety or depression select friends and social situations with whom they are compatible. Cognitive and emotional integration opens up a larger social world with all its possibilities. It is a path that can lead us to identify with the whole of humanity.

I stabilized my brain chemistry by directing my Controller to take charge of the anxiety and depression that I was experiencing; I was suffering from extreme anxiety and considerable depression and experiencing related complications in my studies and life. I knew little about brain chemistry in 1958, I simply implanted routines in my mind at the behavioral level to control anxiety and depression. It was some years later that I began to digest literature in the neural sciences. Self-integration also meant that critical elevations on my MMPI began to disappear and return to normal levels. And, by the time I graduated with my bachelor's degree, MMPI test elevations for paranoid-schizophrenia, obsessive-compulsive, and psychopathic personality areas tested within normal ranges.

Changes in my life style included extending periods of concentrated study from twenty minutes to four or eight hours of unbroken concentration with exceptional recall; recall in the 99 percentile with one reading, for example. I was sleeping full nights without nightmares for the first time in my life and no longer found it necessary to approach sleep through exhaustion. My tendency to become angry at others in irritating situations was almost eliminated. I was intense, as described by my friends, and the hyper-vigilance I had learned from my father and mother's brutality was gone. Most of these changes took place within a year of my newly conditioned routines through self-hypnosis.

Insight 12: Integration of our psyches comes in stages, but each stage of higher integration improves self-control and tends to increase our social network. As indicated in insight number 11, mental health develops and changes in stages. When I implemented various routines to control anxiety, depression and nightmares, I became conscious of becoming less agitated, anxious and depressed. I began to sleep better, was less exhausted at bedtime, was gaining a much improved level of concentration and had an improved sense of being whole – a sense of unity in my psyche. I consciously developed a sense of wholeness, a new level of intra-psychic integration that I had not previously known.

To continue the metaphor with my Controller, unity, being centered and focused meant that I was expending less psychic energy completing normal daily routines of work and study. Throughout the day, a hyper-vigilant individual wastes a tremendous amount of physical and emotional energy paying attention to all the fine details occurring in his life, and that was definitely true for me. As my self-therapy was implemented, I no longer had to deal with the energy demands of anxiety, depression, and hyper-vigilance; I truly became a new person.

Insight 13: Social maturity occurs when cognitive and emotional integration reaches a level that permits harmonious interpersonal contact and life-goal realization, but adult maturity has many additional levels that we can achieve. As a child and young adult who moved on average three times every two years, I often found myself in situations of physical confrontation: geography where boys and young men solved interpersonal conflicts physically. As I integrated my psyche during my first year at the University of Minnesota, I found this physical history distasteful and vowed to give it up. And I did. Over the following two to three decades I became increasingly pacifistic as I passed through higher levels of maturity, less restless and slowly projected the intra-psychic peace I was experiencing onto the world around me. Gradually, I came to realize that emotional integration expresses itself in interpersonal harmony, and vice versa.

Insight 14: Humanity becomes one unit of people at higher levels of mind-brain integration and maturity, and we come to personally experience the Moral Code. Continuing the insight from number 13, my integrated psyche has come to experience all humanity as one family. I believe this personal feeling of being part of one human family is inevitable once we tear down the cultural walls of prejudice and discrimination taught by our respective cultures. However, these cultural walls fall away by themselves as we reach higher levels of self-integration and maturity; what has often been presented as mystic phenomena in various religions and philosophies. It is at this point of our personal development that the Moral Law of C. W. Lewis comes into being. From this perspective, the Moral Law is in our DNA, but not something that automatically occurs. It requires a stable environment, loving family and personal opportunities for each one of us to integrate cognitively and emotionally. The Moral

Law is unknown to the fragmented or corrupted self. The fragmented self must become integrated before it can experience what is meant by do unto others as you would have others do unto you. But, there is no limitation to this maturity level imposed by trauma and neglect if we have most of our physical brain left intact.

Insight 15: Most forms of punishment, especially those of harsh imprisonment, do not permit the individual psyche to move closer to the moral code that is dependent upon emotional and cognitive integration. Harsh punishment fails due to brutal living conditions that require hyper-vigilance, on the assumption that deprivation alone produces character. It does not. Righteousness is not obtained by just appealing to an external god; righteousness is obtained through love and nurturing of the soul. It is obtained by acknowledging and supporting how the moral law is expressed though normal, healthy living conditions. We cannot deny what is built into our DNA. If by God, so be it.

The atheist sees this source of the Moral Law as occurring naturally without God; the theist sees this source as coming from God; nevertheless, we are bound by the same human condition when we recognize that the Moral Law comes from our DNA and how this DNA is expressed in our environment - when it is nurtured properly. It does not occur through direct appeal as is evidenced by American religious conversions taking place in prisons. When these individuals return to community their rate of reconviction is as high as those who have not experienced being born again while confined. There is no conflict on this point then, between the atheist and the theist. The only difference being the assumed source of our DNA code. Conflict between the atheist and the theist comes from assuming that the Moral Law works from an external source, rather than observing how it emerges from our own psyches. (The argument is where the Law comes from, God or nature). I never understood why some believers insist that God can only work as an external source rather than through what is considered His natural design. Once we get rid of the idea that God has limited abilities, or can only work in magical ways, this conflict is eliminated for many of us.

"I have known true alchemists," the alchemist continued.

"… They understood that when something evolves, every-thing around that thing evolves as well."

BIBLIOGRAPHY

Andrews, D., Bonta, J. (1998). The Psychology of Criminal Conduct. Cincinnati: Anderson Publishing Company.

Aristotle. (1996). The Nicomachean Ethics. Hertfordshire: Wordsworth Classics of World Literature.

Barber, B. (1952). Science and the social order. Glencoe: The Free Press.

Barkalaja, A. Shamanism as Information Design (21-55)) in Leete, A., Firnhaber, R.P., eds. (2004). Boca Raton: Brown Walker Press.

Bloom, F.E., Beal, M.F., Kupfer, D.J. (2003). The Dana Guide To Brain Health. New York: Free Press.

Casti, J. (1994). Complexification. New York: Harper Collins.

Cohen, J.B. (1985). Revolution in Science. Cambridge, Massachusetts: Harvard University Press.

Collins, F.S. (2007). The Language of God. New York: Free Press Paperback.

Comte, A. (1855). The positive philosophy of Auguste Comte. Trans. Harriet Martineau. New York: Calvin Blanchard.

Darby, J. Shamanism in Science (14-20) in Leete, A., Firnhaber, R.P., eds. (2004). Boca Raton: Brown Walker Press.

Damasio, A. R. (1994). Descartes Error: Emotion, Reason, and the Human Brain. New York: Grossman/Putnam

Damasio, A. R. (1999). The Feeling of What Happens. Orlando: Houghton Mifflin Harcourt Publishing.

Damasio, A. R. (2003). Looking for Spinoza: Joy, Sorrow, and the Feeling Brain. Orlando: Harcourt Publishers.

Davies, P. (2007). Cosmic Jackpot: Why Our Universe Is Just Right for Life. New York: Houghton Mifflin Company.

Dawkins, R. (1989). The Selfish Gene. Oxford: Oxford University Press.

Dawkins, R. (2006). The God Delusion. New York: Houghton Mifflin.

Ehrman, B. D. (2003). Lost Christianities: The Battle of Scripture and the Faiths We Never Knew. New Oxford: Oxford University Press.

Evans, B. (1947). The Natural History of Nonsense. New York: Alfred A. Knopf.

Firnhaber, R. P. Mapping the ASC: A Cultural-Physiological Construct (84-119) in Leete, A., Firnhaber, R.P., eds. (2004). Boca Raton: Brown Walker Press.

Frank, P. (1947). Einstein, his life and times. New York: Alfred A. Knopf.

Freud, S. (1997). The Interpretation of Dreams. Hertfordshire: Wordsworth Classics of World Literature.

Gardner, J. (2007). The Intelligent Universe. Franklin Lakes: New Page Books.

Gibran, K. (1979). The Prophet. New York: Alfred A. Knopf.

Green, B. (2000). The Elegant Universe. New York: Vintage.

Green, B. (2004). The Fabric Of The Cosmos: Space, Time, And The Texture Of Reality. New York: Vintage Books.

Griffin, D. R. (1989). Archetypal Process: Self and Devine in Whitehead, Jung, and Hillman. Evanston: Northwestern University Press.

Guth, A. (1997). The Inflationary Universe. Reading: Perseus.

Hare, R. (1993). Without Conscience: The Disturbing World of the Psychopaths Among Us. New York: Guilford Press.

Hawking, S. (1988). A Brief History of Time. London: Bantam.

Hemingway, E. (2004). For Whom the Bell Tolls. London: Arrow Books.

Hoeller, S. A. (2003), Gnosticism: New Light On The Ancient Tradition Of Inner Knowing. Wheaton: The Theosophical Publishing House.

Hooper, D. (2006). Dark Cosmos: In Search of Our Universe's Missing Mass and Energy. New York: Smithsonian Books, HarperCollins.

Humphrey, N. (2002). The Mind Made Flesh: Frontiers of Psychology and Evolution. Oxford: Oxford University Press.

Kaku, M. (1994). Hyperspace. New York: Oxford University Press.

Kaku, M. (2005). Parallel Worlds: A Journey Through Creation, Higher Dimensions, and the Future of the Cosmos. New York: Anchor Books.

Kauffman, S. (1993). The Origin of Order. Oxford: Oxford University Press.

Kirsch, J. (2005). God Against The Gods. Penguin Books: New York.

Kuhn, T.S. (1962). The structure of scientific revolutions. Chicago: The University of Chicago Press.

Lakoff, B., Johnson, M. (1999). Philosophy In The Flesh: The Embodied Mind And Its Challenge To Western Thought. New York: Basic Books.

LeDoux, J. (1996). The Emotional Brain: The Mysterious Underpinnings of Emotional Life. New York: Simon & Schuster Paperbacks.

LeDoux, J. (2003). Synaptic Self: How Our Brains Become Who We Are. New York: Penguin.

Leete, A., Firnhaber, R.P., eds. (2004). Shamanism in the Interdisciplinary Context. Boca Raton: Brown Walker Press.

Mead, G. H. (1936). Movements of thought in the nineteenth century. Chicago: University of Chicago Press.

Mero, L. (1998). Moral Calculations: Game Theory, Logic, and Human Frailty. New York: Copernicus.

Penrose, R. (1994). Shadows of the Mind: A Search for the Missing Science of Consciousness. Oxford: Oxford University Press.

Piaget, J. (1962). Play, Dream, and Imitation in Childhood. New York: Norton.,

Picknett, L. (2004). Mary Magdalene. New York: Carroll & Graf Publishers.

Prigogine, I. (1980). From being to becoming: time and complexity in the physical sciences. San Francisco: W. H. Freeman and Company.

Radin, P. (1957). Primitive Man as Philosopher. New York: Dover Publications.

Robinson, J.M. (1990). The Nag Hammadi Library. New York: HarperCollins Publishers.

Schneider, L. C. (2008). Beyond Monotheism: A Theology of Multiplicity. New York: Routledge.

Smolin, L. (1997). The Life of the Cosmos. Oxford: Oxford University Press.

Spinoza. (1955). The Ethics. New York: Dover Press.

Stanford, C. (2001). Significant Others: The Ape-Human Continuum and the Quest for Human Nature. New York: Basic Books.

Star, C. G. (1991). A History of the Ancient World. New York: Oxford University Press.

Steltenkamp, M. (1993). Black Elk: Holy Man of the Oglala. Norman: University of Oklahoma Press.

Tipler, F. (1994). The Physics of Immortality. New York: Doubleday.

Weatherford, J. (2004). Genghis Khan and the Making of the Modern World. New York: Three Rivers Press.

Wilhelmi, B. Differentiations: A Shamanic Reading of the Gospels (142-148) in Leete, A., Firnhaber, R.P., eds. (2004). Boca Raton: Brown Walker Press.

Wilson, E. O. (1999). Consilience: The Unity of Knowledge. New York: Vintage

www.ingramcontent.com/pod-product-compliance
Lightning Source LLC
Chambersburg PA
CBHW030919090426
42737CB00007B/253

* 9 7 8 0 6 1 5 3 9 5 6 2 3 *